EVIL

Spine-Tingling True Stories
of Murder and Mayhem

Published in the United States and its territories and Canada by
HAMMOND WORLD ATLAS CORPORATION
Part of the Langenscheidt Publishing Group

36-36 33rd Street, Long Island City, NY 11106

EXECUTIVE EDITOR Nel Yomtov

EDITOR Kevin Somers

Produced for Hammond World Atlas Corporation by

MOSELEY ROAD INC.

129 MAIN STREET

IRVINGTON, NY 10533

WWW.MOSELEYROAD.COM

MOSELEY ROAD INC.

PUBLISHER Sean Moore

ART DIRECTORS Gus Yoo, Brian MacMullen

EDITORIAL DIRECTOR Lisa Purcell

PHOTO RESEARCHERS Ben DeWalt, Neil Dvorak

CARTOGRAPHY Neil Dvorak

ASSISTANT EDITORS Jo Rose, Zain Taufiq

EDITORIAL ASSISTANTS Rachael Lanicci, Natalie Rivera

COVER DESIGN Linda Kosarin

COVER PHOTO © Joseph / Shutterstock Images LLC

Printed and bound in Canada

ISBN-13: 978-0843-708769

EVIL

Spine-Tingling True Stories of Murder and Mayhem

Colin Wilson and Damon Wilson

L HAMMOND World Atlas

Part of the Langenscheidt Publishing Group

Contents

A Gallery of Evil

How does one define "evil"? Is it a man who lures a child away from her parents, only to rape her, torture her, and then ultimately kill her? What about the assassin who kills an individual, sure that one death will save the lives of many? Then, of course, there are the mass murderers and serial killers, men (for they are almost always male), who pile up the bodies in unthinkable numbers. Surely all of the above can be called evil. But then that raises another question—why are we all so captivated by the subject? What draws the reader to disturbing tales of true crime?

When I was a child, my father brought home from work a book called *The Fifty Most Amazing Crimes of the Last Hundred Years* and unknowingly introduced me to a subject that has continued to fascinate me all my life.

The cases all had a sketch of the murderer at the head of the article—Dr. Crippen, Henri Landru, and so on. But the one that fascinated me most was the one on Jack the Ripper, which had only a huge black question mark. The notion of a man who killed and disemboweled women struck me as so horrific as to be almost unbelievable.

My grandfather, who had been a small child at the time of the murders in 1888, remembered being warned by his mother not to stay out after dark, "or Jack the Ripper might get you."

What baffled me, of course, was the problem of why a man should want to disembowel women. I was totally unable to grasp that the attack itself should satisfy sexual desire. And that, unfortunately, explains why so many of the "monsters" in these pages were obsessed by cruelty. All living animals are possessed by a desire to express themselves freely, to avoid frustration. But here we encounter a strange mystery. Why is it that a simple and straightforward desire for sex, a biological urge, which after all is an expression of affection—like a kiss—should turn into cruelty? And yet this is precisely what happens again and again in cases of sex criminals. It would seem that once human desire reaches a certain point of intensity, it mutates into something evil.

Now the Marquis de Sade, who was an expert on such matters, has a frighteningly simple explanation. He claims that nature itself is based on cruelty, from a cat tormenting a mouse to a tiger ripping its prey to pieces. We "civilized" humans prefer to close our eyes to this cruelty and declare that religion has taught us higher values. But, says Sade, these values are pure self-delusion. And to prove his case, he would point to some of the "monsters" in this book as examples of the natural cruelty of those with power—Vlad the Impaler, Ivan the Terrible, and Elizabeth Báthory.

But if Sade is correct in saying that people with power tend to misuse it, then why do mothers not beat their babies? Why did Sade himself not misuse it when he had the chance, for he was on a revolutionary tribunal and could have taken revenge on his mother-in-law, who had been responsible for having him thrown into the Bastille? Sade himself demonstrates that there is a force of natural decency in human beings.

Or, as Jung put it, "The soul has a religious function."

In the following pages, you will read many stories of evil, including historic true crimes, from the assassination of Julius Caesar in ancient Rome to the assassination of Archduke Franz Ferdinand that set off World War I. In these pages you will meet the monsters of evil—from medieval nobleman Gilles de Rais, the first recorded serial killer, to the infamous Manson Family of hippie-era California. There are also classic cases, that I would define as ones in which the killers choose murder as a way to solve problems, often caused by their own tangle of lies or self-indulgence, from the lawless gangsters of the Great Depression to Buck Ruxton, a successful English doctor, who killed his wife in a fit of jealousy. Of course, we include the serial killers, so many of whom are now household names: Ted Bundy, John Wayne Gacy, Henry Lee Lucas. We also take a look at some notable unsolved cases, including the Boston Strangler and Jack the Stripper.

And of course, the one who started it all: Jack the Ripper.

Colin Wilson
2009

Historic Evil

The death of Caesar

The Assassination of Julius Caesar

(Ides of March, 44 BCE)

Judging the young Gaius Julius Caesar, nobody in ancient Rome expected him to develop into a great national leader. He spent his youth (he was born in July 100 BCE) as a fashionable fop: writing poetry, perfuming and curling his hair, and indulging in numerous love affairs—with men as well as women, according to his enemies. His fellow Romans regarded him as a clever socialite but not a man likely to achieve high office. For all his artistic pretensions, however, Caesar was, at heart, a warlord.

The Radical Fop

In 65 BCE Caesar was elected as an *aedile*: the master of ceremonies in public celebrations. The Roman Senate still thought of him as a fop and a political lightweight, but Caesar put the posting to good use. He borrowed large sums from Crassus, a millionaire friend, and staged some spectacular public shows. One of them featured 320 pairs of gladiators.

Caesar was already immensely popular with the plebeians (the teeming, non-noble population of Rome) because, although of a high patrician (noble) house himself, he seemed to genuinely care about the lot of Rome's poor. That's why Crassus was willing to bankroll his friend almost without limit—Caesar wielded considerable political clout with the reformist *populares* party.

Rome's foremost military hero, Pompey the Great, came back from his conquests in the East in 62 BCE. Caesar suggested an alliance. He was the most popular man in Rome, Crassus was the richest, Pompey was its greatest hero; together they could do what they liked. This oddly assorted trio—the ambitious millionaire, the egotistical general, and the still rather foppish man of the people—entered into a partnership that would make them masters of Rome.

Bust of Julius Caesar. Caesar began his public life in the post of master of ceremonies in the Roman republic . He proved to have a gift for organizing dazzling spectacles for celebrations and holidays.

ATLANTIC OCEAN

EUROPE

Black Sea

Rome

AFRICA

THE ROMAN EMPIRE 44 BCE

Roman possessions

The Three-Headed Monster

Pompey, shown above, formed the triumvirate with Crassus and Caesar.

The people *could* overrule the Senate, if the plebeian leaders spoke with one voice—an event so rare that the Senate had never made any real attempt to strengthen its position against the *populares*. Their friends knew Pompey, Crassus, and Caesar as "the triumvirate"; their enemies called them "the three-headed monster."

In the following year, 59 BCE, the three-headed monster achieved the first of its aims: in the teeth of bitter opposition from the patricians, Caesar was elected consul (the name given to the two leading magistrates who ruled the Roman Republic). Caesar then used his power to get Pompey what he most wanted: land for his retiring soldiers. Then Pompey and Crassus were appointed heads of a commission to administer new laws—positions that allowed them to target their enemies with selective legislation. Thus the three triumvirs emerged as the most powerful men in Rome.

Caesar battles the Britons on the shores of the English Channel.

Conquest

The Senate's endless backbiting and infighting wearied Caesar, so he marched off to Gaul (present-day France) looking for adventure and glory. He found both over the next seven years. His army, in a stunning series of battles, subdued the Gauls from the border of Spain to the North Sea, then crossed the English Channel and defeated the southeastern Britons.

Back in Rome, Pompey and Crassus viewed these triumphs with mixed feelings. The three-headed-monster could only remain stable as long as none of the heads grew too big. So Crassus, determined to win some military glory, tried to outdo Caesar by invading the Parthian Empire (in what is modern-day Iran).

The campaign proved a disaster; Crassus badly misjudged the situation. Sweltering in heavy armor beneath the blazing sun, Roman legionnaires stood defenseless against mounted enemies, who fired volleys of arrows and then rode away before any chance of counterattack. The Parthian army's hit-and-run tactics destroyed the Romans. Crassus himself was captured and executed.

Traitor or Liberator?

In 49 BCE the Roman Senate appointed Pompey (far right) sole consul, setting the stage for Caesar's revolt.

On hearing the news of Crassus's defeat and seeing that now was their chance to break the *populares* stranglehold on government, the patricians offered to make Pompey sole consul of Rome. The aging Pompey must have feared that he couldn't handle Caesar without Crassus to balance matters. Pompey decided to betray his political partner. The Senate ordered Caesar to leave his army and return to Rome.

Despite all he had done for the Republic, Caesar knew just how vindictive the patrician Senate could be: if he returned to Rome without his army to protect him, he'd be dead within days. He decided to disobey orders and marched part of his army to the banks of the river that divided Gaul from Italy—the Rubicon. There he waited, hoping that matters might still be smoothed over. But when Pompey and the Senate threw down the gauntlet, ordering him to disband his army or be considered a public enemy, Caesar gave the order to cross the Rubicon. It meant civil war.

Lone Ruler

Pompey and his army made a tactical withdrawal to Greece—why battle on home territory when you can devastate somebody else's land? Caesar entered Rome in triumph and had himself reappointed sole consul by what remained of the Senate—naturally, his most implacable enemies had fled with Pompey.

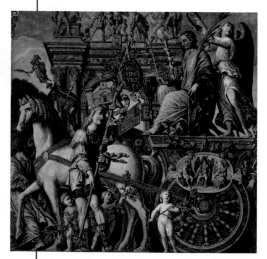

Caesar, honored with a banner reading VENI, VIDI, VICI, during his victory parade.

Caesar then pacified the rest of Italy. The Roman armies of Spain had sided with their old commander, Pompey, so Caesar defeated them before turning to the greatest task. In Greece Caesar defeated Pompey's vastly superior forces at the Battle of Pharsalus. Pompey escaped to Egypt, but as he stepped ashore, his Egyptian hosts stabbed and beheaded him. Egypt wanted nothing to do with defeated generals, even ones as legendary as Pompey the Great.

In 45 BCE Caesar sailed back to Rome to a magnificent victory parade. The leading chariot bore the words VENI, VIDI, VICI: "I came, I saw, I conquered." The Senate voted Caesar the title of *dictator* (then a term that simply meant that he was the sole consul—with no co-consul who might veto his decisions). It was a post that few imagined he would ever give up voluntarily.

The Great Reformer

Now 65 Caesar was growing increasingly imperious and distant in his manner. Many feared that the once fun-loving dandy had developed delusions of grandeur or even kingship.

Yet if he himself was cold, most of his works as dictator of Rome were reforming. He altered the calendar by adding a "leap year" to fix the yearly slippage of a few hours that meant that the midsummer festival was slowly edging into autumn. He settled new towns with his battle-weary ex-soldiers, giving each a generous land grant. He enacted laws that curbed the power of the rich and alleviated the misery of the poor. He also extended Roman citizenship to former barbarian lands, such as areas of southern Gaul. To represent these new citizens, he expanded the number of seats in the Roman Senate, diluting the power of the old patrician families.

Caesar also chose to forgive his surviving enemies, rather than kill them. He clearly meant to smooth over the ruptures of the civil war, and, perhaps, he had developed an aversion to spilling more Roman blood.

The Assassination

Less than a year after Caesar's victory, a conspiracy formed, spearheaded by former enemies of Caesar but also backed by those he considered allies and friends. On the morning of March 15, 44 BCE, a group of senators called Julius Caesar to the Forum, on the pretense of reading a petition. As Caesar began to read, one of the conspirators, Tillius Cimber, pulled at Caesar's toga. The outraged Caesar cried out, but Casca, another member of the plot, came at Caesar with a dagger, landing a glancing slice on the dictator's neck. Caesar had no bodyguards, and his friends did nothing to help him. Soon the entire group pounced on him. He initially fought off his 23 attackers until, seeing one called Marcus Junius Brutus stab at him, he exclaimed, *"Et tu, Brute?"* Then, throwing a fold of his robe over his face, he succumbed to the blades. Brutus, the son of Sevilia, a former lover, was a particular favorite of Caesar's, and history has remained muddied over Caesar's last words. Most historians believe he exclaimed, "You too, Brutus?" But the Roman historian Suetonius reported that he actually cried, "You too, my son?"

Much has been made, by William Shakespeare and others, of the "noble" aims of the conspirators—that Caesar hoped to make himself a king, and they wanted to defend republican freedoms. But was this true?

Death of Caesar by Vincenzo Camuccini (1773–1844) depicts Caesar's former friends and allies stabbing him in the Roman Forum.

Who's Your Daddy?

Was Marcus Junius Brutus (one of the leading conspirators in Julius Caesar's assassination) actually Caesar's illegitimate son? The answer is almost certainly "no." Caesar was only 15 years old when Brutus was born; a bit too young for even the amorous Julius to conduct an affair with another man's wife.

After cremation outside the building, Caesar's ashes were buried in the heart of the Forum.

The Reason for Murder

Caesar had all the power he needed as "dictator for life" (a position the Senate awarded him only a month before his death), and he had no legitimate children upon which to pass a hereditary monarchy.

Caesar was actually, at the time of his murder, preparing a military expedition against a minor insurgency in Spain. After that he planned to execute a major attack against Parthia to avenge the death of his friend Crassus. It is likely, knowing Caesar's military genius, that he would have won at least a partial victory in the East, increasing Rome's wealth and power yet again. And while away fighting, Caesar would have been in no position to cruelly tyrannize Rome, even if his character ever changed enough to make him want to do so.

So by killing him when they did, the conspirators achieved little or nothing and also lost much for Rome . . .

Murder in the Cathedral
(April 26, 1478)

Giuliano de' Medici

When Lorenzo de' Medici, the wealthiest banker in Florence, went to Mass on Easter Sunday 1478, he had no suspicion that killers stalked him and his younger brother and co-ruler, Giuliano. A professional hit man named Montesecco had been hired to do the job by a rival banker, Francesco de' Pazzi, and when Lorenzo was dead, Montesecco was supposed to invade the city with a hired army and wipe out the rest of the Medici family.

The Pazzi Conspiracy

Giuliano was the first to die—but he should not have even been in the cathedral. Pazzi had persuaded him to rise from a sickbed to attend High Mass at the cavernous Basilica di Santa Maria del Fiore. At the closing of Mass, as Pazzi stood with Giuliano near the altar, he gave Giuliano a friendly squeeze—he was really checking for a concealed dagger. Then an accomplice, Bernardo Bandini Baroncelli, shouted, "Here, traitor!" and plunged his dagger into Giuliano's side. Giuliano staggered back into Pazzi. Pazzi began slashing, stabbing Giuliano 18 more times. Giuliano fell dead.

Meanwhile the priest slated to kill Lorenzo placed a hand on Lorenzo's shoulder. Lorenzo twisted around in a flash, and the priest lunged, slicing Lorenzo's neck. Drawing his own sword, Lorenzo fought off his attackers before his friends hustled him to safety behind the massive bronze doors of the sacristy.

Chaos erupts in the nave of the Basilica di Santa Maria del Fiore as perpetrators of the Pazzi conspiracy attack the Medici brothers.

"Palle! Palle!"

Unaware that the plot had misfired, the head of the Pazzi family, Jacopo, rode around the piazza waving his sword and shouting, "Liberty and the republic!" in an effort to raise the populace against the Medicis. The crowd, who loved the Medicis, replied with shouts of *"Palle! Palle!"* or "Balls! Balls!"—not a lewd riposte but a reference to the Medici coat of arms. Jacopo fled.

Within an hour the bodies of most of the plotters, including Francesco de' Pazzi, were hanging out of the Bargello, also known as the Bargello Palace or Palazzo del Popolo ("Palace of the People"), and other government palace windows with ropes around their necks. Some were simply tossed from towers to die broken on the ground. Jacopo, after capture, begged for mercy. "Allow me to commit suicide," he pleaded. His capturers denied him. They beat him until he could not walk before hanging him naked.

The Medici coat of arms

Leonardo da Vinci's sketch of Bernardo di Bandini Baroncelli, hanging from the Bargello

The Scene of the Crime

The Basilica di Santa Maria del Fiore is the cathedral church (Duomo) of Florence. Construction began on the Duomo in 1296, with its major construction completed in 1436. With a variegated exterior in various shades of green and pink marble, it features a magnificent dome, which was designed by Filippo Brunelleschi. It was in its peaceful but imposing setting that Giuliano de' Medici bled to death from the knife wounds inflicted by Francesco de' Pazzi and Bernardo Bandini Baroncelli.

Until the murder in the cathedral, the Pazzi family had had an honorable history with the Duomo. Francesco's ancestor, Pazzo ("the madman") had returned from the First Crusade with a stone from the Basilica of the Holy Sepulchre in Jerusalem. His descendants were given the distinction of striking a light from this stone on Holy Saturday, when all fires in the city were extinguished. From this spark, the altar light of the Duomo was rekindled annually. On Easter Sunday a dove-shaped rocket would slide on a wire from above the altar to a fireworks-laden oxcart waiting in the Duomo's piazza. The fireworks not only entertained the populace, they also provided the sparks that relit the city's hearths.

Golden mosaic in baptistery of Santa Maria del Fiore in Florence, Italy

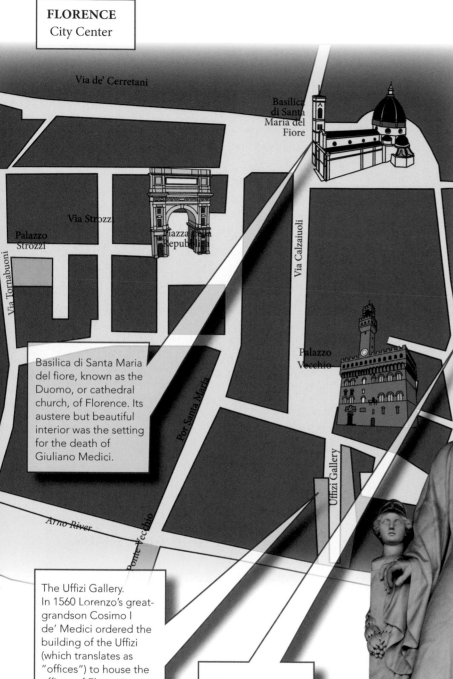

Via de' Cerretani

Basilica di Santa Maria del Fiore

Via Strozzi

Via Tornabuoni

Palazzo Strozzi

Piazza della Repubblica

Via Calzaiuoli

Palazzo Vecchio

Bargello

Por Santa Maria

Arno River

Ponte Vecchio

Uffizi Gallery

Basilica di Santa Maria del fiore, known as the Duomo, or cathedral church, of Florence. Its austere but beautiful interior was the setting for the death of Giuliano Medici.

The Uffizi Gallery. In 1560 Lorenzo's great-grandson Cosimo I de' Medici ordered the building of the Uffizi (which translates as "offices") to house the offices of Florentine magistrates.

The perpetrators of the Pazzi plot were sentenced to die by hanging from the Bargello Palace.

LORENZO IL MAGNIFICO

Twisting the Pope's Tail

Lorenzo de' Medici was a brilliantly gifted "Renaissance man" who, before his early death (at the age of 43) had made his city, Florence, the most celebrated in Italy. Lorenzo was the patron of great artists like Michelangelo, Leonardo da Vinci, and Botticelli. His grandfather Cosimo the Great had accumulated the family wealth, and Lorenzo became head of the family in 1470, when he was only 21.

Eight years later he became the target of the murder plot, dreamed up by men he trusted: Pope Sixtus IV, who had once been his friend and client, and Francesco de' Pazzi, the town's second-richest banker. When the pope decided to buy a strategically placed town called Imola, Lorenzo had secretly asked Pazzi not to lend him the money. Pazzi immediately told the pope. The pope removed the papal account from Lorenzo and transferred it to Pazzi.

Lorenzo now made the mistake that cost his brother's life. A wealthy man named Borromeo lay on his deathbed, and his only relative, his daughter, was married to a Pazzi. Lorenzo quickly passed a law that said that male heirs should be preferred over females. Borromeo's money went to Lorenzo's nephew instead. Pazzi swore revenge.

Among the statues of famous Florentines that grace the facade of the renowned Uffizi Gallery is one of Lorenzo de' Medici.

Papal Sinners

It seems astonishing to us that a pope could be part of a murder plot. But in Renaissance Italy, few people would have raised an eyebrow. More than one medieval pope had proved immoral.

Sixtus IV was born in 1414 into the modest Rovere family. He entered the Church and became a Franciscan friar. Intellectual brilliance brought him to the papal throne in 1471, but he was also power-mad and corrupt—and soon infamous for his greed and nepotism.

To do him justice, Sixtus was not willing to countenance murder. "No killing," he warned Pazzi as they hatched their plot to overthrow the Medicis. But both Pazzi and the pope knew perfectly well that there was no way of getting rid of the Medicis without murder.

When the plot failed the pope was beside himself with rage, not simply because his enemy was still alive but also because one of his own favorites had been killed—Francesco Salviati, the archbishop of Pisa.

It had been Archbishop Salviati's job to murder the chief justice, Petrucci, when he was eating lunch. But Salviati was unaware that Petrucci's door had a spring lock that would snap closed. When he demanded to see Petrucci, he was without his thugs. When Petrucci grew suspicious and called for the guard, Salviati lost his nerve and tried to run away. Consequently he became one of the corpses dangling out of a window.

Sixtus IV, shown seated at far right, one of the ringleaders of the Pazzi plot

The inner courtyard of the Bargello, once the site of executions. The Bargello now serves as a museum.

In Deep Trouble

The pope now demanded that Lorenzo should be sent to Rome to be tried for Salviati's murder. Florence refused, and the pope placed the whole city under interdict, forbidding Mass and communion, and called for a crusade to destroy it.

There were plenty of the pope's friends who were delighted to answer the call. King Ferrante of Naples was particularly dangerous and had soon routed Lorenzo's half-hearted mercenaries. Then people began dying of plague at a rate of eight a day. Lorenzo knew it would only be a matter of time before Florence handed him over.

Lorenzo now played his masterstroke. In December 1479 he embarked on a journey to Naples. With lavish gifts in hand, he exerted all his considerable charm on Ferrante. His grand gesture worked. The king liked him, and soon the two of them were spending all their time hunting together. Ferrante agreed to peace, and when Lorenzo returned to Florence, crowds cheered themselves hoarse, and every bell in the city rang all day.

The pope was furious—but helpless. And he soon felt obliged to swallow his rage. When the Turks invaded southern Italy, his contemporaries generally believed that Lorenzo was behind it, for he had often claimed that he had some influence over the sultan. When Otranto fell to the Turks, the pope thought they were preparing to march on Rome, and hastily granted Florence absolution. Once again the bells rang out for Lorenzo.

Cesare Borgia

Cesare Borgia

(1475-1507)

If Lorenzo de' Medici is one of the greatest men of the Renaissance, Cesare Borgia has a good claim to be the most evil.

His father, Rodrigo Borgia, who became Pope Alexander VI, may have been the worst pope who ever lived: he was corrupt, ungodly, and obsessed with seducing underage girls. When he was a cardinal, the previous pope had to reprimand him for holding an orgy in his garden with crowds of expensive courtesans.

Rodrigo's mistress, Vannozza dei Cattanei, having produced three illegitimate children, Giovanni (Juan), Cesare, and Lucrezia, felt that her position ought to be legalized. The pope found her a husband—specifying that he was not to engage in sex with Vannozza. When she became pregnant again, the pope suspected that she had reneged but accepted the child, a son named Gioffre (Jofré), philosophically.

A Change of Fate

Alexander VI hoped to become the master of Italy, so he decided that Giovanni was destined for the army. Cesare would enter the Church—and inherit the papacy. Cesare hated the idea. Then one evening Giovanni vanished mysteriously after he and Cesare ate supper with their mother. His body was pulled from the Tiber River with nine stab wounds. It was a long time before people realized that Cesare had chosen the simplest method of stepping into his brother's shoes as the family warrior.

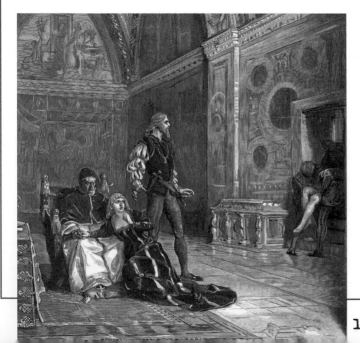

The lifeless body of Giovanni is brought to his family, Alexander, Lucrezia, and Cesare.

Lucrezia Borgia

Lucrezia has a reputation as a poisoner, but this is completely unjustified—she never poisoned anyone. There are many well-known rumors about Lucrezia's complicity in her brother's crimes and misdeeds, but these reports are unsubstantiated. Born in 1480, she was pretty, gentle, and had a temperament that begged to be dominated.

Her father decided to marry her off as soon as possible. She was betrothed twice by the time she was 13, but it was not until after Rodrigo became pope that he selected Giovanni Sforza, scion of a powerful Milanese family. But Giovanni soon realized that with a brother-in-law like Cesare, he was not likely to live long and returned home to Milan.

For safety, Lucrezia, now divorced, went into a convent. Giovanni had resisted divorce on grounds of alleged impotence but gave in when told he would have to demonstrate his virility with a prostitute in front of the College of Cardinals. Even in a convent, however, Lucrezia still managed to become pregnant. The pope solved the problem by marrying her off to Alfonso of Aragon, the son of the king of Naples.

Portrait of a Woman by Bartolomeo Veneto. Most historians agree that the sitter was Lucrezia Borgia.

Murder in the Family

Lucrezia seemed to enjoy marriage. This did not sit well with the possessive Cesare, who was used to a great deal of attention from his sister. Cesare, once known as a handsome man, had become very conscious of his appearance. A bout of syphilis had scarred his face, and he began wearing masks and dressing in all black. Jealous of his sister's good-looking husband, he plotted to rid himself of his rival. One evening a group of Cesare's men repeatedly stabbed Alfonso while he was crossing Saint Peter's Square. Papal guards intervened and carried the bleeding man to his wife's apartment in the Vatican. Lucrezia and Alfonzo's sister Sanchia (who was married to Gioffre Borgia) fought to save his life. But just as he began to recover, he was found strangled in his bed. Cesare, accused of the murder, freely admitted it—he claimed Alfonso had fired a crossbow at him as he walked in the papal gardens. The grief-stricken Lucrezia retired to her castle at Nepi.

A Glass of Wine with Cesare Borgia by John Collier. In Collier's illustration Pope Alexander VI bends over his plate, while Cesare, at left, pours a glass of wine—assumed to be poisoned—for a guest. Lucrezia stands between her brother and father.

The Beginning

In exchange for a divorce decree, the new French king, Louis XII, made a deal with the pope to appoint Cesare as the duke of Valence. In 1499 Cesare married Charlotte d'Albret, the 16-year-old daughter of the king of Navarre. In a scandalous letter to his father, he described, in detail, the pleasures of the wedding night. The French court hated him for his vain, tasteless behavior, and Cesare spent much of his time grinding his teeth at slights and insults. That same year, with Cesare in tow, Louis XII invaded Italy with the pope's approval. Cesare immediately began a campaign against those who had upset him—"friends" of his died suddenly after banquets, or were found stabbed in the Tiber. Finally some Romans recalled the death of his brother Giovanni and saw the light.

The Ducal Palace in Urbino. Cesare held Urbino from 1502 to 1503.

The Conqueror

Cesare marched off to fight in the province of Romagna, south of Venice, which his father wished to add to the papal territories. He had the kind of dash and boldness that brought swift victories. The pope provided the monetary support by selling cardinal's hats to 12 completely unsuitable but wealthy candidates.

Cesare captured Rimini, Fana, and Pesaro. He now had the bit between his teeth—and he seemed unstoppable. After Cesare had subdued Romagna, his father made him duke of the province. Cesare decided that the unruly region needed a firmer hand, so he gave the most ruthless man he knew—Remirro de Orco—full authority to restore law and order by whatever means necessary. De Orco carried out the task with ferocity and soon had the whole region cowering. Cesare—to avoid the blame for this cruelty—had de Orco captured, hacked into two pieces, and left out in the public square at Cesena. A brutal end to someone whose brutality he'd sanctioned.

In summer 1502 Cesare displayed his cold-blooded qualities on the field of battle. His latest objective was the town of Camerino. This was well to the south of his other conquests in Romagna, and the large town of Urbino lay between them. Urbino's duke, Guidobaldo, was a friend and ally, so he saw no reason to worry about his exposed position. Cesare marched on Camerino from the south—and then unexpectedly seized Urbino. Guidobaldo had to flee to Mantua. If anyone had accused him of treachery, Cesare would have replied that if an ally is in a position to stab you in the back, it is common sense to strike first.

Lucrezia— Marriage 4

While Cesare was conquering Italy, Lucrezia had remarried. The pope was aware that his health was failing and wanted to see his beloved daughter settled. For an enormous dowry, the duke of Ferrara agreed to permit the marriage between Lucrezia and his son Alfonso d'Este. It was Cesare who suggested the alliance. He had morphed from a possessive malcontent into a methodical madman.

Disaster

With shattering suddenness, the whole edifice of power came tumbling down. On Friday, August 11, 1503, the pope and Cesare attended a party at a vineyard just outside Vatican City; their host was cardinal Adriano Castelli da Cornetto. The next day, the pope and Cesare lay ill in bed with all the signs of fever. For a few days, they were both at the point of death. The pope briefly rallied, only to have a relapse and die.

Cesare, still lying ill in bed, knew he was in trouble. His career would be at an end if one of his father's enemies became pope. A harmless and aged cardinal was elected Pius II but died within a month. And the man who replaced him—as Julius II—was a member of the Rovere family, old enemies of Cesare and his father. On the day Julius was elected, Cesare told Niccolò Machiavelli that he never thought that at his father's death he would be dying himself.

A nineteenth-century print, showing the accidental poisoning of Alexander and Cesare.

Few Tears for Cesare

Cesare had only three mourners: his mother, Vannozza; his sister, Lucrezia; and his adviser, Niccolò Machiavelli.

The Castel Sant' Angelo in Rome was built by the Roman emperor Hadrian (117–138) as a mausoleum. A corridor connects it to the Vatican, and beginning in the thirteenth century, Roman Catholic popes used it as a fortress, a prison, and a place for torture. It is now a museum.

Plague in a Bottle

Cesare took refuge in the Castel Sant' Angelo to avoid the daggers of his enemies. Lucrezia, safe in Ferrara, wrote to the king of France begging him to allow Cesare to take up his dukedom there. But Cesare was now an embarrassment to the French. The new pope ordered Cesare arrested and brought back to the Vatican—he was locked in the room where he had Lucrezia's second husband strangled. Cesare escaped from Rome and hurried to his allies in Naples, only to face arrest again.

Imprisoned on the island of Ischia, he was forced to give up his conquests in Romagna. Everything he had gained was now lost. He was allowed to go to Spain, but he'd forgotten that his brother Giovanni had left a widow—a bitter widow determined to avenge her husband's murder. Cesare landed in a Cincilla jail.

The Spaniards had only one reason for keeping him alive: he was a valuable pawn to use against the pope. To have Cesare in prison was like having a plague germ in a bottle. In 1506 Cesare escaped and joined his brother-in-law, the king of Navarre, who was engaged in a territorial dispute in Spain. Cesare again took up a position as a commander—but of a mere 100 troops.

He rode ahead of the rest of the army and engaged the enemy first to prove that he was as bold as ever. This time his luck deserted him. Badly wounded, he was left to die of thirst. He was only 31.

Jean Marat

Charlotte Corday and the Assassination of Jean-Paul Marat

(July 13, 1793)

On July 13, 1793, the French revolutionary leader, Jean-Paul Marat, sat in his bathtub. A crate was propped next to it, serving as a makeshift writing desk so that Marat could lean on it to pen an article for his fiery leftist newspaper *L'Ami du Peuple* (*The Friend of the People*). One of the greatest intellectuals and scientists of his age, Marat suffered from a debilitating skin disease, which itched fiercely and left his skin covered in blisters. The condition made it more comfortable for him to write in a medicated bath.

Charlotte Corday, just after stabbing Marat in his bath

One Death to Save Many

At just after seven in the evening Marat heard women's voices outside his door. One was his future sister-in-law, Catherine Evrard, and the other a more cultivated voice, obviously that of a "lady." In fact he was half expecting a feminine caller, for a woman named Charlotte Corday had written to him earlier in the day, begging for an interview. Marat now called out to Catherine to let her in.

Corday, who came from Caen in Normandy, was a pretty young woman in her mid-20s. Her purpose, she had explained in the letter, was to tell Marat about a group of conspirators who belonged to the moderate Girondist faction and were plotting against Marat's own extreme leftist faction, the Jacobins. (The Girondins had actually started the French Revolution in 1789, but the Jacobins now regarded them as reactionary fuddy-duddies.)

Marat asked her to name names, and as Corday, sitting by the bath, started to dictate, Marat began writing them down, remarking, "They shall all be guillotined." He then asked his fiancée, Simonne, to fetch some more of the kaolin solution he used in the bath. Charlotte knew that this was her only chance. As she stood up, she took a knife out of the top of her dress and plunged it into Marat's right breast near the clavicle. Marat slumped back. The blade had severed the carotid artery, and he died almost immediately. And Corday, believing she would be killed too, sat there quietly as Marat's crimson blood flowed into the milky bathwater.

Revolution!

The French Revolution was a bloodbath waiting to happen. Since the beginning of the eighteenth century, France had experienced a population explosion, which filled the towns with unemployed farm laborers and beggars. But while the poor died of starvation, the aristocracy did not even pay taxes.

You could say the Revolution began in December 1725, when the hired ruffians of the Chevalier de Rohan, with whom he had exchanged angry words, beat up Voltaire, the writer and philosopher. When Voltaire complained, Rohan had him thrown into prison and released only on condition that he left the country. This treatment filled him with rage and hatred. He went to England, where there was a tradition of free speech. And from then on he devoted his considerable wit and brilliance to trying to destroy people like Rohan.

By 1787 things were so bad that the Marquis de Lafayette, who had fought in the American Revolution, suggested to the king that he ought to call a parliament. Louis XVI refused, but the newspapers set up such a clamor that he finally had to give way and call a parliament (or Estates General). This started by suggesting that the aristocrats should pay taxes.

Jacques-Louis David painted *The Death of Marat* just days after the journalist's death. David deliberately depicted Marat as a healthy man, cut down as a martyr for the revolutionary cause.

Marat's Bathtub

After Marat's death, the infamous bathtub disappeared. Evidence suggests that Simonne Évrard sold it to her neighbor, a journalist. In the ensuing years it changed hands a few times, and in 1885 a *Le Figaro* journalist tracked it down to a parish church in Brittany. The parish curé realized that he had a hot commodity. After offers from both Madame Tussaud's waxworks and Phineas Barnum, the curé sold the tub for 5,000 francs to the Musée Grévin, another waxworks in Paris. It is there still.

The Bastille Falls

On July 14, 1788, a starving mob surrounded the Bastille, Paris's greatest prison. The governor agreed to surrender, but as he marched out at the head of his troops, someone grabbed him and hacked off his head with a butcher's knife.

The king then behaved stupidly. He decided to escape from Paris and return at the head of an army. Revolutionaries caught him and forced him to return to the city—but at least they allowed him to live.

Then Marat began to demand the king's death. So did his fellow revolutionary leaders Robespierre and Danton. In January 1793 a guillotine removed Louis' head. His was followed by that of his infamous queen, Marie Antoinette. And the Girondins, also driven out of government, were forced to flee to places like Caen in Normandy. Many also lost their heads.

The storming of the Bastille

Detail from David's *Death of Marat*, showing the lifeless hand of Marat, still clutching Charlotte Corday's letter of introduction

Enter Mademoiselle Charlotte Corday

On July 7, 1793, rebel Girondins held a parade in Caen. And Charlotte Corday, daughter of an aristocratic family, watched it. She had been about to enter a religious order when the Revolution broke out and nunneries were abolished.

Corday was not a royalist. On the contrary, she was an admirer of Jean Jacques Rousseau, the writer who stated: "Man is born free, and is everywhere in chains."

Her mother had died in childbirth. And the priest who had administered the last rites had been forced to flee into the woods; he was hunted down with dogs and executed. As far as Corday was concerned, the man who was basically responsible for this was the immensely influential editor of the *Friend of the People*, Jean-Paul Marat.

Charlotte in Paris

On July 9 Corday took a carriage called a diligence to Paris. On arrival she took a room at the Hôtel de Providence before heading to the Palais-Royal, where she bought a 6-inch kitchen knife with "a dark wooden handle and a silver ferrule." She intended to stab Marat at the national assembly, but she was disappointed to learn that Marat was ill, so he could not be killed in front of his fellow deputies, as she had imagined. She went to his lodging in the morning and was told he was too ill to see anyone. She left him a letter, promising to reveal the names of traitors in Caen. And when he returned later in the day she was lucky— newspapers and fresh bread were just arriving, and she was able to slip upstairs. There she encountered Catherine, who told her she could not possibly see Marat. So as she pleaded, Corday deliberately raised her voice so that Marat could hear her. And his voice called: "Oh, let her in . . ."

Just Who Was the Monster?

Corday proved a remarkably composed murderess. In a preliminary interrogation, she plainly stated that she had come to Paris to kill Marat. A police commissioner noted, "Convinced that the flames of civil war were about to be ignited throughout France and certain that Marat was the principal author of these disasters, the prisoner testified that she wished to sacrifice her life for her country." And although the authorities sought to establish that she had merely been the handmaiden of a larger conspiracy, Corday calmly insisted after repeated questioning that she had planned and committed the assassination alone— she simply had no coconspirators and no accomplices. At her trial she never deviated from her story, asserting, "I told my plans to no one. I was not killing a man, but a wild beast that was devouring the French people."

It was a vain hope, though. Rather than uncovering the evil of Marat, she instead turned him into a martyr.

A copperplate print, published in England just 10 days after the assassination of Marat, shows Charlotte Corday, with her wrists linked by a chain, pleading her case before the Revolutionary Tribunal. Marat's body lies between Corday and the judges, who appear shocked and alarmed by her forthright declaration of murder.

Corday stares out from behind prison bars.

The guillotine was intended to provide a fast, humane method of execution.

Off with Her Head

Corday never shirked from her guilt, admitting, "I killed one man to save 100,000." Four days after she stabbed Marat, on July 17, she faced the guillotine. Immediately after her head fell, one of the executioner's assistants lifted her head from the basket and slapped it on the cheek. But even executions have a code of etiquette—and slapping a decapitated head was a breach of it. The assistant spent three months in prison as punishment.

Her body, after it had been autopsied to verify her virginity, was tossed into a trench next to Louis XVI.

Unleashing the Terror

Charlotte got only one thing wrong. Her bold act did not save France from further bloodshed. On the contrary, after her execution, it unleashed the period historians call "The Terror," in which thousands of people died on the guillotine.

The Death of Napoleon Bonaparte

(May 5, 1821)

Napoleon Bonaparte

In late winter 2002, workers bulldozing an abandoned army barracks outside Vilnius, Lithuania, stumbled upon a mass grave. The bodies had not been thrown in haphazardly; they were laid out in rows and layers with military neatness. And many of them were still covered by the shreds of dark-blue uniforms.

The dead men were the remains of one of the most successful armies in European history: the French *Grand Armée* of Napoleon Bonaparte. They had defeated larger armies again and again, winning France an empire that, at one time or another, stretched from Egypt to Sweden and from Portugal to Russia. And there, in the frozen Lithuanian earth, lay two thousand of them—none showing evidence of death through violence. All had died of a combination of starvation, disease, exhaustion, and, especially, bitter cold. They had followed the tremendous vision of their commander, only to be killed by an enemy even his strategic genius could not outmaneuver: the Eastern European winter.

At the height of his power, Napoleon had earned the nickname "the Monster"—so frightening was his reputation. Yet he died suddenly on his exile island of Saint Helena at the age of just 52. Little surprise then, that some still believe that he was murdered to prevent his escape to terrorize the world again.

The Rise of the Monster

Napoleon was born on Corsica in 1769, the son of a petty aristocrat. In his teens Napoleon attended the Parisian Military Academy. He rose rapidly through the ranks of the French army, joining the republicans during the revolution and becoming a national hero after he led the Revolutionary army to victory over the Austrian occupying forces in northern Italy.

He then invaded Egypt, seeking to strike from there at British territories in India, but he was defeated by Admiral Nelson at the Battle of the Nile and was forced to return to France. There he seized power over the flagging revolutionary government and made himself First Consul—dictator in all but name—in 1799. He had himself crowned emperor of France in 1804.

Conquest then followed conquest: by 1809 Napoleon ruled almost all of Western Europe.

Napoleon Bonaparte at the Battle of the Bridge of Arcole. During this battle with Austrian troops in 1796, Napoleon proved to be a brilliant tactician.

Napoleon's Empire at Its Height in 1811

- French Empire
- Conquered "Rebellious" States
- Conquered "Allied" States

KINGDOM OF SWEDEN

KINGDOM OF DENMARK AND NORWAY

North Sea

UNITED KINGDOM

Baltic Sea

PRUSSIA

DUCHY OF WARSAW

R U S S I A N   E M P I R E

English Channel

CONFEDERATION OF THE RHINE

ATLANTIC OCEAN

• Paris

FRANCE

F R E N C H   E M P I R E

Vienna •

• Budapest

AUSTRIAN EMPIRE

SWITZERLAND

ITALY

ILLYRIAN PROVINCES

O T T O M A N   E M P I R E

Black Sea

PORTUGAL

• Madrid

SPAIN

Rome •

Adriatic Sea

KINGDOM OF NAPLES

Aegean Sea

Mediterranean Sea

The Fall of the Monster

Then came the defeats, culminating with the retreat from Moscow to France, during which 570,000 of the 600,000 soldiers of the *Grand Armée* died in the snow.

The French Empire was finished. Napoleon's own generals persuaded him to surrender and hand himself over to the victorious allied nations. They sent him into exile on the Mediterranean island of Elba with a ceremonial guard of 2,000 men. But within a year he and his tiny army escaped and marched on Paris. The French collaborator armies sent to kill him instead joined him, and within weeks Napoleon was once again master of France.

Napoleon now asked his enemies for peace, but they would not trust him. So he attacked their forces in Belgium before they could invade France. He narrowly lost the Battle of Waterloo, defeated only by a combination of thick mud, the Duke of Wellington's generalship, and the doggedness of British, Dutch, and Prussian troops.

His new place of exile was the dreary Longwood House on Saint Helena—an island off the African coast in the mid-Atlantic so remote that even he could not escape from it.

Napoleon, after his abdication in Fontainebleau

Napoleon in exile on Saint Helena off the African coast. He moved to Longwood House on the island in December 1815. In letters to the governor, Napoleon complained that the house was ill maintained and damp. By May 1821 his health had deteriorated dramatically.

The Death of the Monster

So was Napoleon Bonaparte murdered to prevent a second escape and a third attempt at creating a lasting French empire?

When he died in 1821 the autopsy listed the cause of death as "stomach cancer." Certainly this sounded convincing at the time. Paintings of Napoleon famously showed him habitually holding his right hand under his waistcoat, cradling his stomach, because he suffered from stomach ulcers—a condition brought on by constant stress but later made worse by the terrible cold on the retreat from Moscow. Such severe ulcers are often a precursor to stomach cancer.

Hints of Murder

Napoleon had not spent his last days alone, and one man in particular remained close to the fallen dictator—his valet, Marchand, who recorded his master's agonized ending. This memoir, however, did not see print until 1955.

It was then that the conspiracy theories truly arose. Just how did Napoleon die? Was it the purported cancer—or something far more sinister?

Around the time of the memoir's publication, Swedish dentist Sten Forshufvud launched his own investigation. Studying Marchand's account of Napoleon's last days on Saint Helena and comparing its descriptions of his symptoms with various possible diagnoses, Forshufvud came to a striking conclusion. The symptoms were far more consistent with a slow, incremental poisoning by arsenic, than they were with stomach cancer. But how could he prove his hypothesis?

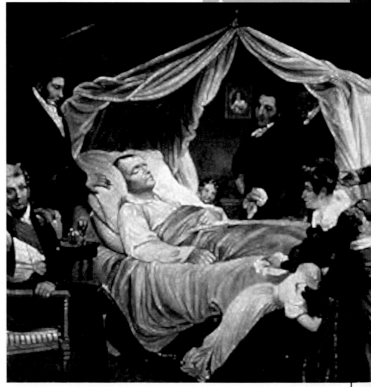

Death of Napoleon by Charles de Steuben. Francesco Antommarchi, Napoleon's physician, performed the autopsy. Antommarchi did not sign the official statement that declared the cause of death to be stomach cancer. Some felt that evidence of the emperor's well-known stomach ulcer gave the British a convenient explanation for his death, therefore dodging some of the criticism they received for the quality of the care they gave him during his exile on Saint Helena.

Arsenical Evidence

Forshufvud first tracked down hair samples, a feat made possible by the nineteenth-century practice of snipping the locks of famous people for keepsakes. He then persuaded Hamilton Smith of the University of Glasgow to use his new testing procedure for detecting arsenical poisoning on the hair samples. Initial tests did detect higher than normal levels of arsenic. Additional tests erased all doubt—at least for a small group of investigators. Napoleon had been the victim of murder by arsenic.

The debate raged for decades, with various characters named as possible suspects, until in 2007 new tests on samples of Napoleon's hair found significant amounts of the poison arsenic. Death by slow arsenic poisoning and death by stomach cancer are very similar, right down to the damage done to the stomach lining by both afflictions.

A Theory in Doubt

Despite the evidence, doubt still remained. Then, in 2008, further tests on hair samples of Napoleon's family and other, unrelated contemporaries, found similar amounts of trace mineral arsenic. The poison was used in many products in the eighteenth and nineteenth centuries, so natural environmental seepage seems a likely cause of the high levels of arsenic found in Napoleon's hair.

There are many who still debate these prosaic findings and insist that there is a solid case to accuse his British jailors or disgruntled retainers of assassination. But, because of the high levels of the poison in his environment, we will probably never be able to prove it.

Below, Napoleon's remains are hoisted onto a ship leaving Saint Helena.

The Assassination of Abraham Lincoln

(April 14, 1865)

John Wilkes Booth

The story of how a pro-Confederate actor, John Wilkes Booth, came to murder the 16th president of the United States is rather more complex than is generally thought. Most people know that Booth shot Lincoln while the president was watching a play at Ford's Theatre in Washington, D.C.—and many thus assume that Booth was just an opportunistic killer, perhaps even an actor in the play itself.

In fact the plot to kill Lincoln was multifaceted. Booth and his fellow conspirators planned multiple murders, ultimately aiming at creating total chaos in the federal government of the United States and perhaps thus giving the Confederacy time to reorganize and fight back from defeat in the Civil War.

Let's Steal the President

The original plan, hatched by John Wilkes Booth, was not actually to kill Lincoln but to kidnap him. Ransoming the president, the conspirators would demand the immediate release of thousands of Confederate prisoners of war. This, they hoped, might give the South enough men to fight back from the brink of defeat.

Booth planned to waylay and abduct Lincoln on a quiet stretch of road as the president returned from watching a play at the Campbell Military Hospital on the evening of March 17, 1865. But Lincoln changed his plans at the last minute and instead attended a political junket at the National Hotel. Booth was doubly furious because, ironically, the National was the hotel in which he himself was staying.

One of the last photographs shot in what was the last official photo session for President Abraham Lincoln. The session was long thought to have taken place on April 10, 1865, just days before his death. Recent research, however, indicates that the session took place earlier that year, on February 5.

A Change of Plan

On April 9, 1865, General Robert E. Lee of the Confederate States of America surrendered to General Ulysses Grant, commander of the Union army at Appomattox Court House: the Civil War was officially over. Two days later Lincoln gave a speech on the White House lawn mentioning, among other things, his belief that African American males should be allowed to vote. An incensed Booth was in the audience and was heard snarling: "That's the last speech he'll ever give."

But the planned assassination was not just an act of revenge; Booth still believed that the South could rise up again and win the war. He wrote in his diary after the announcement of the surrender: "Our cause being almost lost, something decisive and great must be done."

He and the conspirators from the botched kidnap attempt—Lewis Powell, George A. Atzerodt, David E. Herold, John Surratt, and a few others—planned now to kill not only Lincoln but also Vice President Andrew Johnson and Secretary of State William Seward. They also aimed to kill General Grant. This, they hoped, would plunge the government and military of the Union into chaos, allowing the still fleeing and uncaptured government of the Confederacy to re-form and restart the war.

It is evident, from the harebrained optimism of the plot, that none of the conspirators had witnessed the utter desolation of the Confederate states in the latter part of the war: the South had no chance of rising again, even if the entire government of the Union were to suddenly drop dead.

Three of the conspirators in the plot to incapacitate the government of the United States. Above left, George A. Atzerodt; above right, David E. Herold; and right, Lewis Powell. Powell also used the names Paine and Payne. Most of the conspirators were photographed in irons aboard the U.S. monitor *Saugus*, where they were taken after capture.

The Best-Laid Plans

Aiming to kill all four targets on the same night, Booth gave Lewis Powell the job of murdering Secretary of State Seward; George Atzerodt was to assassinate Vice President Johnson. Booth himself would kill the hated President Lincoln and General Grant.

During the afternoon of April 14, Booth went to see Mary Surratt, mother of coconspirator John Surratt, and asked her to bring a package to her tavern in Surrattsville, Maryland, where Booth had stashed guns and ammunition. She was to tell the innkeeper to make ready the weapons. By seven that night he met with the rest of the conspirators.

But the plan went wrong from the start. Powell managed to break into Seward's bedroom and stabbed wildly at him with a knife—but, in the dark, he only landed a few nonfatal cuts before

making his escape. Atzerodt—who had already tried to back out of the plot after the failed kidnapping—simply got drunk and did not even try to kill the vice president.

Meanwhile General Grant and his wife, Julia, were supposed to attend the showing of the comedy play *Our American Cousin* at Ford's Theatre, sitting in the same box with the president and his wife. But the habitually unsociable Grant ducked out of the invitation at the last minute. Thus Lincoln was the only target present when John Wilkes Booth stepped into the box at 10:15 PM on April 14, 1865.

Powell attempts to kill Seward.

Sic Semper Tyrannis!

The Lincolns joined their companions for the evening, Major Henry Rathbone and Clara Harris, a bit late but settled in comfortably, with the president and first lady in velvet-covered rocking chairs, to enjoy the evening's entertainment.

Booth entered the theatre at about 9:00 PM and, knowing the layout well from his stints performing there, made his way to a narrow hallway between Lincoln's box and the theatre's balcony. He chose his moment carefully, waiting for a line from the on-stage actor that he knew would draw a laugh from the crowd. Wrestling past the military officer on guard, Booth fired a one-shot pistol into the back of Lincoln's head. He then pulled a knife, stabbed the guard in the arm, and climbed up on the box's balcony rail. Booth had meant to make a dramatic leap to the stage but caught his foot in a flag hanging from the box and landed awkwardly,

Booth enters the presidential box and fires point blank at Lincoln.

breaking his ankle. Nevertheless the actor managed to shout, "*Sic semper tyrannis!*" (Latin for "Thus always to tyrants!" and the state motto of rebel Virginia) before hobbling off, waving the bloody knife over his head. Although several theatergoers gave chase, Booth escaped through the back door of the theatre. He managed to throw himself onto his horse and rode out toward Navy Yard Bridge to meet up with Herold and Powell.

A Hopeless Effort

The cries of alarm from the presidential box drew the attention of Charles Leale, a young army surgeon. He rushed to help out but found the door to the box jammed—Booth had cleverly notched a dent in the door earlier in the day and had managed to jab a wooden brace against it as he entered the box to kill Lincoln. Although blood was gushing from his upper left arm, Rathbone, inside the box, managed to free the brace, allowing Leale to enter. The president was slumped forward in his chair, held up by a sobbing Mary. By the time Leale had lowered Lincoln to the floor, another doctor had joined him. They worked feverishly, but each of them knew that their efforts were hopeless.

Yet another doctor had joined them, and the three of them, along with some soldiers in attendance, carefully carried the president out of the theatre and across the street to William Petersen's boarding house. There began the vigil that would last until 7:22 AM the next day.

Shocked but resigned to the worst, officers and doctors surround President Lincoln as he lies on his deathbed.

Useless

Abraham Lincoln was the first U.S. president to die by assassination, but his death led to no chaos in the government. Vice President Andrew Johnson was simply sworn in as the 17th president of the United States.

Lewis Powell and George Atzerodt were quickly caught, tried, and hanged. Would-be presidential kidnapper John Surratt escaped to Europe but was later extradited to the United States. He was acquitted of direct involvement in the assassination and lived a long life—unlike his unfortunate mother, Mary, who was hanged for preparing the weapons used by the plotters.

Union soldiers cornered John Wilkes Booth and his guide, David Herold, in a barn in Maryland, 12 days after the assassination. Herold surrendered—and was later hanged—but Booth held out, even after the barn was set on fire. A sniper shot him in the neck, and he died two hours later.

Paralyzed from the neck down and in great pain, Booth's last words were accurate: "Useless . . . Useless . . ."

A crowd gathers to witness the executions of Mary Surratt, Lewis Powell, David Herold, and George Atzerodt on July 7, 1865.

The thick black line shows the route of the train bearing Lincoln's casket as it made its 1,700-mile (2,700 km) journey from Washington to Springfield, Illinois. Millions of people lined the route to view his body and funeral train.

Millions of people came to Lincoln's funeral procession in Washington, D.C., on April 19, 1865.

Lincoln was buried in the Oak Ridge Cemetery in Springfield on May 4, 1865.

An Act of Kindness

Abraham Lincoln's last official act as president was to commute the death sentence on George Vaughn, a convicted Confederate spy. The signing of all the necessary papers, for this act of humane generosity, made Lincoln a little late for the play at Ford's Theatre.

MAP
SHOWING THE
Birthplace and Course of Life
OF
ABRAHAM LINCOLN,
ALSO OF HIS
GREAT FUNERAL CORTEGE.
Prepared expressly to accompany
THE LIFE OF LINCOLN
AND
History of the National Lincoln Monument,
BY JOHN CARROLL POWER.

Explanation.—The smaller line, with the white line in the centre, shows the course from his birthplace to the Capital of the Nation. The heavy dark line is the route traveled by the funeral train. The smaller line is merged into the larger where both pass over the same route.

RAND, McNALLY & CO., PRINTERS AND ENGRAVERS, CHICAGO.

The Assassination of Archduke Franz Ferdinand

(June 28, 1914)

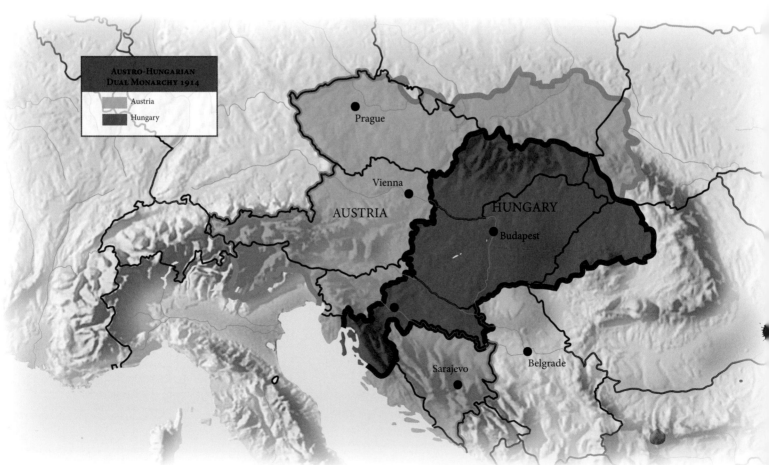

Gavrilo Princip

It was described as "the shot that rang around the world": a single act of terrorism that, it is generally believed, catapulted the planet into its first world war. The 1914 murder of Archduke Franz Ferdinand certainly shocked the planet, much as the murder of President John F. Kennedy did in 1963. It also sparked a diplomatic battle that quickly collapsed into total war. But was the shot fired by the young Yugoslav nationalist, Gavrilo Princip, really the cause of millions of deaths? Most modern historians reject such a simplistic view—one equivalent to blaming the cow that kicked over a lamp in Patrick O'Leary's barn for the destruction caused by the subsequent Great Chicago Fire.

AUSTRO-HUNGARIAN DUAL MONARCHY 1914

Austria

Hungary

Prague

Vienna

AUSTRIA

HUNGARY

Budapest

Sarajevo

Belgrade

The Balkan Tinderbox

By the beginning of the twentieth century, the small eastern European states of Serbia and Bosnia and Herzegovina had spent much of the previous 50 years as political footballs between the three hulking empires of Austria-Hungary, the Turkish Ottomans, and Tsarist Russia. Indeed the Balkan region as a whole was a buffer zone between these menacing states, with Austria holding most of the area in virtual serfdom, and the Ottomans and Tsarist Russia making expansionist territorial claims on those same regions.

To add to the dangerous mix, the ruling class of all three empires were reactionary and corrupt—heavily reliant on draconian laws and military force to maintain control over their territory. But Europe was no longer in the Middle Ages; the people that the aristocrats of all three empires derisively dismissed as "peasants" were becoming increasingly educated and, as a direct result, increasingly aware of just how subjugated and oppressed they were.

One such "peasant" was Gavrilo Princip. He was the son of a rural postman who, as a small child, had been sent to live in Zagreb with his older brother because his parents couldn't earn enough to feed him. Six of Gavrilo's nine siblings had not survived past infancy—a common death toll among poor families in the Austro-Hungarian Empire.

Three emperors of Europe in 1914, from the left: Nicholas II of Russia, Wilhelm II of Prussia, and Franz Joseph I of Austria-Hungary. Europeans before the war were all related to one another. Most of them had grown up in unimaginable luxury, sure that their way of life was secure.

Too Small and Weak

Princip's elder brother had enough money to put him through high school, but when Gavrilo was 17, in 1912, he was expelled over his involvement in a protest against Sarajevo authorities. Seeing how little the rotting Austrian Empire did for them, it was only natural that many young Serbs, Croats, and Muslim Bosnians hoped that self-determination might better their lot, but all such political activity was strongly suppressed by the imperial authorities.

He moved to Belgrade to try to enter another college but was rejected. He then tried to join a guerrilla combat unit that was fighting Ottoman expansion into Macedonia, but they too rejected Princip—this time because poor nutrition as a young child had meant that he grew up to be "small and weak." It seems likely that his involvement in the violent arm of the Serb nationalist movement was a reaction to all this endless rejection. Gavrilo wanted to prove to the world, and especially to his fellow activists, that he wasn't just a worthless weakling.

A Good Man Expecting to Die

By comparison to the impoverished and unwanted Princip, Archduke Franz Ferdinand—the heir presumptive to the throne of the Austro-Hungarian Empire—had been brought up in a life of unimaginable luxury. Born in 1863 he had undergone a strict education but thereafter was free to indulge in such eccentric hobbies as jousting—as if he were a medieval lordling.

Yet the sad irony is that the archduke was actually a forward-looking, humane, and liberal man. He saw that political self-determination must be the future for many of the regions of his empire, and argued vigorously with the backward-looking policy makers who believed that all Austria needed was more crushing laws, more soldiers, and more killing of troublemakers.

But if he hoped that when he inherited the Austrian throne he might be able to roll back centuries of misgovernment, the archduke was also realistic enough to see the dangers of the growing situation. He told a friend in early 1914: "The bullet that will kill me is already on its way."

The Morganatic Wife

In 1895 the archduke had met Countess Sophie Chotek and fallen in love. Although she was an aristocrat, she was not a member of one of the reigning or formerly reigning dynasties of Europe and therefore was an unsuitable mate for the heir to the imperial throne. Franz Ferdinand would have no other wife, though. Eventually his uncle, Emperor Franz Joseph, agreed that the pair could enter into a morganatic marriage.

Their children would have no succession rights to the throne. Sophie herself would not share her husband's rank, title, precedence, or privileges. And ironically, she would not normally appear in public beside him.

The agreement Franz Ferdinand made with his uncle Emperor Franz Joseph meant that his wife, Sophie, rarely appeared at his side for public events. The joint appearance in Sarajevo was a rare occurrence.

Mistakes on Both Sides

The archduke and Sophie were invited to witness a military parade in Sarajevo on June 28, 1914. But by going he was being uncharacteristically tactless—this was the date of a Serbian nationalist holiday. To die-hard nationalists like Gavrilo Princip, the Austrian parade and the archduke's presence seemed like calculated insults.

There were six primary conspirators who plotted the killing of Archduke Franz Ferdinand, all members of Young Bosnia, an offshoot of the Black Hand, a nationalist movement that favored a union between Bosnia and Herzegovina and Serbia. Serbs, Croats, and Muslim Bosnians made up the Young Bosnia group, which committed itself to the independence of the South Slavic peoples of Austria-Hungary. Earlier that morning one of the Young Bosnia members, Nedeljko Cabrinovic, threw a bomb at the open, horse-drawn carriage in which the archduke and his wife were riding. They both escaped unharmed, although several onlookers were injured in the blast. The archduke and wife visited all of the injured at the hospital before they began to make their way back to the palace.

The royal couple was transferred to a car—also open topped—but the driver took a wrong turn in the thronging, cheering crowds. As he stopped and tried to reverse, Princip stepped up to the car, raised a Browning pistol, and fired two shots from a distance of just a few feet. Sophie was hit in the stomach and then Franz in the neck. Princip then tried to shoot himself, but a passerby stopped him. The police then quickly stepped in and took him in alive.

After firing seven shots into the royals' car, Princip tried to shoot himself. But police captured Princip, shown above second to right, before he managed to commit suicide.

The Quick-Burning Fuse

Although their aides tried to save them, both Franz Ferdinand and Sophie died within minutes. Princip and his fellow student conspirators were thrown in jail. But how did the assassination lead to war?

The Austrian government demanded the extradition to Vienna of certain Serbian officials who they suspected of helping Young Bosnia plan the attack. The Serbs, despite their underdog status, refused. So Austria declared war on its own province. Russia mobilized its armies to help Serbia, and Austria reacted by declaring war on Russia. Germany and Turkey supported their ally Austria, and Britain and France weighed in for Russia. By the end of the war more than 20 million people had died—including Gavrilo Princip, who died of a combination of tuberculosis and malnutrition in a Bosnian jail in 1918.

But it wasn't Gavrilo Princip's nationalism or the archduke's death that started the war: it was the decades of unrestrained military expansion within the empires of Europe, coupled with the shortsighted and reactionary policies of the imperial governments.

Grim artifacts from the assassination: the 1911 Gräf & Stift touring car in which the archduke and his wife were riding at the time of their assassination, below, and right, Franz Ferdinand's bloodstained uniform can be seen at the Military History Museum in Vienna, Austria.

No Regrets

Gavrilo Princip never meant his actions to start a war. In his own words: "I am the son of peasants and I know what is happening in the villages. That is why I wanted to take revenge, and I regret nothing."

Shoko Asahara

Shoko Asahara and the Aum Shinrikyo
(March 20, 1995)

On March 20, 1995, soon after seven in the morning, commuters on the Tokyo subway began to experience a tickling in the throat and soreness in the eyes and nose; soon they smelled a stench like a mixture of mustard and burning rubber. Within minutes dozens of people were choking or falling to the ground.

It was happening all over the Tokyo underground system. No one had any idea what was causing it. Fleets of ambulances ferried gasping or unconscious passengers to hospitals—the number of injuries reached 5,500. Many seemed to be temporarily paralyzed, and a dozen would die. Yet it was not until mid-morning that a military doctor made a cautious and incredible diagnosis: the victims were suffering from poisoning by a nerve gas called sarin, once used by the Nazis in their death camps.

Suspicious Activities

A national police investigation soon turned up a likely suspect: an immensely wealthy religious cult known as *Aum Shinrikyo*, or "Aum Supreme Truth," led by a 40-year-old guru who called himself Shoko Asahara.

During the previous six months, police had received dozens of phone calls accusing the cult of fraud, abduction, brutality, and murder. Now Aum Shinrikyo was the chief suspect in the nerve gas attack. In spite of his protest—"We carry out our religious activities on the basis of Buddhist doctrines, such as no killing"—police raided Asahara's headquarters on the slopes of Mount Fuji. Most of the cultists had left, taking crates of documents, but the police found a huge stockpile of chemicals like sodium cyanide and peptone for cultivating bacteria. One of the chief suspects was a young cultist called Yoshihiro Inoue, the guru's intelligence chief, who was caught driving a car that contained chemicals for manufacturing high explosives.

On May 16 there was another police raid on the Mount Fuji headquarters; this time they found a secret room, inside which a large, bearded figure sat cross-legged on the floor in the meditation posture. He told the police imperiously, "I am the guru. Don't touch me. I don't even allow my disciples to touch me."

Kasumigaseki Station was one of the many stations affected during the sarin nerve gas attacks on the Tokyo subway system. The attacks took place just at rush hour, killing 12 commuters and sickening 5,000 more.

The Guru's Progress

Asahara, whose real name was Chizuo Matsumoto, had been born blind in one eye and partially blind in the other. He was raised in a poor home, but had been a brilliant pupil at school. He thought of becoming a radical politician, like Mao Zedong, then began to meditate and claimed that one day he felt the *kundalini* (the sacred energy that electrifies and enlightens the soul) mounting his spine.

Asahara founded a yoga school, which became so profitable that he opened several more. Then he went to the Himalayas to meditate and even had himself photographed with the Dalai Lama. There in the Himalayas Asahara claims he experienced enlightenment and achieved psychic powers.

He changed the name of his yoga school to Aum Supreme Truth (*Aum* is a Sanskrit syllable pronounced during meditation). Teaching a mixture of Buddhism, Christianity, and Hinduism, Asahara was soon surrounded by hundreds of followers. Because he assured them that large cash donations would hasten their spiritual enlightenment, he was soon a very wealthy man.

Make War, Not Love

In 1993 Asahara instructed his chief engineer, Kiyohide Hayakawa, to try to buy an atomic bomb. In fact, during 1994, Hayakawa made eight trips to Russia to try and buy a nuclear warhead.

When Hayakawa failed, Asahara decided to buy land in Australia. There cult members began testing nerve gas on sheep whose skeletons were later found by police.

Hayakawa, shown right, was sentenced to death for his role in two murders and for building a sarin nerve gas factory

No One Accepts Responsibility

But what possible point could there be to gassing hundreds of people in the Tokyo subway system?

Ashara's trial failed to enlighten the public. Placed on the stand in 1996, he refused to enter a plea of either guilty or not guilty. For almost nine years, as the trial ground along, the ex-guru flatly refused to answer questions with anything but incomprehensible mutterings. In February 2004 he was sentenced to death on multiple counts of murder and attempted murder. Twelve of his followers were also sentenced to execution.

All appealed their death sentences, knowing that given the slowness of the Japanese justice system, they might avoid execution for many years, even if their appeals were ultimately unsuccessful.

So, why did they do it? The followers, predictably, say that they were acting on the guru's orders and were not privy to his divine plan. Asahara, through his lawyer, claims the followers cooked up the whole scheme themselves, without his knowledge. He says that he has no idea why they tried to murder so many people.

A wanted poster in Japan listing three of the perpetrators of the Sarin gas attack on the Tokyo subway. From left, Makoto Hirata, Katsuya Takahashi, and Naoko Kikuchi.

Quake-Inducing Terror

Rumors abound about other "doomsday weapons" that Aum Shinrikyo was supposed to be experimenting with: one was even said to be an "earthquake inducer"—a terrifying thought in quake-prone Japan.

Monsters of Evil

The First Serial Killer

(1404-1440)

Who was the first serial killer? The answer to that question is a matter of historical debate. The term *serial killer* itself is, of course, a twentieth-century coinage, but it describes a certain psychological mind-set—an addiction to killing—that is all too common throughout the pages of history.

The earliest and most often mentioned name that fits the serial killer mold is that of a fifteenth-century French aristocrat. He was a warrior for his people's freedom; he was a famously handsome man of exquisite taste; he was a gifted courtier and diplomat; he was comrade-in-arms to a famously virtuous woman who would later be canonized as a saint. And he was probably one of the most monstrous serial killers ever known . . .

Gilles de Rais

Bluebeard

Gilles de Rais was born in 1404, the eldest son of the baron of Rais. France, at the time of Gilles's birth, had already suffered greatly in what was later to be called the Hundred Years' War with England, but worse was to come.

Gilles was orphaned when he was 11 and was raised by his maternal grandfather. We know that Gilles's grandfather found it difficult to marry him off when the time came. This was not because he was in any way ugly—not that appearance mattered much in aristocratic matchmaking. He was actually quite striking, sporting a dapper beard so black that people swore that in certain lights it looked blueish. This earned Gilles the nickname "Bluebeard."

A nineteenth-century illustration of the fairy tale *Bluebeard*. Although Gilles de Rais is a likely source for the tale, none of de Rais's victims were his fiancés or his wife.

A Stolen Bride

Gilles's marital misfortunes were probably a matter of bad luck. Two potential brides died before marriage alliances could be cemented, but sudden death was not uncommon in the disease-ridden Europe of that time. Certainly there is no suspicion that the then teenaged Gilles had anything to do with the deaths. A third marriage attempt proved more fortunate.

In 1420 de Rais married a very wealthy heiress, Catherine de Thouars, and so became one of the richest men in Europe. The courtship did not go entirely smoothly—Catherine had to be kidnapped at one point in order to get the deal settled. France was in chaos at that time—with English armies conquering or laying waste to large swathes of the north—so the bandit matchmaking tactics of Gilles's grandfather were probably seen as in step with the times.

The Namesake

It may be that the fairy tale *Bluebeard*—in which the eponymous villain marries repeatedly, only to murder his new wives the morning after the honeymoon—is the result of a mixing up of Gilles de Rais's story, the dying fiancés, his striking nickname, and his later murders.

Choosing the Losing Side

We first see Gilles acting on his own account when he arranged the release of the captured John VI, Duke of Brittany. He did this with such subtle aplomb that the Breton parliament awarded the young baron with a sizable financial reward, thus making him even richer. We can also see from this that, even in his early 20s, Gilles was evidently a smooth talker and a diplomatic courtier. We next hear of him attending the court of the Dauphin Charles, the heir to the French throne.

Gilles was taking an enormous chance by siding with Charles. The Dauphin was a singularly ineffectual man—he was unable to get the military and political backing to have himself crowned king of France. In the 1420s the likeliest outcome seemed to be England's total conquest of France.

Charles VII of France. The heir to the French throne found a friend in Gilles de Rais, who chose to fight the British alongside the Dauphin.

The Girl from Lorraine

Something extraordinary then happened. In 1428 Joan of Arc (*Jeanne d'Arc* in French), a young woman from the French province of Lorraine, heard voices in her head that she believed to be the messengers of God speaking to her. The voices told Joan to go to the Dauphin and declare that Heaven was on his side. Charles, bankrupt and terrified, was willing to try anything, so he sent Joan to lead his armies.

With Joan at their head they started a comeback that first recaptured the city of Orléans and eventually hurled the English out of France completely. Joan did not live to see this: she was captured by the Burgundians, sold to the English, and then burned as a heretic by the Catholic Church in 1431.

Not surprisingly, much has been made of the relationship between Gilles de Rais and Joan of Arc: the savage monster side by side with the saintly virgin. Much of this seems to have been wishful thinking by later chroniclers. De Rais certainly knew Joan and probably fought alongside her in some battles, but he was not her bodyguard, as some have claimed, or even one of her key supporters.

Joan of Arc, also known as the Maid of Orléans, is credited with inspiring the French army to win their long war with England.

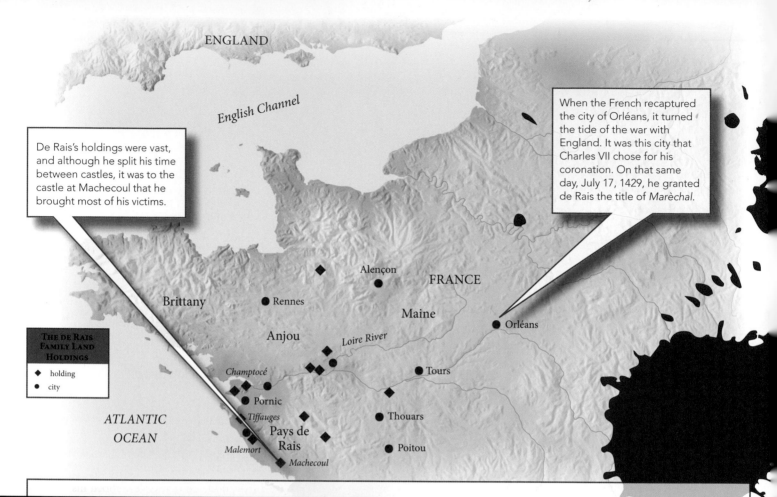

ENGLAND

English Channel

De Rais's holdings were vast, and although he split his time between castles, it was to the castle at Machecoul that he brought most of his victims.

When the French recaptured the city of Orléans, it turned the tide of the war with England. It was this city that Charles VII chose for his coronation. On that same day, July 17, 1429, he granted de Rais the title of *Marèchal*.

FRANCE

Alençon

Brittany

● Rennes

Maine

Anjou

Loire River

● Orléans

The de Rais Family Land Holdings

◆ holding
● city

Champtocé

● Tours

◆

◆ Pornic

Tiffauges

ATLANTIC OCEAN

Pays de Rais

● Thouars

Malemort

◆ *Machecoul*

● Poitou

The Spendthrift

De Rais's military title, *Marèchal*, was largely an honorary designation, bestowed upon him in 1429 by the former Dauphin—now King Charles VII. It was more a reward for Gilles's financial loans than for his martial prowess. After the new king's coronation in Orléans, and despite the fact that the war was still raging, de Rais retired to his comfortable estates, gadding between castles at Machecoul, Malemort, Champtocé, Tiffauges, and his other holdings.

He lived extravagantly, keeping a bodyguard of 200 knights, a private chapel, and one of the finest manuscript libraries in Europe. But soon these huge expenditures ate up his vast fortune.

Gilles was facing bankruptcy, so he turned to alchemy to mend his fortunes. Like many others of the time, he was seeking the fabled Philosopher's Stone, which could supposedly turn all base metals to pure gold. In 1439 Gilles employed a defrocked priest, Francesco Prelati of Florence. It was probably Prelati who turned Gilles to the practice of black magic and invocations of the Devil, using the blood of young children.

An alchemist in his laboratory. Gilles, bleeding money because of his lavish lifestyle, became obsessed with finding the formula that would turn base metals into precious gold.

Killing for the Devil of It

Over the next six years de Rais is said to have used his position as a baron to secretly kidnap dozens, perhaps hundreds, of peasant children, all of whom he tortured and killed. He was certainly a serial killer: the sheer numbers of children involved, and the hideously cruel methods used to murder them, do not point to a man whose only interest was the magical production of gold.

De Rais's downfall began with what would have been, to a baron, a minor misdemeanor. He sold his estate at Malemort to the treasurer of Brittany, Geoffroi le Ferron, but then refused admission to Geoffroi's brother, Jean le Ferron. When Jean insisted on his family's rights, de Rais had him beaten and then imprisoned. But Jean le Ferron was a priest, and Bishop Malestroit seized on this pretext to try to have Gilles declared a heretic.

Only the ruins of Gilles de Rais's castle at Tiffauges still stand, perched on a strategic hilltop position. These days re-creations of medieval weapons and alchemy equipment are on display inside the castle walls.

Trial by Torture

Preliminary hearings began on September 28, 1440, and Gilles's accusers were so certain of finding him guilty that the authorities actually disposed of some of his lands before the trial even began. De Rais was charged with the abuse of a priest, conjuring demons, and sexual perversion involving children. The most shocking of the charges was "spurning the natural way of copulation." Gilles had committed sodomy with young boys and girls . . . and his victims were sometimes alive, sometimes dead, and sometimes even in their death throes when he mounted them.

The formal trial opened on October 15, 1440. The dismembered, rotting bodies of about 50 children that had, it was said, been found in an abandoned tower at de Rais's estate at Machecoul served as the key evidence. Gilles was himself tortured on October 19, as were his servants and four alleged accomplices.

Judicial torture as part of the examination process, it should be noted, was then so common as to be a virtual formality in all capital trials. Many, for example, had been shocked at Joan of Arc's trial when she was *not* tortured, but was merely intimidated by being "shown the instruments [of torture]."

Execution by Rope and Fire

One servant, under extreme duress, declared that Gilles rubbed his penis against the thighs and bellies of children and, after achieving orgasm, took pleasure in seeing their heads cut off or in decapitating them himself. It was also alleged that he took great pleasure in watching the death throes of children, sometimes sitting on their chests while they were dying. It was said that, on one occasion, de Rais tortured and killed one boy in front of his brother, and then did the same to the remaining child.

His own torture apparently had less effect on Gilles than the threat of excommunication: the latter made him break down completely and confess everything. On October 26, 1440, de Rais was hanged, using a knot that garroted him slowly while his feet dangled and scorched in a blazing fire—a fate he shared with two of his associates. No final figure was ever arrived at for the number of children Gilles de Rais tortured and murdered: estimates ranged between 80 and 200.

Child killer de Rais met as gruesome a fate as his victims. After being tortured and threatened into a confession, he was hanged and burned to death.

Vlad Dracula

Vlad the Impaler

(1431–1477)

The Wallachian prince Vlad Dracula can boast of a reputation as one of the worst sadists in world history. Some chroniclers estimate that in his brief reign—a mere six years—he killed 100,000 people, often by his favorite method of execution: impalement via the anus or vagina on a sharp pole.

Born in 1431 in the citadel town of Sighisoara, Transylvania, Vlad was the son of Vlad II Dracul, who received his last name when he entered the Order of the Dragon. *Dracul*, in the Romanian language means "dragon," although it is also sometimes translated as "devil." The surname Dracula therefore means "son of the dragon" or "son of the devil." Vlad Dracula is also known as Vlad Tepes, Romanian for "Vlad the Impaler."

A Well of Hatred

Vlad's grandfather, Mircea the Elder, has been described as a kind of Romanian Charlemagne; Vlad's father was one of Mircea's bastard sons, and he was placed on the throne of Wallachia (southern Romania) in 1436 with the aid of the Hungarians. But Vlad II had a problem: he had to remain equally friendly with two powerful neighbors—Hungary and the Ottoman Empire. This was no easy task. He lost his throne to the Hungarians in 1442 and regained it with the aid of the Turks the following spring.

Two years later, to gain the trust of the Turkish sultan Murad, Vlad II sent his two younger sons, Vlad and Radu, as hostages to the Ottoman Empire. Prince Vlad was convinced that he had condemned them to death; in fact, the Turks allowed them to live, largely because Sultan Murad had conceived lustful designs on Radu. Radu, known as Radu the Handsome, resisted strenuously at first, holding the sultan at bay with a dagger. But he finally gave way and became Murad's "protégé." Vlad remained a difficult prisoner; his harsh treatment hardened his character, making him vengeful.

Immortality of a Sort

In 1897, 410 years after his death, Vlad achieved a kind of dubious immortality as the namesake of the vampiric villain in Bram Stoker's famous novel *Dracula*.

Vlad's grandfather, Mircea the Elder, sat on the throne of Wallachia from 1386 to 1418. Romanian historians consider Mircea one of the most important rulers of Wallachia, often referring to him as Mircea the Great.

Chindia Tower, built by Vlad, is a symbol of Tirgoviste, Romania, once the capital city of the Wallachian princes.

The Prince

While Radu and Vlad remained in Turkish custody, the Hungarians attacked Vlad II again. Betrayed by his boyars (noblemen) he was defeated near Tirgoviste. His eldest and favorite son, Mircea, was buried alive. Vlad II himself was hunted down and killed. When the Turkish sultan heard that the Hungarians had killed their father, he gave the two boys their liberty. Meanwhile the Hungarian leader Janos Hunyadi had seized Vlad's throne. But in new battles against the Turks, Hunyadi was defeated, and the 17-year-old Vlad entered Tirgoviste and appointed himself prince—Vlad III of Wallachia.

Vlad's first taste of power lasted less than two months. After losing a battle to Vladislav II, who also claimed the throne of Wallachia, Vlad fled. For the next eight years, he was a virtual wanderer. In 1456 he made a second bid for the throne of Tirgoviste; this time his small army defeated Vladislav, and for the second time Vlad held the throne of Wallachia.

During the next six years he perpetrated the horrors that earned him the sobriquet "the Impaler."

Vlad the Puritan

His first act as ruler was to rebuild the ancient Poenari Castle on the River Arges, 20 miles north of Tirgoviste; after years of insecurity, he wanted an impregnable stronghold.

After his years in the Ottoman Empire, where Muslim women kept their faces covered, he was probably shocked to find that Christian women allowed themselves far more freedom. In reaction he announced that unfaithful wives were to have their sexual organs cut out, and then they were to be skinned alive and exposed in a public square. Girls who lost their virginity before marriage were to meet the same fate. Lesser sexual offences were punished by cutting off a nipple.

A chronicler describes how, when one of Vlad's mistresses declared that she was pregnant, he had her examined by a doctor, who found it to be untrue. Vlad felt that her lie had exposed him to ridicule and ordered her to be cut open from the vagina to the breasts. He then looked at the dying woman's exposed womb and remarked, "Now everyone can see where I have been."

Vlad built his Poenari Castle high on a mountaintop above the city of Tirgoviste. To reach Vlad's fortress, visitors must climb 1,500 steps.

Banquet Among the Corpses

In 1459 Vlad decided to invade neighboring Transylvania. His first objective was the city of Brasov. Most of its inhabitants met their fates impaled on a hill near the church of Saint Bartholomew. After the impalements Vlad set up tables and held a banquet among the corpses. One boyar found the smell of blood and entrails too much for him and held his nose; Vlad immediately sent for a particularly long pole and had him impaled. He then invaded Sibiu, a town that had offered him refuge in his early years of wandering, and slaughtered 10,000 of his former fellow citizens. His Transylvania campaign continued into the following year. Two more towns that had defied him—Fagaras and Amlas—were burned, and more than 20,000 of the citizens impaled. Many surrounding areas were so completely destroyed that they simply vanished off the map. Vlad returned to Tirgoviste well satisfied with his triumphal campaign.

The First Blow

Vlad knew that sooner or later he would have to wage war against the Turks. Although they had helped him regain his throne in 1456, they demanded a tribute of 10,000 gold pieces a year and 500 children for their army. Vlad signaled his intention when invited to the Danube port of Giurgiu to meet the governor, Hamza Pasha. Certain that this was a trap, he approached the town with an army of 20,000 men—dense forests allowed them to make their approach unseen.

Vlad's army overwhelmed the garrison and forcibly marched the enemy soldiers back to Tirgoviste. Vlad ordered that the Turks be executed by impalement in a meadow outside the town. Hamza Pasha met his fate impaled upside down on a stake.

A woodcut from Vlad's time depicts him enjoying the sight of his victims' suffering from his favorite method of execution—impalement on a stake.

War Against the Turks

As an old hand at warfare, Vlad understood the importance of striking the first blow. In winter 1461 his army burned down the city of Giurgiu and massacred its inhabitants. He counted 23,809 heads, noses, and ears. He then sent off messages to the Pope and to King Mathias of Hungary for help, but his reputation was so black, they ignored him. By the following spring, he had

recognized that his only hope was to fight on alone. He advanced along the Danube (which divides Wallachia from Bulgaria), and then into Bulgaria, where many peasants, who were tired of Turkish oppression, joined him. But the need to besiege Turkish forts slowed him down. And in April Mohammed II set out from Byzantium to meet him.

Vlad was forced to retreat into Wallachia, leaving scorched earth behind him. By mid-June 1462 the Turkish sultan was approaching Tirgoviste. But on the way, in a narrow gorge, Mohammed came upon a forest of stakes, 20,000 of them, with rotting corpses impaled on them, many of them Turks.

When Mohammed II advanced into Tirgoviste the next day, he found a city reduced to burning ruins, and roads lined with the macabre sight of bodies impaled on stakes. Mohammed is said to have groaned: "What can one do against a man like this?" And because plague had appeared in his army, he decided to turn home. But he appointed Vlad's brother Radu to continue the fight. Radu was now the prince of Tirgoviste.

Vlad and his soldiers mount a daring night attack against the Turks.

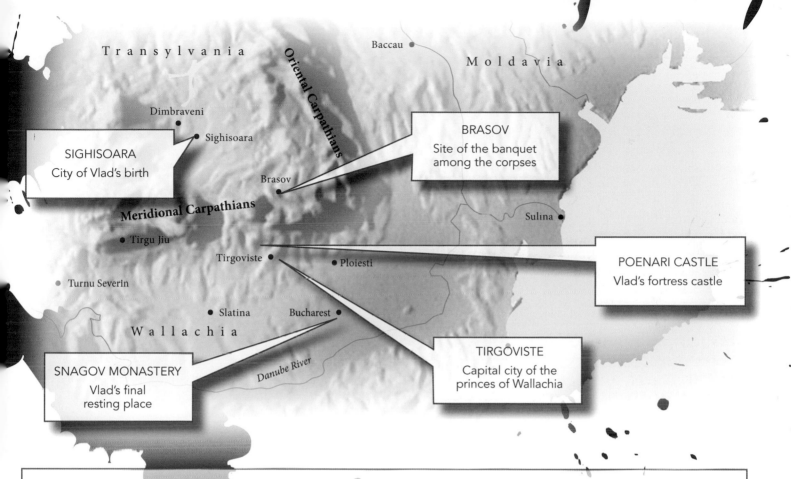

Map labels:

T r a n s y l v a n i a

Oriental Carpathians

Baccau

M o l d a v i a

Dimbraveni

Sighisoara

SIGHISOARA
City of Vlad's birth

BRASOV
Site of the banquet
among the corpses

Brasov

Meridional Carpathians

Sulina

Tirgu Jiu

Tirgoviste

Ploiesti

POENARI CASTLE
Vlad's fortress castle

Turnu Severin

Slatina

Bucharest

W a l l a c h i a

SNAGOV MONASTERY
Vlad's final
resting place

Danube River

TIRGOVISTE
Capital city of the
princes of Wallachia

Vlad in Decline

Vlad retreated to his stronghold above the Arges River. His wife is said to have committed suicide by throwing herself from the battlements into the river. Vlad himself escaped over the Fagaras Mountains. The next morning, from the crest, they were able to look down on the Turkish assault on Poenari Castle.

His aim was to reach King Mathias of Hungary, whose forces were encamped at Brasov. But Mathias received him coolly, and within weeks, Vlad had been taken prisoner.

Vlad spent 12 of the remaining 14 years of his life in Hungary, first in Buda, then Visegrad, 20 miles away. His guards kept him supplied with small animals—birds, mice, rats, and toads—that he could torture or impale. (He is said to have filled his cell with their skewered corpses.) Then, after only 4 years, Mathias not only decided to free him but also allow him to marry one of his own relatives. In order to do this, Vlad was made to renounce his Orthodox faith and become a Roman Catholic; he apparently did this without misgivings. He fathered two children and was given a house in Pesth.

In summer 1476 he set out to retake Wallachia, together with Hungarian armies led by Stephen Báthory and a Moldavian army led by his cousin Stephen. On November 8 he reentered Tirgoviste; he captured Bucharest a week later.

In January 1477 the Turks surprised Vlad's small army of about 4,000 near Bucharest, and Vlad himself was killed in battle. A Slavic narrative claims that his own men assassinated him, but this is unconfirmed. We only know that his head reached Byzantium in February 1477, where it was publicly displayed. Those who went to gaze on the "monster" must have been surprised to see an ordinary looking man with a full mouth under a huge moustache. The headless body had been buried in an unmarked grave in the monastery of Snagov, on an island in a lake near Bucharest.

Insignia of
the Order
of the Dragon

Ivan IV

Ivan the Terrible
(1530-1584)

Ivan IV, the grandson of Prince Ivan the Great (1440–1505), was born in 1530; his father, Vassili III, died when he was three. His mother—who became regent—spoiled and pampered the young Ivan. When she died (probably poisoned), the 7-year-old Ivan quite suddenly found himself ignored and treated with contempt. A council of boyars—Russian nobles—took over the government, chief among whom were the Shuiskys.

Ivan had always been rather a brutal child. One of his favorite games was "splattering dogs," dropping them from the top of a high tower into the courtyard far below. Now neglect and disdain hardened him into a bully and a sadist, who inflicted pain on anyone too weak to fight back.

The First Tsar

In the Christmas of 1543, when he was 13, Ivan summoned the boyars before him and delivered a lecture. He disdainfully pointed out that they were misruling Russia and they were utterly corrupt. But this time, he said, only one of them would be punished. He turned and pointed his finger at Prince Andrew Shuisky. Ivan then ordered the hunting dogs set on him; the dogs tore Shuisky to pieces.

At 17 he decided to have himself crowned, and instead of calling himself "prince," he chose the title "tsar," derived from *caesar*, signifying that he was absolute ruler.

Ivan the Awesome
Known as Ivan Grozny in Russia, Ivan IV Vasilyevich has long been known as Ivan the Terrible in the English-speaking world. Modern English, however, doesn't quite capture the original meaning of the word *terrible*, which now connotes "bad" or "evil." A better translation of its intended meaning? "Ivan the Awesome."

Ivan sits by the deathbed of his first wife, Anastasia Romanova.

Choosing a Wife

Ivan loved reading, but when his eyes tired he pursued sexual pleasures, treating the wives and daughters of the merchants as his private harem. But when it came time to wed, he summoned 2,000 girls from all over Russia. Midwives examined all of them; his bride had to be a virgin. He settled on Anastasia Romanova, a tall, striking girl of gentle disposition; they were married on February 3, 1547.

For the next 13 years Ivan was an admirable tsar, surrounding himself with good counselors. It all ended in 1560, with the death of his wife. This sweet-natured girl had always soothed him; but she had borne seven children in 10 years and her health had deteriorated. Her death revived his natural paranoia; he convinced himself that she had been murdered. Inevitably, there was a bloody purge of those he suspected.

Paranoia and Torture

Ivan's paranoia reached a climax in the destruction of the city of Novgorod. He had an idea that Novgorod intended treason, so he marched there with an army, burning, raping, and looting on the way. He arrived at the city in early 1570 and ordered a timber wall built around it to prevent any inhabitants from fleeing. Then, for the next five weeks, he directed an orgy of sadism. Every day several thousand were tortured to death while the tsar and his depraved son Ivan watched. The torturers invented all kinds of refinements: husbands and wives were roasted alive or beaten to death in each other's presence; children were murdered in front of their mothers. More than 60,000 people perished.

By the time he arrived at his next destination, Pskov, his bloodlust had evaporated, and Ivan pardoned the city.

Ivan cradles the body of his son. Ivan's unpredictable temper cost him what was most dear to him: his son Ivan Ivanovich. Judging the attire of his pregnant daughter-in-law as immodest, he flew into a rage and beat her. When his incensed son confronted him, Ivan struck out with a pointed staff, killing his heir.

The Death of Ivan

Ivan's death, at the age of 54, somehow suits his legend. He summoned a number of soothsayers to the court, and they forecast his death for March 18, 1584. Characteristically, Ivan told them that they would be burnt alive on that day if he still lived. Toward midnight on the 17th, Ivan reminded the soothsayers that they were to die the next morning. They pointed out that the day could not be said to have ended until the setting of the sun. The next evening, Ivan fell backwards, and a few minutes later, he was dead.

Ivan, on his knees, beseeches the hegumen, or abbot, of Pskovo-Pechorsky Monastery to allow Ivan to join as a monk. In his last years Ivan displayed extreme mood swings, becoming increasingly violent and unbalanced. It wasn't unusual for him to devote himself to days of fasting and fervent prayer after indulging himself in long nights of decadent orgies and bouts of gluttonous feasting.

The Blood Countess

(1560-1614)

Countess Elizabeth Báthory

In Hungary a female descendant of Stephen Báthory, the general who had helped Vlad the Impaler to reconquer Wallachia, continued Vlad's tradition of gore.

Countess Elizabeth Báthory was born in 1560 in a part of Hungary close to the Carpathians; her cousin Juraj Thurzó was palatine, or prime minister, of Hungary. At the age of 15 Elizabeth married Count Ferenc Nádasdy; his gift to her was his home, Cachtice Castle in the Little Carpathians. The count was a soldier and spent much of his time fighting against the Turks. But while the count was away fighting, his passionate young bride was left alone in the castle, her newly awakened sexuality doomed to frustration.

Bloody Hands

Her childhood nurse, Ilona Jó, had some knowledge of witchcraft, but it seems to have been one of her husband's manservants, Thorko, who introduced her to practical "occultism." She wrote to her husband: "Thorko told me how to catch a black hen and beat it to death with a white cane. Keep the blood and smear a little of it on your enemy." Life in the castle bored her. She hated her mother-in-law and surrounded herself with astrologers and "magicians," including a "witch" named Dorottya Szentes. And, inevitably, she was unfaithful to her husband. Little is known of the affair except that she eloped with a young nobleman who was reputed to be a vampire. Her husband forgave her, which would seem to indicate that he was under the spell of his young bride.

Between 1585 and 1590 she gave birth to three boys and a girl. In 1600 her husband died, and once again his bride was condemned to sexual frustration. On the other hand, as she was now mistress of the castle, she lost no time in sending away her hated mother-in-law. She also began to indulge in lesbian practices with her two maids, Barsovny and Otvos, chosen for their beauty.

Her sadism began by accident when she lost her temper with a maid who pulled her hair while combing it. Elizabeth slapped her so hard that she drew blood, probably making the girl's nose bleed, and staining her own hands crimson. She was convinced that the skin where the blood had fallen was fresher and whiter. Had she discovered the secret of eternal youth? She ordered her servants Thorko and János Újváry to murder the maid and drain her blood into a bath. Elizabeth then stripped and immersed herself in the blood, rubbing it all over her body.

Finding Victims

Her servants kidnapped children and teenage girls from the surrounding area, and they locked some of the girls in dungeons, where they were fattened up—Elizabeth believed that the fatter they were, the more blood they had in their veins. She was completely convinced that her baths in blood were keeping her young. During the course of 10 years, she killed about 50 girls—at least, this is the number of corpses eventually discovered buried in the castle grounds.

Did Elizabeth bathe in the blood of her victims?

Caught

The turning point in the countess's career came when one of her victims escaped and went to the authorities. Elizabeth's cousin, Juraj Thurzó, the palatine of Hungary, led a band of soldiers to Cachtice Castle on the night of December 30, 1610; in the main hall they found a girl whose body had been drained of blood, and another who was covered with small punctures made by a sharp instrument. In the dungeons there were more girls in the same condition. It seems clear that the countess had "milked" them like blood cows until they died.

Thurzó had no choice but to place his cousin under house arrest.

Whatever Works . . .

Strangely enough, her recipe for eternal youth seemed to work, and the countess remained remarkably youthful.

Nonetheless there is a great deal of doubt surrounding the veracity of the claims that Elizabeth Báthory killed so that she could bathe in blood. It is more likely that the killing and torture just gave her sadistic pleasure.

In her own time she was known not as the Blood Countess but as the Tigress of Cachtice.

Trial and Sentence

Her trial took place at Bitcse in January and February 1611, although she herself never appeared in the courtroom and refused to plead either innocent or guilty. The majordomo, János Újváry, testified that he knew about 37 girls who had been killed, 6 of whom he brought to the castle with promises of jobs. Their bodies were then pierced and the blood drained into dishes.

At the conclusion of the trial, Judge Theodosius de Szulo pronounced sentences of death on Thorko, Újváry, and the two maids, Barsovny and Otvos; all were to be beheaded. Ilona Jó and Dorottya Szentes were to have their fingers torn out one by one before they were burned alive. The countess herself was not sentenced; although the king had demanded the death penalty, he finally agreed to Thurzó's demand that it should be delayed indefinitely. Instead they sent stonemasons to Cachtice Castle, and they walled up Elizabeth Báthory inside her own chamber, with only a small aperture through which she might receive food. She lived on for another three years, until she was 54. On August 21, 1614, a new guard peeped through the aperture and saw that the countess was lying still on the floor; Elizabeth Báthory was dead.

Cachtice Castle, sited high above the village of Cachtice, was built in the mid-thirteenth century. Elizabeth's husband gave her the castle and its surrounding lands and villages as a wedding gift in 1575. It was first her home and then, in the last three years of her life, served as her prison. It now sits in ruins.

The West Port Murders

(1827-1828)

William Hare

In the early nineteenth century, Edinburgh, Scotland, had some of the best medical schools in the world. The city also had a serious ongoing problem: a shortage of cadavers on which the many schools' numerous medical students could practice their skills in dissection. This cadaver shortage was so acute that many professors of anatomy were disinclined to ask questions when they were offered a fresh corpse. After all no one bothered too much if "body snatchers" had disinterred it the day after it was buried.

Tanner's Close

In a remote part of town there was an alley just off the West Port called Tanner's Close, which contained a boarding house for vagrants. A widow, Margaret Laird, ran it in company with William Hare, a tall, thin Irish immigrant. One of the lodgers, Irishman William Burke, lived there with his mistress, Helen MacDougal. In 1828 the two men became partners in a profitable joint enterprise—selling corpses.

At first, murder was far from their thoughts. Then a Highlander known as Old Donald died in his room in the house, owing rent. Hare thought that a medical school would probably be willing to pay for the body. So Donald's coffin was filled with tanbark and his body sold to an unofficial anatomist, Dr. Knox, of 10 Surgeon's Square, for £7, a profit of £4 over and above the rent Donald owed.

Murder for Profit

With the happy—for them—outcome of earning some respectable profit, Burke and Hare decided that selling corpses was an ideal way of making a living. Still, body snatching was a more dangerous occupation than Burke's trade of cobbling. They may have realized that obtaining the "merchandise" put them at risk. At which point Joe the Mumper fell ill. His fever was a serious inconvenience; it kept away other lodgers. So Burke and Hare decided to hasten his end with the aid of a pillow pressed over his face; Hare sat on his legs while Burke suffocated him. They obtained another £10, in gold, for the corpse.

Gruesome Rhymes

A well-known rhyme of the period ran:

Burke's the butcher,
Hare's the thief,
And Knox the boy who
buys the beef.

The University of Edinburgh, 1827. Known for its medical school, one of the oldest in the world, this was but one of the schools that needed cadavers for students to dissect.

Into Their Stride

On February 11, 1828, they lured Abigail Simpson, a hawker of hearthstone and salt, into the house and plied her with whisky. The killers were still novices, which explains why Abigail lived through the night, was made drunk again the next day, and *then* killed. Dr. Knox asked no questions and paid £10 for her body.

Burke and Hare had now perfected their method—getting the victim drunk—and stuck to it. The stream of victims continued steadily: in May they murdered an Englishman with jaundice. Their next victim, a good-looking young prostitute named Mary Patterson, was a risk because she was with another girl, Janet Brown, when Burke picked her up. When Helen MacDougal showed up unexpectedly, she assumed the worst—that Burke was enjoying the girls' services, and she burst into such abuse that Janet left in a hurry. Then Hare arrived, and they soon dispatched Mary. One of Knox's students recognized her as a girl he had patronized, but Burke explained that he had just bought the body from an old woman.

Next came an unnamed cinder woman. Burke and Hare plied her with whisky until she was half-conscious before suffocating her. Their next victim was an elderly prostitute, Mary Haldane. When Haldane's daughter later met Hare in the street and asked if he knew where her mother had gone, he offered to take her to join her. And in due course, the daughter's corpse joined her mother's in a dissection room. On one occasion Burke and Hare killed an old woman and her 12-year-old grandson and raked in £16 for the pair of corpses.

As they had recognized Mary Patterson, the dissecting medical students also recognized the next victim: a mentally retarded teenager, known as "Daft Jamie." Still they did not turn in the cadaver sellers.

A newspaper illustration of the house in Tanner's Close shows the back court. The window marked "A" was Burke's. "B" shows the entrance where Burke and Hare brought the bodies out.

Execution, Confession, and a list of all the Horrid Murders committed by Burke, also the decision of Hare's Case.

Caught at Last

The final murder victim—probably the 14th—was a widow, Marjorie Campbell Docherty. Lodgers at the boarding house, James and Ann Gray, found her body under a bed and went to the police. By the time the police arrived, Burke and Hare had already sold the body, but they told contradictory stories and were arrested.

The trial opened on December 24, 1828, and was the sensation of the year. Only Burke was tried, while Hare entered what is now called a plea bargain. Burke was found guilty and hanged to death in front of a record crowd on January 29, 1829. Hare died as a blind old beggar in London.

A contemporary newspaper headline announces the verdict in Burke's trial for the "horrid murders" that he committed with his partner, Hare.

H. H. Holmes

The Murder Castle
(1893-1895)

The most notable American multiple murderer of the nineteenth century was a man named Herman Webster Mudgett, who (understandably) preferred to call himself Harry Howard Holmes. Like so many con men, the charming, good-looking Holmes was a natural. He provides a powerful argument for the belief that certain people are just born bad—in fact, downright rotten.

He was born in 1860 in Gilmanton, New Hampshire, the son of a post-master. He studied medicine at the University of Michigan and practiced his first swindle in his early 20s—involving the faked death of a patient he had insured and the theft of a corpse (from the medical school) that the insurance company believed to be the dead man.

Vanishing Women

After graduation, Holmes moved to Englewood, Illinois, just south of Chicago, where he came across Dr. E. S. Holton's drugstore. Holton, too sick from cancer to mind the store, had turned it over to his wife. Slick Holmes soon worked as Mrs. Holton's assistant; within three years Mrs. Holton had vanished, and Holmes owned the store. He did so well that he built himself a three-story, block-long "castle" across the street. He moved the drugstore into the ground floor, along with other shops. The second floor held a labyrinth of small rooms, some windowless. Holmes equipped his castle with chutes leading from most rooms to the basement—where a large furnace sat—and a network of pipes arranged so that he could flood any room with gas. When the World's Fair came to Chicago in 1893, he claimed that he had built a mansion to house the Fair's numerous guests.

During the next three years, the "Murder Castle" hosted an orgy of death. Holmes seduced Julia Conner, whose husband rented space in the drugstore; when the husband found out and left, Julia stayed on with Holmes. So did her sister, Gertie, who also became Holmes's mistress. When Gertie became pregnant, she vanished. So did pretty 16-year-old Emily Van Tassell, who often came into the shop with her mother. When Julia objected to Holmes's new secretary, Emily Cigrand, Julia disappeared. And soon after, so did Emily. The following year another mistress, Minnie Williams, and her sister, Nannie, also disappeared. These and other victims met grisly fates; some died locked in rooms flooded with deadly gas, others suffocated in a large bank vault. Bodies exited by the basement chutes, where they were cremated in the furnace or left in quicklime and acid pits. Holmes sold some of the corpses to medical schools. Body count estimates—based on missing persons reports—range from 20 to 230.

Bird's-eye view of the Chicago World's Fair. The massive fair brought an influx of transients to the city and surrounding areas, such as Englewood, making it hard for the police to estimate the number of Holmes's victims.

Mass Murder

Holmes had furnished his castle on credit, and when he fell behind in the payments, the lending company went to reclaim its furniture. The house proved to be empty, but, acting on a tip, the lenders found the furniture walled up in a sealed room.

Holmes then left his castle and Chicago and landed in jail for petty fraud, where he met Marion Hedgepeth, a convicted train robber. He asked for Hedgepeth's advice on finding a crooked lawyer, offering to cut Hedgepeth in on an insurance fraud he had in the works. The swindle was similar to the "corpse fraud" he'd committed in Michigan. An accomplice, Ben Pitezel, was supposed to "die" in a laboratory explosion. Holmes, having insured his life, would substitute a medical school cadaver and share the insurance money with Pitezel.

In fact Pitezel's death was all too real. Holmes assured Mrs. Pitezel that her husband was now in hiding; in reality, his plan was to kill Mrs. Pitezel and her five children and then keep the $5,000 insurance payment.

Hedgepeth ruined this plan. Enraged that Holmes had failed to pay him his "cut," he subsequently squealed to the police. Police exhumed Pitezel's body—chloroform had killed him.

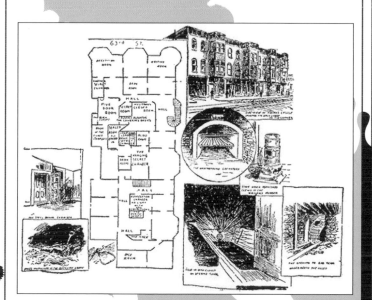

The *Chicago Tribune* ran a plan of the second floor of the "Murder Castle," with insets showing the chutes, quicklime pits, and furnace. Holmes hired and fired builders weekly so that no one but him knew the exact layout of the structure. The second floor contained secret hallways and closets that connected the warren of bedrooms. Some of these were soundproof and had peepholes so that Holmes could watch his victims' agony. There is evidence that Holmes held many of his victims captive for months before he finally killed them.

HOLMES' OWN STORY

PRICE, 25 CENTS.

which the Alleged Multi-murderer and Arch conspirator tells of twenty-two Tragic Deaths and Disappearances

in which he is said to be Implicated, with Moyamensing Prison Diary Appendix

H. W. Mudgett M.D.
H. H. Holmes

ACCUSED OF MORE CRIMES THAN ANY OTHER MAN LIVING

PHILADELPHIA
BURK & McFETRIDGE Co.
1895

The Holmes case received wide publicity. After his conviction, the Hearst newspaper syndicate paid Holmes $7,500 to write his story.

On the Run

The search was on for Holmes. He was missing and so were three of Pitezel's five children: Alice, 15; Nellie, 11; and Howard, 9. Holmes had taken them off "to rejoin their father."

The law caught up to Holmes before he could complete his plan and murder the rest of the Pitezel family. Investigators sadly unearthed the girls' bodies from the cellar of a rented house in Toronto; they located Howard's charred remains in a stove in Indiana.

Tried in October 1895, Holmes was found guilty and sentenced to death. He wrote a "confession" for the Hearst newspapers, claiming 27 murders, and then withdrew it and declared innocence. Executed in May 1896, he choked slowly at the end of a poorly tied noose.

Fritz Haarmann

The Butcher of Hanover
(1919-1924)

Defeated in World War I, Germany sank into a terrible depression after the Armistice in 1918. Hanover, in Saxony, was one of the hardest-hit places. It was there, in a ravaged and starving city, that Fritz Haarmann committed one of the most horrific series of crimes in modern times.

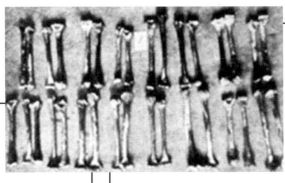

Some of the bones recovered from the river Leine. They were identified as those of at least 27 of Haarmann's victims.

Bad Beginnings

Haarmann, born in October 1879, was the sixth child of a morose locomotive stoker and his invalid wife, seven years his senior. Fritz was his mother's pet, and he hated his father. He liked playing with dolls and detested games. At 16 his family sent him to a military school at New Breisach, but the school soon released him when he showed signs of epilepsy. He then went to work for his father, but he proved lazy and inefficient. Accused of indecent behavior with small children, he was sent to an asylum for observation. Released after six months, he took to petty crime and continued his indecent assaults on minors. Even though he was jailed several times for burglary and confidence trickery, his father tried to give him respectable work, setting him up as the keeper of a fish-and-chips shop. Fritz promptly stole all the money he could lay his hands on.

After four years in jail for theft, he joined a smuggling ring in 1918. From his Hanover headquarters at 27 Cellarstrasse, he conducted business as a smuggler, thief, and police spy. This last assured him immunity for his illegal activities, and Haarmann enjoyed illicit commercial success.

Terror in Saxony

After the war many refugee trains came into Hanover, providing easy prey for Haarmann. Haunting the train station, he picked up incoming youths and offered them a night's lodging.

One of the first of these young men was 17-year-old Friedel Rothe. After they reported him missing, the lad's worried parents learned that he had been friendly with "Detective" Haarmann. The police then searched Haarmann's room, but found nothing. (Haarmann later admitted that the boy's head lay wrapped in newspaper behind his stove at the time.) Then they caught Haarmann engaged in sodomy with another boy, and he received nine months in jail for indecency.

In 1919 Haarmann met the young Hans Grans, a pimp and petty thief. Although Grans's original intent was to make some money off the openly homosexual older man, the pair struck up an odd friendship. Soon Grans moved in with Haarmann, and the two formed a sinister alliance. Their method of murder was always the same: they enticed young men from the railway station back to Haarmann's rooms, Haarmann sodomized them and then killed them (according to his own account, by biting through their windpipes while in the throes of lust). The pair then dismembered the victims' bodies, which they later sold as meat. The victims' clothes were sold and the useless (in other words, inedible) body parts thrown into the river Leine. At the trial, a list of 28 victims emerged, their ages ranging between 13 and 20. One boy was killed only because Grans liked his trousers.

Arrest and Trial

In May 1924 two skulls were found on the banks of the river Leine. Two detectives from Berlin arrested Haarmann and again searched his lodgings, removing many articles of clothing. Soon after, boys playing near the river discovered a sack full of bones. A police pathologist calculated that they represented the remains of at least 27 different bodies.

The police subjected Haarmann to intense questioning. It took them a week—and quite a few rages on Haarmann's part—but finally he decided to make a full confession. And with the confession came a change of attitude. Haarmann was now utterly helpful—even taking police through the streets of Hanover, pointing out where he had disposed of bodies. Based on what Haarmann was telling them, the police also arrested Grans.

Haarmann's trial opened on December 4, 1924, at the Hanover Assizes. It went on for 14 days and took in the testimony of hundreds of witnesses. During the proceedings Haarmann, who chose to represent himself, was unexpectedly merry and nonchalant—and often completely irresponsible. He frequently interrupted witnesses, he complained that there were too many women in the courtroom, and he hurried up witnesses whom he found dull. The judge was oddly lenient, though, and rather than remonstrating Haarmann, he apologized that he could not keep women out of the room and even let the defendant light up a cigar during one distraught mother's broken-hearted testimony.

Haarmann persisted to the end in his explanation of how he had killed his victims—biting them through the throat. Some boys he denied killing—for example, Hermann Wolfe, whose photograph showed an unattractive, badly dressed young man. Haarmann declared that Wolf wasn't his type; he was far too ugly. What he did do was implicate Grans—some say he wanted to make sure that his companion followed him into death.

Haarmann was found guilty and sentenced to death by beheading. Grans was found guilty of inciting murder. He also received a death sentence. Before he died Haarmann produced a full confession; it is an explicit account full of sexual violence that makes clear the pleasure he took in committing the murders.

The mass grave of the 27 identified victims of Fritz Haarmann. A memorial to them stands in the Cemetery Hannover Stoecken. Haarmann was convicted of killing 24 of these young men.

Buckets of Blood

Haarmann had some narrow escapes. Once, a suspicious buyer asked the police to analyze some meat from one of Haarmann's sellers, but the analysis judged it to be pork. On another occasion, a neighbor stopped to talk to him on the stairs when some paper blew off the bucket he was carrying; it seemed to contain blood.

Marcel Petiot

Dr. Marcel Petiot, Amateur SS Man

(1940-1944)

France in the aftermath of World War II was a divided country. The Allied defeat of the German occupiers and the honor earned by the bravery of the French Resistance still could not efface the shame that so many French citizens collaborated with the Nazis. Then news broke of the capture of a man who had not just supported the fascists but had apparently also copied their homicidal methods. Doctor Marcel Petiot was a con man, an egotist, and a sadist. And he was also a serial killer who had murdered refugees from the Nazis in a home-made gas chamber.

Small-Town Politics, Medicine . . . and Murder?

Petoit was born in Auxerre in 1897, son of a minor official in the French Post Office. In 1918 he qualified to study medicine. There can be no doubt of his remarkable mental abilities. He spent part of his three years of medical study in a mental asylum and the rest at home with his mother, yet she later declared that she never saw him study. Nevertheless Petiot successfully qualified as a doctor in 1921.

He became a general practitioner in the town of Villeneuve-sur-Yonne, in the Bourgogne region and in 1928 was elected mayor. Still a bachelor, he employed a strikingly attractive housekeeper. But shortly after she became noticeably pregnant, she suddenly disappeared. She was never seen again.

Not long after, Dr. Petiot married. Later in the 1930s, following a scandal concerning certain other unexplained disappearances in the town, Dr. Petiot moved his practice to Paris.

How to Utilize a War

In May 1940 the Germans invaded France. After six weeks of savage fighting, and after suffering 130,000 soldiers killed in action, France surrendered to Nazi occupation in July 1940. Almost immediately French Jews and other "undesirables" started to be rounded up and sent east to German concentrations camps and, for very many of them, death. A lot of people suddenly needed to get out of France as quickly and quietly as possible. Dr. Petiot evidently realized this. When he moved to Paris, he decided to ruthlessly take advantage of them.

It seems probable that Petiot acquired his Paris house at 21 Rue Le Sueur with the express purpose of committing multiple murders. On his instructions a builder made certain alterations to the structure, completing them in September 1941. Other, more sinister, constructions were made by Dr. Petiot himself in secret. Petiot also bought a flat and a small consulting room at 66 Rue Caumartin, which was where his wife and son lived.

A detailed list of Petiot's victims is not known, but it seems reasonably certain that the first "refugee victim" was a Polish furrier named Joachim Gusbinov—a neighbor of Petiot's in the Rue Caumartin. Fearing Nazi deportation to Poland, Gusbinov had sold his fur business and withdrew two million francs from his bank. Then in January 1942 he called on Petiot at Rue Le Sueur and was never seen again.

Tears fall as Parisians watch German tanks roll in.

Four of Petiot's many victims. From left, Gisèle Rossny, Joseph Réocreux, Annette Basset, and François Albertini

False Hope

Other early victims of Petiot were a colleague of his, Dr. Paul Braunberger, and a whole family of refugees, the Knellers. All these victims were told that Petiot had contacts who could, for 25,000 francs, spirit them out of France to Argentina. None, having entered, ever saw the outside of 21 Rue Le Sueur again.

Petiot employed four men to find his victims. These agents lounged around cafes and bars on the lookout for men and women who wanted to escape abroad. These employees had no idea of the ultimate fate of the doctor's "customers" and probably felt that they were helping to save people from the Nazi occupation.

Imitation is the Sincerest Form of Flattery

The murders continued through 1942 until May 1943. Then, ironically, Petiot was arrested by the Gestapo under suspicion of helping saboteurs to escape from France. His arrest was preceded by a nasty incident: the Gestapo blackmailed a Jewish man into calling on Petiot to inquire about escaping. When the man disappeared, the Germans assumed that he had taken advantage of Petiot's escape facilities. In fact, of course, the Germans had accidentally sent yet another Jew to his death.

Although all Gestapo records were later destroyed by the retreating Germans, it seems likely that Dr. Petiot confessed that he was not helping refugees escape, but killing them instead. His interrogators must have thus been placed in an odd position—did they shoot him as a mass murderer or give him a medal for so enthusiastically embracing the Gestapo ideology? In the end they took the middle route and, in December 1943, released him without charge or comment. Petiot continued his career of murdering refugees, this time without fear of Nazi intervention.

Gestapo Fears

The Gestapo did not have it all their own way in Occupied France. Between early 1943 and summer 1944, the Toulouse Resistance group kidnapped, tortured, and killed so many Gestapo men, that the feared German secret police eventually didn't dare to go outdoors without numerous bodyguards.

Black Smoke

On Saturday, March 11, 1944, Petiot's neighbor in the Rue Le Sueur, Jacques Marcais, became sickened by the greasy black smoke that poured from his neighbor's house and complained to the police. Two policemen called and found a card pinned to the door that directed inquiries to Rue Caumartin. They telephoned Petiot, who replied that he would be over immediately. But in the meantime the filthy smoke belching from the chimney so enraged the police sergeant that he called the fire brigade.

The chimney was on fire thanks, in part, to all the vaporized human fat that had previously passed through it. When the firemen forced an entry, they found the offending stove in the cellar. They also found the remains of 27 bodies lying around the cellar, most of them partly dismembered. As the police searched the house, Petiot entered and calmly walked around introducing himself as the owner.

When the police sergeant told him that he was under arrest in suspicion of multiple murder, Petiot showed his unpleasant streak of genius once again. He took the policeman aside and quietly told him that what he had discovered was the secret execution chamber of the Parisian French Resistance; the bodies were all those of pro-Nazis, collaborators, and other traitors, he assured him. This was a risk, of course, because if the sergeant had himself been a pro-Nazi it would have guaranteed Petiot's arrest. But most Frenchmen were pro-Resistance, so the risk was not so great. The sergeant let the doctor go.

Forty-Seven Suitcases

Petiot returned to the Rue Caumartin, packed some suitcases, and fled with his wife, Georgette, and 17-year-old son. The Gestapo joined the quisling French authorities in hunting the murderer, but they too had no luck in catching him.

Further investigation of the house on Rue Le Sueur showed just how Petiot had killed his victims. The triangular-shaped cellar was a homemade gas chamber. The doctor would get his victims to enter—doubtless claiming that it was a safe place to hide from the Germans until transport out of the country could be arranged. He then sealed the ceiling hatch from the outside and gassed them. Much of the "empty" upstairs of the house was filled with the belongings of his victims, including 47 empty suitcases.

Further investigation suggested that he had sold many portable valuables, like jewelry, on the black market, gaining perhaps a million francs as a result.

But financial gain was clearly not the doctor's main reason for killing men, women, and children. He had built a periscope into his gas chamber, allowing him to watch his victim's death agonies.

The chief of police inspects the boiler in the triangle-shaped death chamber at 21 Rue Le Sueur. The boiler caused the smoky black fire that drew the police's attention.

Doctor on the Run

In June 1944 came D-day, and on August 24 Paris was liberated. And Dr. Petiot remained at large.

He was arrested on November 2, 1944, as he left the Metro station at St. Mande Tourelle in the eastern outskirts of Paris. It turned out that he had been hiding in a flat in the Rue Faubourg, St. Denis, and had grown a beard. Because of a habit of standing at the open window with a hairy, bare chest, he became known locally as "Tarzan," and a complaint had even been made to the police about his seminudism.

Petiot told the police that the 27 bodies found in his cellar were mostly those of German soldiers. He admitted that he had killed 63 people, but declared that he had done so on the orders of the Resistance and that he had also helped many patriotic Frenchmen to escape. Unfortunately, he said, none of these could vouch for him since, of course, they were all away in South America. He even named several famous Resistance leaders as his colleagues . . . and again unfortunately, they all just happened to be dead.

Above right, Petiot in court during his trial. Despite a hard-fought defense, a jury sentenced him to death. Below right, workmen in the La Santé Prison courtyard clean and dismantle the guillotine, after it carried out the execution of Petiot. Blood still stains the pavement.

Execution of the Executioner

His trial opened after 17 months of investigation, on March 18, 1946. A key moment was when a Resistance officer was called to prove that Petiot was completely ignorant of many matters in which he claimed inside knowledge. In his own evidence to the court Petiot put up a spirited defense, but also came across as arrogant and egotistical. When the jury eventually convicted him, Dr. Petiot bellowed with rage and fought with his guards. He was guillotined on the morning of May 26, 1946.

The final number and identities of Petiot's victims are unknown. He himself admitted to 63 murders, but the figure is probably higher. We do know that he killed entire families at the same time—just as the SS did in the extermination camps.

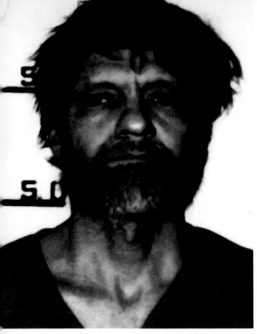

Theodore Kaczynski

The Unabomber

(1970s-1990s)

What is now called "eco-terrorism"—that is, militant action taken against people or organizations that are believed to be damaging the environment—has been taking place since the 1960s. Most such actions are, fortunately, relatively harmless—animal rights activists set laboratory test animals free, demonstrators trespass into restricted areas to make protests, and antiglobalization riots occasionally wreck multinational-owned burger outlets. But such "eco-terrorists" generally revere human life as much as they do all life on the planet, so rarely try to harm other people. One exception, however, stands out . . .

Striking from a Distance

The so-called "Unabomber" terrorized the United States for most of two decades. For much of that time investigators believed that he was simply a serial killer with an unusual method of killing victims. It was only toward the end of the Unabomber's reign of terror that his ecological excuse for murder became plain.

On May 25, 1978, a small parcel bomb wounded a security guard at Northwestern University in Illinois. This was the first—and amateurish—attack made by the serial killer who later became known as "the Unabomber." Over the next 18 years, the Unabomber would send homemade, but increasingly sophisticated, parcel bombs to educational establishments, technology companies, and corporate businesses.

Police were doubly flummoxed by this method of attack: not only was the killer murdering apparently random strangers—the first and greatest problem in serial crime investigation—but he or she was also striking from a distance, using the unwitting U.S. Postal Service as an accomplice. There were no personal links to lead to the killer from the victims and no possibility of chance eyewitnesses identifying the murderer.

Between May 1978 and December 1985, the Unabomber sent out nine, fortunately nonfatal, parcel bombs. Two were intercepted and defused, but the others injured 18 people, some seriously. One of these bombs—which wounded United Airlines president Percy A. Wood—earned the bomb maker the media nickname "the Un.A. bomber," later simplified to "the Unabomber."

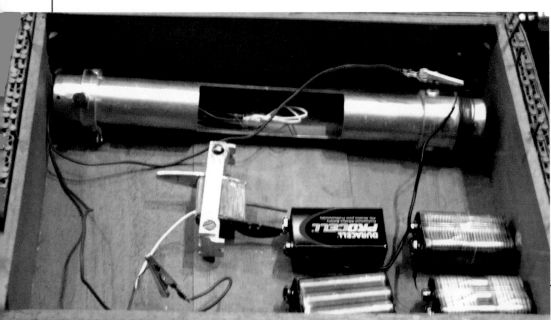

A Unabomber-style bomb, reproduced by the FBI, is on display at the Newseum in Washington, D.C.

Hand Delivered

December 1985, in Sacramento, California, saw the first fatal Unabomber attack. Hugh C. Scrutton tried to remove a package left lying in the car park behind his computer rental shop. It exploded, killing him.

This bomb had not been delivered by the postal service; it had been simply left in the parking lot. It seemed likely, therefore, that the killer had put it there in order to watch, from a distance, the result of his or her handiwork. Unfortunately nobody had seen the booby-trap bomb being planted. The next bombing followed the same pattern.

On February 20, 1987, the killer left a bomb in the parking lot outside a computer firm in Salt Lake City, Utah. This time, however, a secretary in the firm spotted the bomber placing the booby trap. She thought it odd that the tall man in the hooded sweatshirt and aviator sunglasses should leave a lump of wood—with nails sticking out of it—right where it might damage somebody's tires. Unfortunately, before she could alert anyone, her boss, Gary Wright, drove into the lot, got out of his car, and kicked the lump of wood out of his path. The resulting explosion blew off his leg but did not kill him.

Lying Low

Police were delighted to have even a sketchy description of the Unabomber and plastered the artist's reconstruction all over the national media. Any doubt that the Unabomber intended his bombs to kill had been removed by the last two attacks: both bombs had been packed with metal fragments, designed to shred their victims with flying shrapnel. But at least he seemed to have given up killing from a distance—the temptation to see the results of his murders had obviously been too great.

Unfortunately the publication of the witness description inadvertently removed this advantage. The Unabomber stopped sending bombs for six years—presumably frightened that the police might identify him—and when he struck again he did so using his older and (for him) safer method of delivery: the U.S. Postal Service.

On June 22, 1993, a parcel bomb badly injured Professor Charles Epstein, a leading geneticist at the University of California, San Francisco, partly destroying his hand and sending shrapnel through his chest and across his face. Only swift medical aid saved his life.

The next day a similar parcel bomb seriously critically injured computer scientist David Gelernter of Yale University. He lost most of his right hand and the sight and hearing on his right side. He too survived, but only after he underwent extensive medical treatment.

Police widely circulated this composite sketch of the Unabomber, made from the first witness's description.

Oklahoma

On December 10, 1994, a parcel bomb killed New York advertising executive Thomas Mosser. There were doubts that this was a genuine Unabomber attack until someone pointed out that one of Mosser's corporate clients was the Exxon oil company—responsible, in many people's eyes, for recklessly polluting the environment. Less than five months later, on April 24, timber industry lobbyist Gilbert B. Murray picked up a parcel, supposedly sent by a firm called Closet Dimensions. As Murray picked up the package, one of his staff members joked: "It's heavy. Must be a bomb." The blast was particularly powerful, destroying Murray's head and upper body but not killing anyone else. Fortunately he was to be the Unabomber's last victim.

American domestic terrorism, however, was about to enter a deadly new chapter. No longer would it be dominated by the work of the Unabomber. On April 19, 1995—on the second anniversary of the federal raid that led to the deaths of David Koresh's Branch Davidian cult—a bomb, hidden in a parked truck, demolished much of the Alfred P. Murrah Federal Building in Oklahoma City. One hundred and sixty-eight people, including 19 children in a daycare center on the ground floor, were killed.

One British newspaper echoed the suspicions of many in the immediate aftermath of the Oklahoma bombing with its headline: IN THE NAME OF ALLAH. It came as something of a shock to many who believed the complicity of Muslim terrorists, therefore, when investigators arrested American Gulf War veteran, Timothy McVeigh.

McVeigh confessed to the bombing, citing his violent opposition to federal gun-control laws as his motive. He was executed on June 11, 2001.

Advertising executive Thomas J. Mosser died when he opened a package bomb sent by the Unabomber to his New Jersey home.

Bomb Envy

In the wake of the Oklahoma bombing, the Unabomber sent a "manifesto" to the *Washington Post* and the *New York Times*—threatening to blow up a passenger jet if it were not promptly published. The Unabomber, it seemed, resembled a lot of serial killers in his fantasy that he was the most feared man in the world. The Oklahoma bomb had evidently made him feel inadequate, so he was upping the stakes.

The manifesto proved to be a rambling screed that attacked big business, environmentally damaging government policies, scientific research, and progress in general. The opening paragraph read:

The Industrial Revolution and its consequences have been a disaster for the human race. They have greatly increased the life-expectancy of those of us who live in "advanced'" countries, but they have destabilized society, have made life unfulfilling, have subjected human beings to indignities, have led to widespread psychological suffering (in the Third World to physical suffering as

well) and have inflicted severe damage on the natural world. The continued development of technology will worsen the situation. It will certainly subject human beings to greater indignities and inflict greater damage on the natural world, it will probably lead to greater social disruption and psychological suffering, and it may lead to increased physical suffering even in "advanced" countries.

Both the *Washington Post* and the *New York Times* published the Unabomber's manifesto, in an effort to prevent further violence.

A Hero in His Own Lights

It was plain that the Unabomber believed that all development since the Industrial Revolution was dangerous and damnable. He was evidently a well-educated, well-read man, and many of the things he stated in his manifesto were simply extreme extensions of mainstream environmentalism.

But he was also delusional and self-justifying, insisting that his bomb campaign had been the only way to make the media pay attention to his message. It may have been true that there were few avenues to attack modern technology through the conventional, pro-technology U.S. media, but killing to get people's attention completely undermined his own cause.

And the fact that he had almost certainly watched the explosions that killed Hugh C. Scrutton and crippled Gary Wright placed the Unabomber firmly in the serial killer category. Whatever environmental and political self-justification he offered, he was not an ecological activist: he was a homicidal sadist.

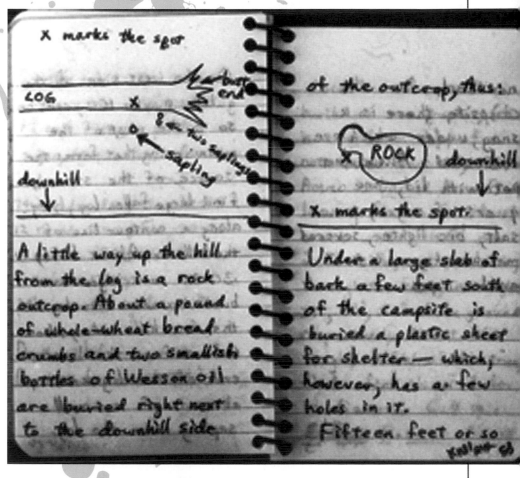

Pages from the Unabomber's handwritten notes, showing a map with info on hidden supplies

A Brilliant Maniac

Fortunately, the manifesto was the last terror package the Unabomber was ever to send. David Kaczynski, in Montana, read the Unabomber's manifesto and realized with horror that it sounded exactly like the rantings of his hermit-like older brother, Theodore. Most telling was the reversal of the old homily: "you can't have your cake and eat it too."

The Unabomber, insisting that the positive uses of technology were not worth the negative side effects, wrote: "you can't eat your cake and have it." This was a family habit of phrasing the well-known quotation, picked up from their mother, and its inclusion convinced David that Theodore was the Unabomber. With natural misgivings David Kaczynski informed the FBI, who raided Theodore's isolated Montana cabin and found plenty of proof that he was the Unabomber.

Theodore J. Kaczynski had been a brilliant academic—in 1967, at just 25, he had been appointed an assistant professor of mathematics at the University of California, Berkeley. But two years later Kaczynski suffered a total emotional breakdown and had subsequently become a recluse in Montana. Living in an isolated log cabin, Kaczynski believed he followed a life that was in tune with nature—making bombs with parts carefully hand-carved from wood and roiling in hatred for the modern world.

In 1996 Ted Kaczynski was sentenced to four life sentences, with parole permanently denied.

Charles Manson

The Manson Family
(August 1969)

The hippie movement energized and defined the culture of the late 1960s in North America and Europe. The hippie belief in free love and pacifism seemed to many to be the route to a new golden age in human history. But then one hippie guru went power mad, and the nightmare publicity from the resulting atrocities marked the beginning of the end for hippiedom as a leading mass movement.

The Making of a Cult Leader

Charles Milles Manson was born in 1934 to Kathleen Maddox, an unmarried, teenaged alcoholic. He began committing petty crimes by the age of 9, and by his 30s Manson had spent more than half of his life in jail.

In 1967 Manson, now 33, was released from prison. Moving to San Francisco—the unofficial capital of the growing hippie movement—he turned to panhandling. Then he met a young librarian from Berkeley, Mary Brunner, and was soon living with her. Manson persuaded her that the enlightened, free-love thing to do would be to allow him to bring other women back to their flat. Soon he had 18 new female flat-mates/lovers, most of whom saw him as a hippie guru.

Three of Manson's followers holding a sit-in outside the Los Angeles County Courthouse. His followers—almost all of them were young women—remained loyal to him even after his arrest for murder.

Beach Boy Dennis Wilson in the early 1970s. In 1968 Wilson found himself having to rid his home of unwanted houseguests, after he took in some of Manson's female followers and then Manson himself. While they lived there, the girls waited on both Wilson and Manson.

Adopting a Family

Charles Manson was a very articulate man, despite his tough past. He took elements from the Scientology he had read about in prison and then mixed them with his own LSD-inspired creed. He gave free talks in the Haight-Ashbury district—the very heart of hippiedom—and soon gathered what he called his "Family." These were young, white, middle-class (mostly female) hippie followers, who came to believe Manson was a prophet.

The Family then went on the road, heading south to Los Angeles and eventually inviting themselves to stay at the Pacific Palisades home of Beach Boys drummer, Dennis Wilson. Wilson generously put up with this invasion and even the cost of having a number of the Family treated for gonorrhoea. Discovering that Manson was an aspiring singer-songwriter, Wilson introduced him to some of his music business connections and even paid for studio time to allow Manson to record a demo tape. But eventually the disruption of housing a hippie commune proved too much, and Wilson kicked them all out.

Helter Skelter

By January 1969 the Family was renting an isolated property, the Spahn Movie Ranch, in the desert outside Los Angeles. Manson was by this time teaching them that a race war would soon break out between blacks and whites across the United States. Given the recent assassination of Martin Luther King and the National Guard suppression of African Americans during the L.A. Watts riots two years earlier, this must have seemed, to some, a reasonable expectation. The race war would lead, Manson prophesied, to a nuclear war that would destroy civilization. After which it was his fate to lead his Family to rule over humanity's survivors in a postapocalyptic golden age.

Manson called this apocalypse Helter Skelter. He lifted this term from a Beatles song of the same name, believing that the Beatles also foresaw the end of civilization and were personally sending him a coded message to escape with his chosen followers. In fact a helter skelter is merely the name of a carnival ride common in Britain.

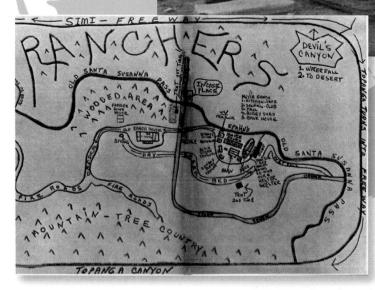

The dilapidated Spahn Movie Ranch, above, had been used from the 1940s to 1960s as a setting for many Western films. In 1968, with Westerns on the decline, George Spahn rented it to the Family. At left is a map of the ranch, drawn by Family member Tex Watson.

Music to Start a War

Manson decided that the Family should record a song album, the hidden messages of which would spark the race war. Although record producer Terry Melcher showed some interest in recording Manson's music and even talked about filming the Family at Spahn Ranch, Manson's attempts to get his music published failed miserably. At one point, while trying to find Melcher, who had formerly lived in the rental property, Manson wandered onto the grounds of 10050 Cielo Drive in Benedict Canyon, Los Angeles, now the home of movie director Roman Polanski and his wife, actress Sharon Tate. Manson left without incident, but Tate later said that she found him "creepy."

Manson then got in a spat over money with Bernard "Lotsapoppa" Crowe, a 300-pound African American drug dealer. Manson shot Crowe and escaped, believing that he had killed him. Crowe survived, but Manson was now convinced that the radical political group the Black Panthers would hunt him down. There was no longer any time to use music to subtly start the race war. The Family would now just have to murder some prominent white people, leave evidence that black radicals had committed the crimes, and then take cover when the apocalypse began. Manson assured his followers that they would be safe; he would lead them to Death Valley, he said, where they would hide in an underground city of gold.

Record producer Terry Melcher, shown above, met Manson through Dennis Wilson. More than once Manson went to Melcher's rented house at 10050 Cielo Drive to discuss recording his music.

Map

HINMAN HOUSE
964 Old Topanga
Canyon Road

SPAHN MOVIE RANCH
1200 Santa Susana
Pass Road

JAY SEBRING HOUSE
9820 Easton Drive

LaBIANCA HOUSE
3301 Waverly Drive

Los Angeles

POLANSKI-TATE HOUSE
10050 Cielo Drive

Off Limits
Public officials gave new street numbers to the Polanski-Tate and LaBianca houses so that ghoulish tourists would stay away. The Polanski-Tate house was pulled down in the 1990s.

Killing Piggies

The Family killed their first victim, Gary Hinman, on July 27, 1969. Hinman was actually a friend of the Family. Manson believed, incorrectly, that Hinman had inherited some money, so he demanded it for the use of the Family. Family members Bobby Beausoleil, Mary Brunner, and Susan Atkins held Hinman captive in his own house for two days. Even after Manson showed up and slashed him with a sword, Hinman continued to deny that he had any money. Manson then ordered Beausoleil to kill him and then hurriedly left. Beausoleil stabbed Hinman to death. He and the girls used Hinman's blood to scrawl the words POLITICAL PIGGY on the wall and a Black Panther symbol to frame nonexistent black murderers.

On August 8 Manson ordered another follower, Tex Watson, to take Atkins, Patricia Krenwinkel, and Linda Kasabian to the Polanski-Tate house at 10050 Cielo Drive. Kill anyone there, he told them, and make it as gruesome as they could manage. His loyal followers complied. They shot to death 18-year-old Steve Parent, who just happened to be leaving from a visit with the building's caretaker. They then broke into the house and stabbed the eight-months-pregnant Sharon Tate to death, along with her three house guests: Wojciech Frykowski, Abigail Folger, and Jay Sebring. Roman Polanski was working in London at the time, and thus escaped. Before leaving the Family wrote PIG on the front door in Tate's blood.

Sharon Tate, shortly before her death, with her husband, Roman Polanski.

No Apocalypse

The next night Manson led his group of killers, Watson, Atkins, Krenwinkel, and Kasabian, now joined by Leslie Van Houten and Steve "Clem" Grogan, to the house of Leno and Rosemary LaBianca—a supermarket executive and his wife—in Los Feliz. Manson stayed for the tying-up of the victims but again left before the stabbing started. And the stabbing was brutal—Watson, Krenwinkel, and Van Houten slashed Rosemary at least 41 times after choking her with a lamp cord. After stabbing Leno to death, one of the killers carved the word WAR into his stomach. Before the band of killers left they wrote RISE and DEATH TO PIGS on the walls in blood, again hoping to implicate the Black Panthers.

The Manson trial turned into a media circus. During the trial, few of the Family members displayed a drop of remorse for their sickening acts of brutality. Shown at right are (from left) murderers Patricia Krenwinkel, Leslie Van Houten, and Susan Atkins mugging for the press as they are transported from prison to the courthouse.

A Persuasive Man

It is a common misconception that Charles Manson is a killer. In fact he has never killed anybody. He got his Family to do that for him.

Remote-Control Killers

The police, media, and public did not fall for the ploy. No race war started and, by December 1969, all the murderous members of the Manson Family were under arrest.

Manson's remote-controlled killers were Susan Atkins, Tex Watson, Bobby Beausoleil, Bruce Davis, Patricia Krenwinkel, Leslie Van Houten, and Clem Grogan. All seven of them were convicted and received death sentences, as did Manson. Mary Brunner and Linda Kasabian only acted as lookouts during the murders and later gave evidence against the others, thus escaping prosecution. The executions were all commuted to life-imprisonment, however, when California voted to abolish the death penalty in 1972. The convicted Family members all remain in jail, as of this writing.

Charles Manson, left, remains incarcerated in a California prison. All of the convicted Family members have been under consideration for parole, but in every case the parole boards have denied them release.

Lake and Ng

(1983–1985)

Leonard Lake

When ex-Marine, ex-con Leonard Lake met Charles Ng, the son of a wealthy businessman from Hong Kong, he had finally found a partner for his delusional survivalist fantasies. But as well as building a bunker that would house them during the coming nuclear apocalypse, the pair built a torture chamber inside a remote Northern California ranch. There they videotaped themselves raping, torturing, and killing their victims. Most of the victims were young families, who had known the perverse pair before they were taken captive. No one knows the exact number of people who died at the hands of Lake and Ng, but estimates rise as high as 25.

Careless Shoplifter

On June 2, 1985, a security guard at South City Lumber in San Francisco observed a young man walking out of the store without paying for the bench vise that he took with him. The guard alerted a policeman, who caught up with the man just as he was putting the vise into the trunk of a car. As soon as he saw the police officer, the young man darted away and disappeared among the parked cars. An older, bearded man, who was bending over the open trunk, explained that it was all a mistake, and offered to pay for the vise.

The police officer insisted on making a routine search of the car and discovered a handgun with a silencer. Possession of this kind of weapon violated California state law, so the policeman told the bearded man that he would have to accompany him to the station. There the bearded man handed over his identification—which belonged to a 26-year-old man named Robin Stapley—and then asked for a glass of water. When it was handed to him, he popped a small capsule into his mouth and swallowed it down with the water. A moment later he slumped forward heavily onto the table. He had popped a cyanide capsule.

He died four days later without regaining consciousness. The Honda he was driving proved to be registered to a used car dealer called Paul Cosner, who had disappeared seven months earlier. A check with fingerprint records revealed that the name of the dead man was, in fact, Leonard Lake, a known burglar, 39 years of age.

The Torture Chamber

Papers found in Lake's wallet led the police to a small ranch in Wilseyville, Calaveras County, about 150 miles northeast of San Francisco. There they discovered a bedroom equipped with chains, shackles, and hooks in the ceiling—it looked ominously like a torture chamber. In an underground bunker with prison cells, they discovered videotapes that showed young women being sexually abused by Leonard Lake and his partner, Charles Ng, the young man who had been caught shoplifting.

In a trench nearby, police unearthed the remains of eight human bodies. Fragments of bone found on the property and photographs from the ranch house brought

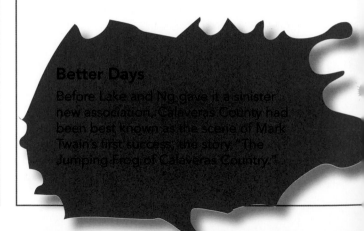

Better Days

Before Lake and Ng gave it a sinister new association, Calaveras County had been best known as the scene of Mark Twain's first success, the story "The Jumping Frog of Calaveras County."

Harvey and Deborah Dubs pose for a portrait with their son, Sean. All three are believed to have been murdered by Lake and Ng.

Literary Inspiration

The journals also made it clear that the inspiration behind the kidnapping of the girls was a novel called *The Collector* by the British writer John Fowles, in which an art student named Miranda is kidnapped by a self-pitying and self-obsessed young man and dies in captivity. Lake labeled his scheme of kidnapping sex slaves "Project Miranda."

the possible total of torture and murder victims to 24, including two very young children. It became clear that Lake and Ng had made a habit of luring people to the bungalow and killing them. The women were held as "sex slaves" and made to cater to the pair's perverted sexual demands before they were murdered.

Lake's voluminous journals described the rapes and murders in detail. He wrote: "The perfect woman is totally controlled. A woman who does exactly what she is told to and nothing else. There is no sexual problem with a submissive woman. There are no frustrations—only pleasure and contentment."

Lake proved to be a Vietnam veteran who was also a "survivalist"—that is, someone who is obsessed with the inevitability of World War III, and who makes elaborate preparations to survive it. This was the original purpose of the underground bunker. The picture that finally emerged was of a man who spent most of his life living in a world of fantasy, indulging in grandiose daydreams of success without any realistic attempt to put them into practice. He was also a man whose whole life had been dominated by sex—a man who, as a teenager, had obtained sexual favors from his sisters in exchange for protecting them from a delinquent younger brother—whom Lake later murdered.

The Accomplice Arrested

On July 6, 1985, police arrested Charles Ng in Calgary, Canada, for shoplifting again. A judge sentenced him to four and a half years in prison. He insisted that he had played no part in the killings in Wilseyville and that the murders had all been carried out by Lake alone.

Eventually California, which had reinstated its death penalty in 1977, extradited Ng from Canada, which has no death penalty. Ng was returned to Orange County, California, for one of the longest and most expensive trials in American legal history, costing $14 million. Ng was convicted on February 11, 1999, of 11 of the 12 murders with which he was charged (six men, three women, and two baby boys) and was sentenced to death. He is now on San Quentin's death row, awaiting execution.

Ng, sitting in a Santa Ana, California, courtroom listens to the defense make its closing arguments in his multiple murder trial.

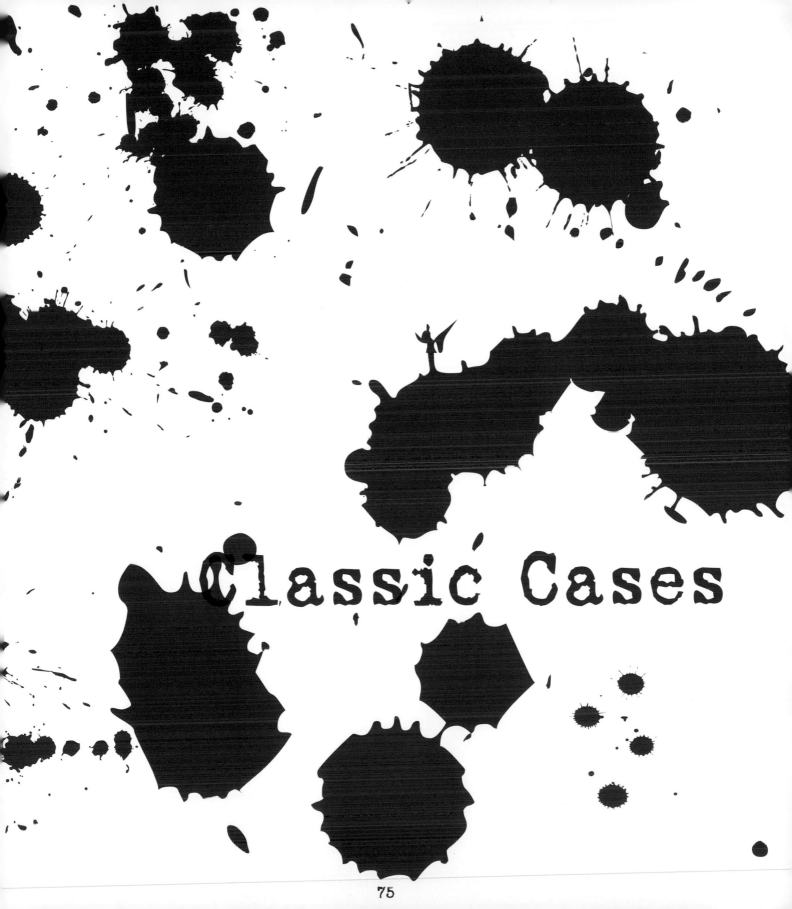

Classic Cases

Professor John White Webster

The Harvard Medical College Murder

(November 23, 1849)

The murder of Dr. George Parkman by Professor John White Webster of Harvard Medical College was Boston's greatest scandal of the nineteenth century, and America's first classic murder case.

Early on the afternoon of November 23, 1849, Professor Webster, goaded to a fury by the sneers of the unlikable Dr. Parkman, picked up a heavy chunk of kindling wood from the side of his stove and hit Parkman with all his strength. He then looked down at the prostrate body of his infuriating colleague. He had killed a man. What was he to do with the body?

Bloody Remains

The solution was near at hand—the assay (testing) furnace he used to analyze mineral samples. He dragged Parkman's skinny body into the adjoining washroom, heaved it into the sink, and proceeded to dismember it with a stout kitchen knife. Then he put the head into the furnace, which was now roaring, and stuffed the rest of the parts into a tea chest lined with tanbark.

A contemporary print offered its version of murder in the laboratory, showing Webster lashing out in anger at the greedy moneylending doctor.

A Classroom Bore

Professor Webster's reputation as an amiable man may have saved him from being as complete a disaster as a teacher as he was as a money manager. When reporting the case, the *Boston Daily Bee* described Webster as "tolerated rather than respected, and has only retained his position on account of its comparative insignificance. As a lecturer he was dull and commonplace, and while the students took tickets to his lectures, they did not generally attend them."

Unlikely Murderer

The disappearance of the detested Dr. Parkman caused a sensation in Boston, and many must have hoped he had come to a bad end. Parkman had abandoned the medical profession to become a moneylender and was known to treat with contempt those who had fallen behind in their payments. Professor Webster was his opposite. Round and plump, with a cherubic face, he looked like a member of Dickens' Pickwick Club.

On November 25 an uneasy Professor Webster called on the Reverend Francis Parkman—George Parkman's brother—and told him that Dr. Parkman had called on him on the 23rd to collect the repayment of a loan. He had left Webster's carrying $483.64, which lent conviction to the notion that a thief must have waylaid the missing man and murdered him for the cash.

Bones in the Walls

The janitor at the college, Ephraim Littlefield, had other ideas. He and his wife lived in the basement of the medical college building, right next to Webster's laboratory. A sour man, jealous of his social betters, Littlefield did not like Webster. And the fact that the professor had given him a turkey for Thanksgiving was enough to arouse his suspicions. Webster had never before given the Littlefields a gift. Littlefield also noted that the furnace burned day and night, and wondered . . .

It so happened that the furnace was on the other side of a wall in a corridor. So with hammer and chisel (and with his wife keeping guard), Littlefield broke through to the furnace. "I held my light forward . . . the first thing I saw was the pelvis of a man and two parts of a leg. I knew it was no place for these things." He went to the police.

When Webster found out what Littlefield had done, he was heard to say: "That villain! I am a ruined man!" When taken into custody for the murder of Dr. Parkman, he attempted to swallow strychnine, but it only made him vomit. He passionately declared

Ephraim Littlefield, the janitor who broke the case, had also been a prime suspect in the Parkman murder. After Professor Webster's conviction, however, Littlefield collected the $3,000 reward that the Parkman family had offered for any information that led to finding the doctor. Littlefield used that money to retire from his janitorial post.

his innocence, however, insisting that he knew nothing about the remains. Investigators had found fragments of false teeth in the furnace, identified as those belonging to Dr. Parkman, but the professor continued to disclaim all knowledge of the murder.

Webster's laboratory was in the basement of the Harvard's old medical college building, shown above. It seems Parkman went there to see Webster that November afternoon on the latter's invitation, raising the suspicion that he had planned to kill Parkman. Most writers on the case (including this one) have been sympathetic to Webster because Parkman was a bad-tempered miser. If Webster planned the murder, this view may be over-credulous.

Sensational Murder Trial

Webster was tried before Chief Justice Shaw. So much of Boston wished to see the trial that a shift system of seating in the public gallery was arranged, thus permitting a change of spectators every 10 minutes or so—it was estimated that 60,000 people witnessed parts of the trial, which lasted 11 days.

Found guilty, Professor Webster initially maintained his innocence. Some time later he admitted to the crime; there had been a violent quarrel concerning Dr Parkman's loan and Professor Webster's continued inability to repay. He confessed: "I felt nothing but the sting of his words . . . in my fury I seized whatever thing was handiest—it was a stick of wood—and dealt him a blow. . . . He did not move . . . he was absolutely dead. I took off the clothes and began putting them into the fire. . . . My next move was to get the body into the sink . . . there it was entirely dismembered. The only instrument was the knife . . . which I kept for cutting corks."

Despite the claim that the killing blow had been struck in momentary anger, so appealing for a new verdict of manslaughter, Webster was hanged in August 1850.

The Colorado Cannibal

(1874)

Alfred G. Packer

In the early 1870s the Free Territory of Colorado was a very daunting place. Made up of featureless plains leading up to the brutal eastern slopes of the Rocky Mountains, the area was, to white settlers, largely uninhabited and unexplored. Wild animals, resentful Indians, brutal weather, and exhausting terrain took their toll on the new interlopers. The perceived reward outweighed any risk, however; most settlers believed that there was gold in those hills.

Alfred G. Packer was a prospector who claimed to know Colorado as well as any man living. He also claimed to know the location of many big gold deposits. Both these claims later proved to be completely untrue . . . and his pretense cost five men their lives.

An Unreliable Wilderness Guide

In autumn 1873 Packer, then in his mid-20s, led a team of 19 prospectors from Salt Lake City, Utah, to the San Juan County area in Colorado, loaded down with supplies and equipment. The weeks passed and the weary men saw nothing but barren country and eventually arrived close to the snow-capped peaks.

On the point of starvation, they stumbled across the camp of members of the Uncompahgre band of the Ute tribe. The tribe's leader, Chief Ouray, learned of their hazardous proposed expedition and succeeded in persuading 10 members of the party to abandon the futile quest. The nine remaining prospectors promised to pay Packer handsomely to continue as their guide. They remained at the Uncompahgre camp until they recovered and were still determined to hunt for gold. All Chief Ouray could do was to supply them with provisions and advise them to follow the banks of the Gunnison River as best they could.

Alfred Packer was now the undisputed leader of the expedition. Confident in his knowledge of the area, he claimed to be able to guide the party to the goldfield by a much shorter route than the one suggested by Chief Ouray. Four of the nine men, however, insisted on following the Gunnison River—without the aid of Packer's "expert knowledge."

Packer led the remaining five, Israel Swan, Frank Miller, George Noon, Shannon Bell, and James Humphrey, to their demise.

Chief Ouray of the Uncompahgre band and his wife, Chipeta. Ouray knew the land far better than Packer did and advised the prospecting group to abandon their dangerous journey. None of them listened.

Dead Giveaway

The most striking physical evidence against Packer was that he had seemed too fit when he made it to the Los Pinos Agency—the Uncompahgre chief Ouray, who saw him soon after, commented: "You're too damn fat!"

The Sole Survivor?

Of the four men who followed the Gunnison River, two died of starvation before reaching the Los Pinos Indian Agency on Cochetopa Creek in February 1874. General Charles Adams, the U.S. agent at Los Pinos, saw to it that the two survivors were nursed back to full health before beginning their trek to civilization.

In March 1874 a wild-looking man appeared at Los Pinos, begging for food. His face was hideously bloated, but he was in surprisingly good physical condition, everything considered. He gave his name as Packer and explained that his five companions had deserted him while he was ill, leaving him with only a rifle to shoot wild game to survive.

After a 10-day stay at the agency, Packer left. In his travels, he stopped at many saloons, drank heavily, and flaunted a considerable quantity of money. The conflicting stories he told in those bars about the fate of his companions led to speculation that he had, in fact, murdered them. General Adams decided to have Packer tracked down. His team located Packer and escorted him back to the agency, where Adams placed him in solitary confinement.

General Charles Adams, shown above, standing at right behind Chief Ouray and Chipeta, took care of the surviving prospectors when they reached the Los Pinos Indian Agency. When Packer reached the agency it was clear that something had gone very wrong.

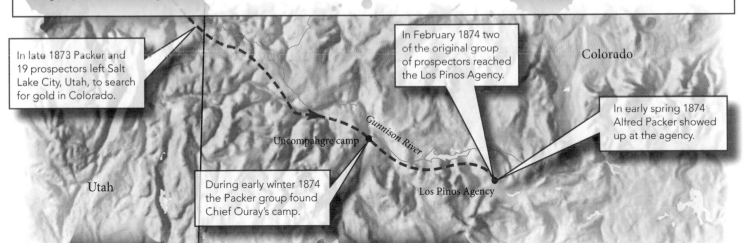

In late 1873 Packer and 19 prospectors left Salt Lake City, Utah, to search for gold in Colorado.

In February 1874 two of the original group of prospectors reached the Los Pinos Agency.

Colorado

In early spring 1874 Alfred Packer showed up at the agency.

Gunnison River

Uncompahgre camp

Utah

During early winter 1874 the Packer group found Chief Ouray's camp.

Los Pinos Agency

Packer's Statement: The First Killing

On April 2, 1874, two Ute men arrived at the agency, holding what they claimed were strips of "white man's meat." They had found it just outside the agency, where the snow had kept it well preserved. It was human flesh. Packer must have been carrying it, then dumped the grisly evidence when he saw that he had reached safety.

When he was shown the flesh, he gave a loud groan of despair and fell to the ground. When he had recovered enough, he made the following statement:

When I and five others left Ouray's camp, we estimated that we had sufficient provisions for the long and arduous journey before us, but our food rapidly disappeared and we were soon on the verge of starvation. . . . One day I went out to gather wood for the fire and when I returned I found that Mr Swan, the oldest man in the party, had been struck on the head and killed, and the remainder of the party were in the act of cutting up the body preparatory to eating it.

Packer's Statement: More Meat

Alfred Packer's "confession" concluded:

This food only lasted a few days and I suggested that Miller be the next victim, because of the large amount of flesh he carried. His skull was split open with a hatchet as he was in the act of picking up a piece of wood. Humphrey and Noon were the next victims. Bell and I then entered into a solemn compact that as we were the only ones left, we would stand by each other whatever befell, and rather than harm each other we would die of starvation.

One day Bell said: "I can stand it no longer!" and he rushed at me like a famished tiger, at the same time attempting to strike me with his gun. I parried the blow and killed him with a hatchet. I then cut his flesh into strips which I carried with me as I pursued my journey. When I espied the agency from the top of the hill, I threw away the strips I had left, and I confess I did so reluctantly as I had grown fond of human flesh, especially that portion around the breast.

A sign points out the site of the massacre. It uses the spelling of Packer's first name that he often used himself: "Alferd," rather than "Alfred."

The *New York City Daily Graphic* sent pen-and-ink artist John A. Reynolds out to Colorado to capture the local color. Reynolds got more color than he expected when he came across five decomposing bodies. He proved his measure as a journalist when he sat down and sketched the gruesome sight. The sketches appeared in *Harper's Weekly*.

The Discovery of the Bodies

In June 1874 a newspaper artist named John A. Reynolds was out sketching in the wilderness when he came across the bodies of five men. Four of them were lying in a row, and the fifth, minus its head, was lying a short distance away. It was the remains of the missing prospectors, Israel Swan, Frank Miller, George Noon, Shannon Bell, and James Humphrey. The bodies of Bell, Swan, Humphrey, and Noon had rifle bullet wounds in the back of the skull, and when Miller's head was found, it had been crushed by a blow from a rifle butt.

The find made complete nonsense of Packer's statement. A path led from the bodies to a nearby hut, where blankets and possessions belonging to the murdered men were found, and it was apparent that Packer had lived in that cabin for many days, making frequent trips to the bodies for his supply of meat. Each body had its breast cut away to the ribs.

A Change of Statement

A warrant was issued, charging Packer with five murders, but in the meantime the prisoner had escaped. The authorities hunted for him, but, showing that he had more wilderness skill than might have been guessed from his previous expedition, Packer vanished completely.

Nine years later, on March 12, 1883, Sheriff Sharpless of Laramie County recognized and arrested Packer and brought him to Lake City, Colorado. Packer's trial began on April 3, 1883, when he was charged with the murder of Israel Swan in Hinsdale County on March 1, 1874.

Packer, in his statement to the court, now claimed that he had only killed Shannon Bell—and that was in self-defense. He told a story of his companions fighting among themselves and of Bell firing at him. This completely contradicted what he had said in his original statement, and the jury did not believe his new account. On April 13 the jury found Packer guilty of murder, and voted for the death penalty. Packer appealed to the Colorado Supreme Court and was granted a stay of execution.

Standing before a painting of Packer defending himself against a hatchet-wielding Bell, David Bailey, curator of the Western Museum in Grand Junction, Colorado, holds the pistol that he believes Packer used to shoot Bell. Bailey and others support Packer's self-defense plea.

A Republican Cannibal

In October 1885 the Colorado Supreme Court granted him a new trial, and the prosecution decided this time to try him on five charges of manslaughter. Packer was found guilty of each charge and was sentenced to serve 8 years for each offense, making a total of 40 years. Sentencing Packer, Judge Melville Gerry gave vent to his feelings along unexpectedly political lines: "There were only seven Democrats in Hinsdale County, and you ate five of them, you depraved Republican son-of-a-bitch!"

Packer served 17 years at hard labor before being released. He proclaimed his innocence throughout all those years. He died on a ranch near Denver on April 24, 1907, aged 65, having been pardoned on January 1, 1901.

The Gunnison River flows through the rough country of Hinsdale County, Colorado.

Serial Killer or Survivor?

Was Alfred Packer, as some have suggested, a serial killer? In both the legal and psychological sense the answer is no. He does not seem to have killed his victims over a prolonged period, as serial killers do, but in a single, frenzied attack. More important, he does not appear to have become addicted to murder—the true sign of a serial killer. In the nine years that he was an outlaw on the run, Packer almost certainly had opportunities to murder people, but there is no evidence that he ever killed (or ate) anyone after the ill-fated expedition.

The truth is that Packer, in a life-or-death situation, acted as a selfish and utterly ruthless survivor.

The Body Beneath the Hearth

(December 24, 1891)

Little is known of Frederick Bailey Deeming's early life. Born in Leicestershire, England, Deeming himself claimed that both his mother and father had been in and out of mental homes and that as a child his own abnormality earned him the nickname Mad Fred.

In 1883, at about 30 years of age, he married and went to Australia to seek his fortune. He tried to make this by swindling jewelers and was arrested for fraud. Released on bail he fled with his wife, Marie, and their children to Port Adelaide and then left for South Africa. On the voyage he succeeded in defrauding two brothers out of £60.

Frederick Bailey Deeming

Selling Gold Mines

The family moved to Cape Town, but Deeming was soon on the move again, supporting himself with jewelry frauds. He was wanted by jewelers in Cape Town, Durban, and Johannesburg for swindles amounting to £1,000. To avoid capture he obtained a post as manager of a gold-mining company at Klerksdorp and offered to sell gold mines to rich financiers. He soon gained a reputation as a cheat, especially after he faked his own death to renege on a deal.

Eventually Deeming sent Marie and the children (there were now four: Mary, Bertha, Sydney, and Leala) to England, and he traveled there separately.

At Hull in Yorkshire he posed as a millionaire and a relative of Sir Wilfred Lawson. There he swindled a jeweler out of £285 (paying with bouncing checks) and hastily embarked for South America. On this trip fellow passengers knew him as the manager of a diamond mine in South Africa. They were startled when detectives at Montevideo, Uruguay, arrested him for fraud.

The Vanishing Family

Back in Hull in October 1890, Deeming was sentenced to nine months in jail. On his release he went to the Commercial Hotel, Liverpool, where he posed as an inspector of regiments in South Africa, who had come to England to take a house for a Colonel Brooks. He found a cottage, Dinham Villa, at Rainhill, and specified that he was going to concrete the kitchen hearth and floor. In July 1891 Marie and the children moved into Dinham Villa and then simply disappeared—under the concrete. Deeming, at that time calling himself "Albert Williams," then married Emily Mathers, a tobacconist's daughter with family money. He took her to see Dinham Villa and danced a little jig on the kitchen floor.

Frederick Deeming, with his first wife, Marie. Marie died at her husband's hand, along with their four young children.

A Murder on Andrew Street

With his new wife, Deeming sailed once more for Australia. Emily appears to have at first been extremely happy with her lively husband. Yet by the time they reached Melbourne, 10 days before Christmas, she must have had her doubts. A neighbor said her eyes were red from weeping. The couple, known to neighbors as the Williamses, took a house on Andrew Street in Windsor, Victoria, a Melbourne suburb. But Australia didn't provide Emily Mathers with a new life—or any life at all. Soon after she moved to Andrew Street, Deeming cemented her lifeless body under the floorboards near their bedroom hearth.

Newspaper illustration of Emily Mathers's body as it was found under the floor in the bedroom she shared with her husband

The One Who Got Away

In January 1892 Deeming hastily left Melbourne and sailed for Sydney. On the boat he met his next prospective victim, a Miss Katie Rounsefell. Believing her new acquaintance to be "Baron Swanston," she quickly agreed to marry him. He traveled to Sydney with Katie, then left her and obtained a job with Fraser's gold mine in Southern Cross, Western Australia. She was actually on her way to join him when chance—in the form of the discovery of Emily's body—saved her. Eight weeks after Deeming had moved out of Andrew Street, the agent went to look over the place, having heard of an offensive odor in the bedroom. The newly cemented fireplace was crumbling—the heat of an Australian summer had dried it too quickly. The policeman who came to check out the odor kicked away a few lumps of soft concrete and found himself looking at the face of a dead girl.

Deeming had left many clues, including a card with the Rainhill address on it. This soon led to the discovery of the bodies in Dinham Villa. Victoria Police traced Deeming to Southern Cross, arrested him, and took him back to Melbourne. At one point he narrowly escaped lynching. He wrote to Miss Rounsefell, declaring his innocence and asking her to believe in him; he also asked for money. (Miss Rounsefell was an heiress.)

His defense tried an insanity plea, and Deeming declared that the apparition of his dead mother frequently appeared to him and had once urged him to kill all his women friends. He also made a speech declaring that Emily Mathers was still alive and that the people in court were the ugliest he had ever seen in his life. The jury found him guilty, and the judge sentenced him to death. Deeming was hanged in the old Melbourne Jail.

Kate Rounsefell

Advice

In late 1892 Edward Thunderbolt organized the reburial of his friend Emily Mathers in Melbourne Cemetery. A tall, urn-topped memorial bears the name "Emily Lydia Mathers" and the details of her murder. Attached to the base is a plaque with the words of a poem "Advice," written by Thunderbolt for his friend:

To those who hereafter come reflecting
Upon this text of her sad ending:
To warn her sex of their intending,
For marrying in haste, is depending
On such a fate, too late for amending

By her friend,
E. Thunderbolt.

Fred the Ripper?

Deeming confessed to being Jack the Ripper—impossibly, because Deeming was in jail at the time of the murders.

Belle Gunness

Lady Bluebeard

(1900–1908)

America's "Lady Bluebeard" was born Brynhild Paulsdatter Størseth near Trondheim, Norway, in 1859, and followed her sister Nellie to Chicago at age 24. Belle, as she liked to be called, married compatriot Mads Sorenson, a department store detective, about 1884. In an effort to escape the poverty imposed by her husband's $15 weekly salary, she took in lodgers and ran a candy store. In 1896 this burned down, and she collected the insurance money.

The Queen of Hearts

Suddenly Belle realized that there were other ways of making money. Her daughter Caroline died the same year and her son Axel two years later, both with symptoms of acute colitis. Both were insured. So was the Sorenson home in the Chicago suburb of Austin, which burned down in 1898. Her husband died in 1900, and the young doctor who saw the body thought its contortions indicated strychnine poisoning. An older colleague said it was due to "an enlarged heart," and when a postmortem revealed an enlarged heart, the matter was dropped.

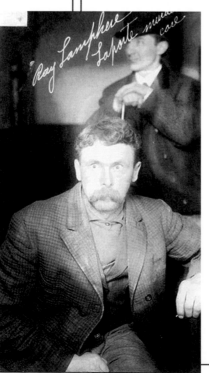

Belle Gunness's jealous hired hand, Ray Lamphere

Black Widow of the Prairie

Mads Sorenson had died with perfect timing, on the day two insurance policies on his life overlapped. With $8,500 of settlement money, Belle was able at last to buy a comfortable farmhouse near La Porte, Indiana, where she moved with her children, including a 10-year-old adopted daughter, Jennie. In April 1902 she married a young widower, Peter Gunness. He had a baby, and when the child died soon after the marriage, the local doctor suspected smothering, but he kept his suspicions to himself. Eight months later, in December 1902, Peter Gunness died in an odd accident—according to Belle, a heavy meat grinder fell off its shelf and smashed his skull. Jennie appeared at the inquest and supported Belle's story, and Belle escaped any repercussions.

Over the next few years, Belle hired a series of handymen. Most of them seem to have been her lovers. Belle had never been pretty, although her blue eyes were striking, and a wide, down-turned mouth carried the promise of sensuality. The few men who slept with her and survived recorded that she had a natural talent for sex that made her addictive. Many of these hired men left unexpectedly—so unexpectedly that Belle was left to finish the plowing. Their relatives later identified some of them in Belle's homemade cemetery.

In June 1907 Belle approached a young odd-job man named Ray Lamphere and told him she wanted a man about the house. He had a droopy moustache and eyes like an anxious koala bear; he gladly accepted. On the first night, Belle joined him in bed.

Just before Christmas 1907, a new man arrived at the farm. Belle explained to Ray that they were engaged. For the next week Ray was in a frenzy of jealousy; then, to his relief, the man disappeared. Not long after, in early January, another man came, Andrew Helgelian. When it became clear Belle had taken him as her new lover, jealousy again tormented Ray. He and Belle quarreled. Ray soon learned that Belle was not to be crossed.

Fire!

On the afternoon of April 27, 1908, Belle went to make her will and told her lawyer that she believed Lamphere intended to burn down the house. That night the new hired man woke up smelling smoke and raised the alarm. He tried to awaken Belle, but her bedroom door was locked and she did not respond. By the time the firefighters arrived, the house was a smoldering ruin.

When it cooled enough to search, the remains of a woman and three children were found in the basement, into which they had fallen as floors collapsed. It was clear that the children had been battered about the head. Oddly enough, the woman's head was missing, and the body seemed too small to be Belle, even though false teeth found in the ashes were identified as Belle's.

Lamphere was arrested and accused of murder and arson. The jury found him innocent of murder but guilty of arson, and he received two years.

When Asle Helgelian came looking for his brother Andrew, searchers began to dig in the hog pen. They found there the remains of 20 men, with skull injuries suggesting blows from a hatchet, as well as a skeleton identified as Jennie.

Was Belle dead, or had she arranged her own funeral pyre and escaped? That mystery has never been solved.

Inspired Lyrics

The story of Belle Gunness inspired a folk song that included the lines:

*She placed in the papers a
lonely hearts ad.
Men came to Belle Gunness
to share food and bed.
Not knowing that soon they'd
be knocked in the head.
But while they were sleeping,
she'd lift the door latch.
She'd kill them and plant
them in her tater patch*

Above: Workers and police comb over the rubble and ruins of the burned-out basement of Belle Gunness's house. At right is the front page of the *Los Angeles Times* of May 6, 1908, which featured a story on the "gruesome mystery." In the shaded area are the details of the "Indiana Woman Believed to Be Guilty of Wholesale Murder," whose "Victims Strangely Drop from Sight."

The Mask Murders

(March 27, 1905)

Henry Faulds

The first murder to be solved in Great Britain using fingerprint evidence occurred in Deptford, southeast London, in 1905.

At 7:15 AM, March 27, 1905, a small girl playing on the pavement outside a shop in Deptford saw the door open slowly and a man with a bloody face peer out. Then he closed the door again. At half past eight, the shop assistant arrived and was surprised to find the door still locked. He found the shopkeeper, Thomas Farrow, lying dead in the back parlor. Ann Farrow, his wife, was lying in a bloodstained bed, still alive but unconscious.

Enter the Fingerprint Experts

By half past nine, Scotland Yard men were at the scene. A milkman said he had seen two men leaving the shop at a quarter past seven.

Medical evidence showed that the Farrows had been violently attacked around seven that morning; the two intruders had been wearing black stocking masks, which they left behind. The door had not been forced, and Farrow was partly dressed, suggesting that he had come downstairs to answer a knock on the door, expecting an early customer. The men had attacked him with a jimmy (a type of crowbar), then gone upstairs and attacked his wife. Then they forced open the cashbox, which was found under the bed.

Local rumor had it that the Farrows kept a large sum of money in the house. They were mistaken; the shop takings—less than £10 a week—were banked regularly.

One of the killers had left a vital clue—his bloody thumbprint on the lid of the cashbox. The box was sent straight to the Yard's fingerprint department. Then they took the fingerprints of Mr. and Mrs. Farrow. A check in the fingerprint records—now amounting to 80,000 or so—failed to identify the bloody thumbprint.

Unsavory Characters

Straightforward detective work made further progress. Two brothers, Alfred and Albert Stratton, were known to the local police as thugs, but had not yet acquired criminal records. They had abandoned their usual haunts. The younger brother, Alfred, had a mistress, and when the police located her, she showed signs of a recent beating. She informed the police that he had left via the window in the early hours of Monday morning—the day of the murder—and returned by the same route after dawn. The landlady of the elder Stratton told police that she had once come upon black stocking masks hidden under his mattress.

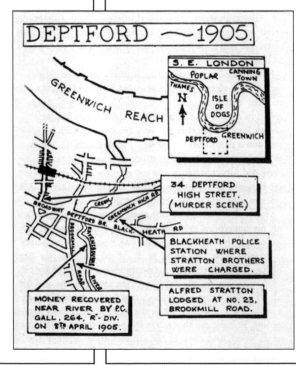

DEPTFORD ~ 1905.

S. E. LONDON

GREENWICH REACH

POPLAR / CANNING TOWN
THAMES
N
ISLE OF DOGS
DEPTFORD / GREENWICH

34 DEPTFORD HIGH STREET. (MURDER SCENE)

BLACKHEATH POLICE STATION WHERE STRATTON BROTHERS WERE CHARGED.

ALFRED STRATTON LODGED AT NO. 23, BROOKMILL ROAD.

MONEY RECOVERED NEAR RIVER BY P.C. GALL, 264, "R"- DIV. ON 8TH APRIL 1905.

A newspaper illustration of the Deptford area of London in 1905, showing the locations of key elements of the Mask Murders, which were also know in the press as the Deptford Murders and the Farrow Murders

Double Murder

Assistant Commissioner Melville MacNaghten gave orders for the arrest of both brothers. When they were taken into custody a week later, Ann Farrow had died at the hospital, turning it into a double murder inquiry.

At the Tower Bridge police court, both brothers were noisy and abusive, and the magistrate felt that there was almost no case against them. Then the brothers were fingerprinted. That afternoon the fingerprint expert came into his chief's office, saying: "Good God, sir, I've found that the print on the cashbox corresponds exactly with the right thumb of Alfred Stratton."

On May 5, 1905, the brothers appeared at the Old Bailey, the Central Court in London, charged with murder. The fingerprint expert for the defense was Henry Faulds, the Scot who had discovered fingerprinting in Tokyo, and beside him was Dr. J. G. Garson, who had developed his own system for classifying fingerprints. Both experts felt that they were not given the recognition they were due and were intent on taking revenge on Scotland Yard by testifying for the defense.

The defense contended that Alfred Stratton's thumbprint and the bloody thumbprint on the cashbox were not identical—there were various small differences. That, replied Detective Sergeant Collins, was natural. He proved his point beyond any doubt by taking the prints of the jurymen several times over, showing that small discrepancies occurred.

Dr. Garson was called to the stand. The prosecutor, Muir, was ready for him. He held out a letter. Had Dr. Garson written him this letter, offering to testify on behalf of the prosecution? Dr. Garson reddened, and admitted that he had. "But I am an independent witness . . ." The icy voice of the judge interrupted him. "I would say a completely untrustworthy one. Kindly leave the witness box."

With no expert witnesses to refute the power of the fingerprint evidence, both Stratton brothers were condemned to death. And the evidence of the bloodstained fingerprint became front-page news throughout the British Isles.

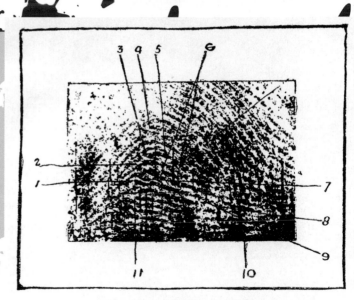

Print found on Cash-box (enlarged).

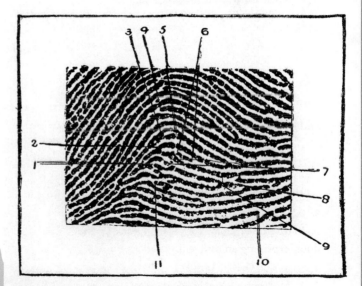

Thumb-print of Alfred Stratton (enlarged).

Fingering the Crook

In 1909 a patrolling constable in Clerkenwell noticed a finger, caught by its ring, on one of the spikes at the top of a warehouse gate. Its owner had slipped when trying to climb the gate, and the spike had gone between the ring and his finger; his struggles had torn off the finger. The fingerprint files identified the digit as that of a burglar, who was duly arrested and charged with an attempt at breaking and entering.

Fingerprint evidence from the Deptford Mask Murders case, from Henry Faulds's *Guide to Finger-print Identification*, 1905. Although Faulds was one of the developers of the forensics fingerprinting system, he chose to side with the defense in the case against the Stratton brothers. He believed that a match established from a single print provided insufficient evidence for a murder conviction. The Scotland Yard's fingerprint expert convinced the jury otherwise, and they found the Strattons guilty of murdering the Farrows.

Al Capone

The Golden Age of American Gangsters

(1920s-1930s)

It is arguable that the cowboy outlaw bandits of the late nineteenth century were the direct forbears of twentieth century mobsters like Baby Face Nelson and Al Capone; and that the early twentieth century was merely the transition period from the age of the six-shooter to the age of the tommy gun. Certainly American gang violence and organized crime were not a twentieth-century development.

Roots in the Old West

The infamous 1881 gunfight at the OK Corral was not, as Hollywood would have us believe, just a battle between the "good guy" Earps and the "bad guy" Clantons. Certainly the Clanton gang were cattle rustlers and barroom hell-raisers, but the Earps were little better. The Earp brothers came to the Arizona town of Tombstone—with the card-sharping gunslinger and dentist, Doc Holiday—primarily to make money, not to uphold the law. In fact it seems likely that the Earps were simply using their deputized positions to gain control of Tombstone for their own ends. The killing of three men in the OK Corral gunfight, and the many killings in the months that followed, was more like a gangster turf war than a genuine attempt to end crime in Tombstone.

Old West "good guys" were as ruthless as the bad ones, such as in the Dodge City peace commission of 1882, which include the West's most fearless gunslingers. Back row, from left: W. H. Harris, Luke Short, and Bat Masterson. Front row, from left: Charles Bassett, Wyatt Earp, F. McClain, and Neil Brown.

How to Create a Breeding Ground for Crime

The prohibition of alcohol in the United States began with the Volstead Act in 1919. The act was pushed through Congress by a political hegemony of religious fundamentalists, moral crusaders, and those people who disliked the increasing urbanization of America (cities were generally believed to encourage drinking). But the result was the exact reverse of what the prohibitionists had wanted the ban to achieve. Secret, illegal alcoholism rocketed. Violent bootleggers (alcohol smugglers) virtually ran many big cities, such as New York, Cleveland, and Chicago, and U.S. society in general became more, not less libertine.

By 1924, only five years after the imposition of Prohibition, the speakeasy trade was one of the biggest money spinners in America. These were illegal, secret alcohol bars: the term *speakeasy* comes from the fact that customers were habitually warned to keep their voices down for fear of police detection. The effect of making a common pastime illegal was to make many ordinary people feel outside the law, with a resulting loss of respect for authority in general.

Fed by bootleg alcohol profits, "mobs" of organized criminals grew vastly in size and power— eventually touching almost every aspect

Detroit police raid a bootlegger's brewery. Prohibition did far more to encourage the growth of organized crime than it did to discourage alcohol consumption.

of American life. Then the Wall Street crash of 1929 rocked the financial base of the country, creating the Great Depression. Suddenly in such a bleak economic climate, the risks of being an outlaw bandit seemed worth taking.

Bonnie and Clyde

Clyde Barrow had just finished a 20-month jail sentence for armed robbery when he first met Bonnie Parker in 1930. She was an out-of-work waitress and doubtless found the life of crime that Barrow offered her irresistibly attractive. The two became lovers and set themselves up as roaming armed robbers.

But Bonnie and Clyde, as the papers dubbed them, were small-time crooks by the standards of the time, cautiously robbing only gas stations, restaurants, and small-town, poorly defended banks. They were certainly not in the league of more daring bank robbers like John Dillinger and Pretty Boy Floyd. Still, during the course of this rather petty criminal career, their gang killed at least nine people.

Yet the romantic appeal of the pair as "gangster lovers" quickly gained them national fame and a largely undeserved legendry status. And this may have been a key factor in the authorities' ruthless determination to apprehend them, dead or alive.

They were betrayed by a friend and ambushed by police near Bienville, Louisiana, on May 23, 1934. Without giving a warning for the pair to surrender, officers riddled their car with machine-gun bullets, killing both within seconds.

Clyde Barrow and Bonnie Parker

The First "Public Enemy Number One"

Born in 1903 there is little clue in John Herbert Dillinger's quiet, rural upbringing to hint at why he later became such a master criminal. From all accounts he was an easygoing, good-natured boy.

At the age of 20 Dillinger joined the U.S. Navy but found life onboard the USS *Utah* so boring that he deserted after only a few months. Being a deserter in peacetime was not a major crime, but life on the run seems to have set the young Dillinger on the path of petty larceny. He was caught trying to rob a grocery store in 1924 and spent the next three years in prison. It was there that he apparently decided to become a real criminal and set about learning everything he could about bank robbery from his more experienced fellow inmates.

On his release Dillinger soon became a legendary, even mythical figure in the public's eyes. A brilliant bank robber (who timed heists with military precision), it was also said that no prison could hold him. Indeed Dillinger once escaped a maximum-security jail wielding a "gun" he had carved out of soap and blackened with boot polish.

J. Edgar Hoover's newly formed Federal Bureau of Investigation riskily placed its reputation on catching Dillinger—who, in a fit of publicity seeking, Hoover titled "Public Enemy Number One." Indeed it is possible that the then unpopular interstate police bureau might have been disbanded if Dillinger had gone unapprehended for much longer than he did.

America's number-one gangster and its top lawman: John Dillinger, left, and J. Edgar Hoover, right. Hoover made catching Dillinger the immediate goal of his newly formed Federal Bureau of Investigation.

A Dubuque, Iowa, newspaper headline of April 23, 1934, proclaims the latest crime spree of Dillinger. In front are items confiscated from the criminal who was by then one of the most feared men in America.

Dillinger Dead?

Dillinger—or a man who looked just like him—was lured into an FBI trap outside the Biograph Theater in Chicago on July 22, 1934. The authorities said that he was shot dead while resisting arrest, but several witnesses claimed that he was shot down without warning. The killing wound, fired at close range into the base of his skull while he was lying prone on his belly, is what is called an "execution shot" in the military.

A rumor that the man killed outside the Biograph Theater apparently had distinguishing marks different from John Dillinger (a correct missing tooth—but on the wrong side of his mouth—and brown rather than gray eyes, for example) led some to believe that the FBI killed a double. They believed that the real Dillinger used the death to change his identity and surgically change his face in order to escape forever.

Whatever the truth to this belief, FBI director J. Edgar Hoover ever afterward kept a death mask of the man killed outside the Biograph Theater on his desk as a grisly memento.

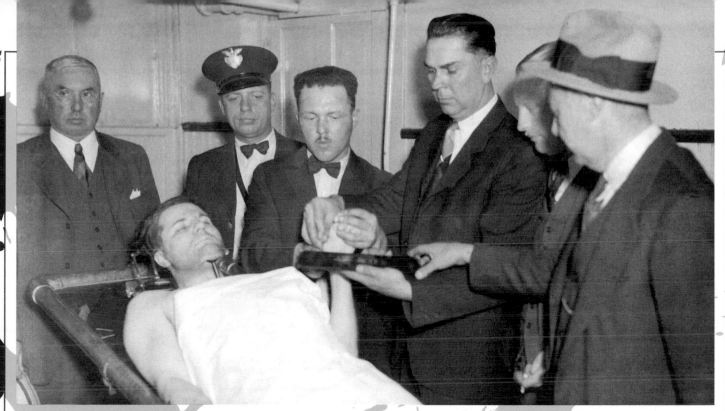

Lawmen surround the body of Pretty Boy Floyd on its mortuary slab after federal agents shot and killed him during a gun battle on an Ohio farm.

Pretty Boy

A farmer, driven to bank robbing by the agricultural disaster of the Great Dust Bowl, Charles "Pretty Boy" Floyd won a genuine Robin Hood reputation by also taking and destroying bank debt papers, thus saving many farmers from financial ruin.

Floyd won the sarcastic newspaper nickname Pretty Boy because a farmer, to whom he'd given money, described him to the press as "kind faced and kind hearted."

Following the death of John Dillinger, the FBI promoted Floyd to Public Enemy Number One. He did not hold the title for long, however. On October 22, 1934, the FBI gunned down Floyd while he was attempting to escape across farmland near East Liverpool, Ohio.

Baby Face

Lester Gillis, better remembered as Baby Face Nelson, was a member of John Dillinger's bank-robbing gang and was named as the new FBI Public Enemy Number One after the death of Pretty Boy Floyd. Dillinger used violence only rarely, but Baby Face took a sick pleasure in shooting bystanders during heists. And he especially liked killing policemen—he gunned down at least a dozen that we know of.

Baby Face died on November 27, 1934, near Barrington, Illinois, when he deliberately started a gunfight with two unsuspecting FBI agents, who just happened to be driving past in the other direction. He killed both of them before bleeding to death himself. Agents later found his lifeless body in a ditch. Ironically one of the agents was Herman Hollis—the man who had fired the killing shot into Pretty Boy Floyd a month earlier.

Like many of his ilk, Baby Face Nelson died in a hail of bullets. Belying his benign nickname, Nelson was a ruthless killer, who unnecessarily provoked the final gun battle that cost him his life.

Scarface

Alphonse "Scarface" Capone was undoubtedly the most infamous American mob boss of the twentieth century.

Born in 1899 in Brooklyn, New York, of Neapolitan immigrant parents, Capone joined a local criminal mob at the age of 11. In 1919 Capone moved to Chicago to work as a pimp and gunman in the profitable prostitution trade. It was at this time that he probably contracted the syphilis that would eventually kill him.

By 1925 Capone had worked his way up to being the crime boss of Chicago's Southside; running prostitution, illegal gambling, and bootlegging rackets and ruthlessly killing any rivals. His wealth in 1927 was estimated at close to a $100 million.

On February 14, 1929, six members of George Clarence "Bugs" Moran's North Sider Gang (plus an innocent dentist who happened to be playing cards with them) were machine-gunned to death in a Chicago garage on Capone's orders. A not untypical act of gang warfare in 1920s' Chicago, the fact that the killing took place on St. Valentine's Day won enormous media coverage and made Al Capone a national villain. The police, however, could not link Capone to the massacre.

Al Capone was finally arrested in 1930 for income tax evasion. After a decade of avoiding arrest on major charges, it had apparently never occurred to Capone to worry about the fact that he was evidently making millions but never paying a dime in taxes.

In 1931 Capone was found guilty and given 11 years. He was released on medical grounds in 1939. His mind already rotten with syphilis, he had no chance of rebuilding his crime empire. He died in 1947.

Al Capone

No Mob?

Incredible as it may seem, for decades many government officials—especially FBI boss J. Edgar Hoover—flatly denied the existence of organized crime associations such as the Mafia. It was only with the increasing public concern about crime in the 1950s, and the FBI's embarrassment at being shown up, that the FBI publically admitted the Mafia actually did exist.

Lucky

Charles "Lucky" Luciano, is a less commonly recognized Mafia figure than Al Capone, but Lucky Luciano was, in fact, a much more powerful boss than Capone ever was.

Starting in petty crime in New York from the age of 10, Luciano soon earned the nickname Lucky by escaping arrest and winning dice games. By 1925 he was a second-in-command to a large mob, run by Joe Masseria. In 1929 he re-earned his nickname when he survived a mob hit. Thugs repeatedly stabbed him with an ice pick and partially slit open his throat.

But unlike most of his contemporary gang bosses, Luciano disliked the violence of the ever-present mob wars, largely because it was scaring away business. In 1931 Luciano had Masseria murdered and took over the dead man's gang. By diplomatically cultivating the younger generation of Mafiosi, Luciano became a *capo di tutti capi* ("boss of bosses") and by 1934 had managed to organize a national "crime cartel"—a loose union of Mafia families.

Crime boss Lucky Luciano

Out of Luck

In 1935 New York special prosecutor Thomas E. Dewey targeted Lucky Luciano and gained evidence of his use of forced prostitution: some of the call girls in Luciano's prostitution empire were forced into "white slavery" by gangster-pimps. Dewey found enough of these "sex slaves" willing to give evidence, and the jury convicted Lucky. A judge sent Luciano down for a 30-to-50-year sentence in 1936.

Despite his imprisonment Lucky Luciano continued to run his crime empire from behind bars. In 1942 he helped the U.S. war effort by utilizing his mob and union connections to stop sabotage on the New York docks. He was released from jail in 1946 (20 to 40 years early) in thanks for this help. Luciano was, however, immediately deported to his native Italy.

He died of a heart attack at a Naples airport in 1962, while waiting to meet a movie director who wanted to make a documentary about his life. It may be worth noting that the mob bosses in the United States had expressly forbidden Luciano from speaking to such people, for fear of the mob secrets he could reveal.

Lucky Luciano's legacy was the greater cooperation between organized crime families in America, which in turn created the modern, semicorporate Mafia of the modern day.

Thomas E. Dewey finally made a case to send Luciano to prison.

Albert Fish

The Brooklyn Vampire

(1910s-1932)

Albert Fish, a seemingly innocuous, mild-mannered man, earned many nicknames, including the Brooklyn Vampire, the Gray Man, the Bogeyman, and the Werewolf of Wisteria, before he was executed for the murder of Grace Budd on January 16, 1936. Grace, unfortunately, was not the only victim of this sadomasochistic pedophilic cannibal.

Evil Charm

A woman who lived in the same lodgings as Fish, testified that he loved playing with children and was extremely popular with them.

Little Grace

In May 1928 Edward Budd placed a classified ad in the *New York World*, looking for country work away from his Manhattan home. It was 58-year-old Fish who answered the ad, visiting the Budd home under the name Frank Howard, a "Long Island farmer." On his second visit to the Budds, after promising Edward a job, Fish offered to take Edward's 10-year-old sister, Grace, to a birthday party for Fish's "niece." Reluctantly her parents allowed the child to go with the seemingly kind man.

Fish, carrying a bundle containing a cleaver, saw, and butcher knife, boarded a train with Grace in tow, traveling north to Westchester County. So excited by his plans for the unsuspecting child, Fish nearly left his "tools" behind—Grace reminded him to retrieve his bundle. He then took her to an empty house known as Wisteria Cottage, where he stripped himself in an upstairs room and then called Grace in. When she screamed, he strangled her. Then he chopped off her head and cut the body in two.

He took parts of her body home with him, cooked them with carrots and onions, and ate them over a period of nine days. During this time he later confessed that he experienced great sexual excitement.

Grace Budd. Little Grace thought that she was going to a birthday party, but Fish had other plans for the bright 10-year-old.

The Hunt

Six years after Grace's death a letter from Fish arrived at the Budds in an envelope that could be traced. In the letter Fish admitted to Grace's murder, gruesomely describing how he feasted on her flesh but declaring that he had not raped her.

A month later, New York City police arrested Fish. Psychiatrist Frederic Wertham was given the task of probing his mental state.

Fish was born in 1870, to a family with a history of mental abnormality. At 5 he was placed in an orphanage; at 15 he left school and changed his first name from Hamilton to Albert. In 1898 he married a girl nine years his junior, and they had six children. Twenty years later his wife eloped with a lodger. Fish, who once said, "I was always fond of children," continued to look after the children and married three more times.

"Unparalleled Perversity"

"Fish's sexual life was of unparalleled perversity," Frederic Wertham says. At 5 he developed a penchant for being spanked because of a teacher. Sadism and masochism were the chief elements in his sexual development. "Experiences with excreta of every imaginable kind were practiced by him. . . . He took bits of cotton, saturated them with alcohol, inserted them in his rectum and set fire to them. He also did that to his child victims." Most disturbing, he developed a craving for cannibalism.

Fish admitted to a lifetime of preying on children, seducing at least 100. His job as a house painter, often working in basements or empty houses, provided opportunities for finding victims. In some cases, he castrated the boys. He developed a habit of sticking needles into himself below the scrotum; an X-ray showed 27 of these needles inside him, some of them eroded into small pieces. He also tried forcing needles under his fingernails, but found this too painful to continue.

Psychiatrist Frederic Wertham worked with the New York City's police department to determine Fish's mental condition. Wertham concluded that Fish's predilection for extreme sadomasochistic behaviors started when Fish was a child.

Visions of Hell

Fish suffered from "religious insanity." He had visions of Christ, as well as of Hell, and believed himself to be a particularly holy man. According to Wertham, Fish "felt that he was ordered by God to castrate little boys." Fish said, "I had to offer a child for sacrifice, to purge myself of iniquities." It is clear that Fish was insane, and that the jury's death sentence expressed its indignation rather than a considered verdict of his total responsibility.

Fish had been arrested many times on criminal charges, including grand larceny. He had also spent 90 days in jail for sending obscene letters and received two suspended sentences for passing fake checks. He was sent to a mental hospital for observation in 1930, more than two years after the Budd murder. The report stated, "at times he showed signs of mental disturbance." Although diagnosed as a sadist (a cat-o'-nine-tails was found in his room), no further investigation was made, and he was released.

Fish was implicated in 15 child murders, but the number may be closer to 100. He may have gotten away with them for so long because, as Wertham noted: "He looked like a meek and innocuous little old man . . . If you wanted someone to entrust your children to, he would be the one you would choose."

The electric chair at Sing Sing Correctional Facility, a maximum security prison in Ossining, New York. Fish was electrocuted in 1936 and buried in the prison's cemetery.

The Murder of Marion Parker

(December 17, 1927)

Edward Hickman

The kidnap-murder of 12-year-old Marion Parker was one of the most horrific crimes of 1927.

On December 15, 1927, a young man went to the registrar, Mary Holt, at the Mount Vernon School in Los Angeles, and explained that the chief cashier at a local bank, Perry Parker, had been seriously injured in an automobile accident and wanted to see his daughter Marion. The man gave his name as George Cooper and said he worked under Mr. Parker at the bank. His manner was so plausible and sincere that the registrar overcame her hesitation and let Marion go with him. Then she found herself wondering why Mr. Parker should ask for just Marion and not for her twin sister Marjorie too, so she rang the Parker's house. Perry Parker was, in fact, at home, and said he had not sent for Marion.

Marion Parker and the Fox

The police were immediately notified. Later that afternoon a telegram arrived for Parker, saying that he would be receiving a special delivery letter and he was to do nothing until he got it. The telegram was signed "Marion Parker and the Fox."

The next day the letter arrived, demanding a ransom of $1,500 for Marion's return. The kidnapper wrote that he would call with arrangements that afternoon, and accordingly when the distraught Parker waited at the chosen rendezvous, police were concealed nearby. It was a futile vigil, and the next morning another letter came from "The Fox." He wrote, "You gave me your word of honor . . . not to tip the police . . . you lied . . . you are insane to ignore my terms." A note in the child's writing was enclosed: "Please, Daddy, I want to come home this morning. This is your last chance . . . come by yourself or you won't see

me again." A further meeting at Manhattan Place Car Park, Los Angeles, was arranged for that evening. The money was handed over to a soft-spoken young man in an open car, who said he would leave Marion (dimly seen at his side bundled to her neck in a blanket) "just down the street."

The man drove off, and when he reached the end of the street, shoved Marion from the car. Parker found his daughter dead. The killer has hacked off her hands and legs, sadistically slashed her body, and wired her eyes open. The missing limbs were found in Elysian Park. The coroner later determined that she'd been disemboweled and stuffed with rags. Marion had probably been still alive when the man began to dismember her.

Marion Parker lived long enough to write a heartbreaking ransom plea to her father.

Foxhunt

A laundry mark on a towel wrapped around the remains led detectives to an apartment house, where they met, during their inquiries, a helpful, pleasant young lodger named Evans. Only after their departure did they realize that the shirt wrapped around the torso of Marion Parker bore the same initials as the one Evans wore when interviewed. Evans was really Edward Hickman, who had recently been imprisoned for forgery while working in the same bank as Marion's father. He was known to blame Mr. Parker for his prosecution.

Hickman fled in a stolen sedan, driving across California, Oregon, and Washington before his capture near Portland. He admitted to abducting Marion but denied the killing, blaming accomplices who were found to have no connection with the crime. (Strange methods were employed to make Hickman talk: once a guard burst into his cell shouting, "I've got a message for you from Marion!") Finally Hickman confessed, stating: "I always wanted to cut up a body, I used a pocket-knife, then drained each piece and washed them in the bathtub . . . then I went out to a cinema . . . I didn't like the pictures, they were too sad and made me cry.'"

Just Too Sensitive to Kill

As a teenager, Edward Hickman worked at two jobs to support his studies. From 5:00 AM to 7:00 AM every day, he worked in a chicken-packaging plant. The idea of killing chickens revolted him, so the manager excused him from that part of the job.

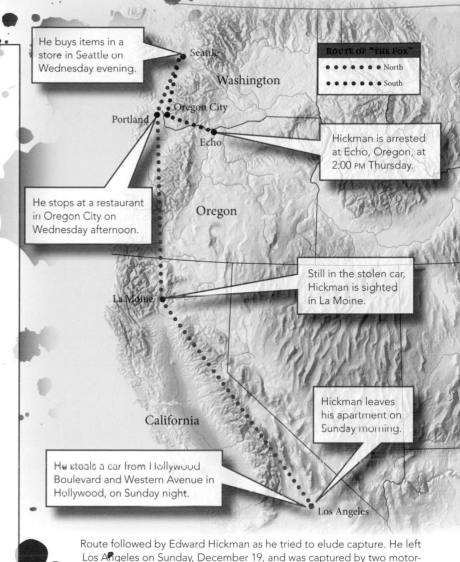

He buys items in a store in Seattle on Wednesday evening.

Hickman is arrested at Echo, Oregon, at 2:00 PM Thursday.

He stops at a restaurant in Oregon City on Wednesday afternoon.

Still in the stolen car, Hickman is sighted in La Moine.

Hickman leaves his apartment on Sunday morning.

He steals a car from Hollywood Boulevard and Western Avenue in Hollywood, on Sunday night.

ROUTE OF "THE FOX"
North
South

Route followed by Edward Hickman as he tried to elude capture. He left Los Angeles on Sunday, December 19, and was captured by two motorcycle cops in Echo, Oregon, on Thursday, December 22.

Madness and Hanging

Hickman's young defense lawyer, Richard Cantillon, found himself in an odd position. With the whole country baying for Hickman's blood, he was quickly convinced that Hickman was guilty—but insane. Hickman's grandmother had died insane, and his mother was periodically confined in a mental home. A brilliant student at his school in Kansas City, he had plunged into schizophrenia after leaving. Deeply religious, he was about to begin studies at a theological college but was obsessed by his belief that he needed $1,500 to complete his studies—hence the kidnap of Marion Parker.

As Cantillon expected, Hickman was found guilty and hanged in San Quentin in October 1928. An incompetent hangman made the rope too short to break his neck, and he strangled to death.

Bruno Hauptmann

The Lindbergh Baby Kidnapping

(March 1, 1932)

March 1, 1932, was a rainy and windy day in Hopewell, New Jersey, and the family of the famous aviator Charles Lindbergh were all suffering from colds—which is why they had decided to delay their departure to the home of their in-laws by 24 hours. At 10 o'clock that evening, the nursemaid, Betty Gow, asked Ann Lindbergh if she had taken the baby, Charles Jr., from his cot. She said no, and they went to ask her husband if he had the baby. Then all three rushed up to the room where 19-month-old Charles should have been asleep. On the windowsill was a note demanding $50,000 for the child's return.

The Ransom

Under the window the police found some smudged footprints; nearby there was a ladder in three sections and a chisel. The ladder, a crude homemade one, was broken where the top section joined the middle one. And there were no fingerprints in the child's room.

The kidnapping caused a nationwide sensation, and soon Hopewell was swarming with journalists. But the kidnappers themselves remained strangely silent.

The kidnap note offered few clues. It had various spelling mistakes, like "anyding" for "anything," and a handwriting expert said that it had probably been written by a German with low educational qualifications. It was signed by two interlocking circles, one red, one blue.

A week after the kidnapping, a well-wisher named Dr. John F. Condon sent a letter to his local newspaper in the Bronx, New York, offering $1,000 of his own money for the return of the child. The result was a letter addressed to Condon signed with two circles—a detail that had not been released to the public. It asked him to act as a go-between, and to place an advertisement reading "Mony is Redy" when he was ready to hand it over.

Lindbergh was convinced by the evidence of the two circles; he instructed Condon to go ahead and place the advertisement. That evening, a man's deep voice spoke to Condon on the telephone. Condon could hear someone else speaking Italian in the background as the deep voice told him that the gang would soon be in touch.

Anne Lindbergh with her infant son, Charles Jr.

"Would I Burn?"

A rendezvous was made with Condon at a cemetery. At the gates a young man with a handkerchief over his face asked if Condon had brought the money; Condon said it was not yet ready. The man took fright and ran away. Condon caught up with him and assured him he could trust him.

The man identified himself as "John," and suddenly asked a strange question: "Would I burn if the baby is dead?" Appalled, Condon asked, "Is the baby dead?" The man assured him that the baby was alive and said that he was now on a "boad" (boat). As a token of good faith, he would send Condon the baby's sleeping suit. In fact it arrived the following day, and the Lindberghs identified it as that of their son.

Shortly thereafter Lindbergh and Condon delivered the ransom money to the kidnappers. Fearful for his son's life, Lindbergh did not inform the police until after the ransom was paid.

On May 12 the decomposing of baby Charles was found in a shallow grave in the woods near the Lindbergh home; he had been killed by a blow on the head, apparently on the night of the kidnapping.

Good and Bad Leads

The police investigation made slow headway. The police strongly suspected nursemaid Betty Gow of being an accomplice, but the Lindberghs had no doubt of her innocence. Suspicion transferred to another maid, Violet Sharpe, when she committed suicide with poison, but again there was no evidence against her.

But the ransom bills—which included "gold certificates" that could be exchanged for gold—had all been marked by the police. Now banks were asked to look out for any of the bills, and in 1933 they began to turn up, mostly in New York, although some as far away as Chicago. This seemed to indicate that the kidnappers lived in New York or thereabouts. In early September 1934, $10 gold certificates began to appear in northern New York and the Bronx. In May of that year, Roosevelt had abandoned the gold standard and called in all gold certificates, but they continued to be accepted by banks and shops.

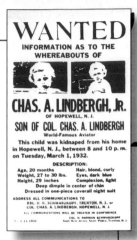

All efforts were made to locate the missing baby, including posters and newspaper ads.

Red Handed

On September 15, 1934, a dark-blue Dodge sedan drove into a garage in upper Manhattan, and the driver, who spoke with a German accent, paid for his fuel with a $10 gold certificate. Because these had ceased to be legal tender, the pump attendant noted the car's number on the back of the certificate. Four days later a bank teller noticed that the certificate was part of the Lindbergh ransom money, and saw that it had a registration number on the back: 4U-13-41-NY.

The police were informed. They quickly discovered that the vehicle was a dark-blue Dodge sedan belonging to Richard Bruno Hauptmann, a carpenter of 1279 East 222nd Street in the Bronx. It proved to be a small frame house, and that night, police surrounded it. The next morning, when a man stepped out of the door and drove off, police followed him and forced his car over to the curb. Hauptmann, a lean, good-looking German in his mid-30s, made no resistance and was found to be unarmed. In his wallet, police found a $20 bill, which proved to be from the ransom money. Concealed in his garage, they found a further hoard of Lindbergh money. Later a further $860 of ransom money and a gun were found concealed in a plank in the garage.

Quick Fact

Charles Lindbergh became world famous for, in 1927, being the first man to fly solo across the Atlantic, from New York to Paris. Later he rather blotted his name by speaking out against American involvement in the war against Nazi Germany.

Charles and Anne Lindbergh

Hauptmann's Story

Richard Hauptmann had come to the United States as a lowly stowaway in 1924. But in America he prospered. He and his wife worked hard, and by 1926 he was in a position to lend others money and even to buy a luncheonette. The day after the Wall Street crash he withdrew $2,800 from his account and began buying stocks and shares at rock bottom prices. Hauptmann had no need to kidnap the Lindbergh baby; even by modern standards he was very comfortable.

Hauptmann protested his innocence. The money, he explained, had been left in his care by a friend, Isidor Fisch, who had returned to Germany in December 1933, owing Hauptmann more than $7,000, on a joint business deal. Fisch had died of tuberculosis in March 1934.

In August 1934, said Hauptmann, he had noticed a shoebox that Fisch had given him for safekeeping before he left. It had been soaked by a leak, but proved to contain $14,600 in money and gold certificates. Feeling that at least half of it was his by right, Hauptmann dried it out and proceeded to spend it. That was Hauptmann's story.

But when Hauptmann's trial opened in Flemington, New Jersey, on January 2, 1935, it was clear that no one believed it.

Conclusive Proof

The most important piece of evidence was the ladder. Not only was there a clear possibility that some of its timber had been purchased at the Bronx yard where Hauptmann bought his timber, but one of the rungs had been traced to Hauptmann's own attic: Detective Bornmann had noticed a missing board, and found what remained of it, with the "rung" sawed out of it. The evidence could hardly have been more conclusive. Moreover, Condon's telephone number had been found pencilled on the back of a closet door in Hauptmann's house.

It was true that there was nothing conclusive to connect Hauptmann with the kidnapping itself. The footprints found outside the child's bedroom window were not Hauptmann's size, and Hauptmann's fingerprints were not found on the ladder. But a man called Millard Whited, who lived near Lindbergh, identified Hauptmann as a man he had seen hanging around the Lindbergh home on two occasions. And Lindbergh himself declared in court that Hauptmann was the "John" whose voice he had heard when delivering the ransom.

The jury was in no doubt whatsoever that Hauptmann was the kidnapper, and on February 13, 1935, he was sentenced to death. By October the Court of Appeals had denied his appeal. On April 3, 1936, Richard Hauptmann was electrocuted, protesting his innocence to the very end.

Framed?

Is it conceivable that Hauptmann was innocent? According to one investigator, BBC journalist Ludovic Kennedy, it is almost a certainty. Kennedy's investigations revealed that Hauptmann's story about his friend Isidor Fisch was true. And Fisch was indeed a swindler; he and Hauptmann were in the fur business together, and Fisch did owe Hauptmann over $7,000.

Then how did Hauptmann, or Fisch, come to be in possession of so much ransom money? The probable answer, Kennedy discovered, is that the Lindbergh ransom money was selling at a discount in New York's underworld; one convict described buying some at 40 cents on the dollar. Nothing is more likely than Fisch, with his underworld connections, bought a large quantity, and left it with Hauptmann when he sailed for Germany. Forensic examination of the money showed that it had been soaked and dried out, confirming Hauptmann's story that Fisch had left it on a damp top shelf in a closet.

The truth was that Hauptmann could easily have been "framed." Soon after her husband's arrest, Anna Hauptmann had made the supreme mistake of moving out of the house, leaving it empty for police and reporters to wander through unobserved. It was only after Anna left, for example that Detective Bornmann "discovered" the missing board in the attic.

Lindbergh testifies at Hauptmann's trial.

Write it Down Exactly

Ludovic Kennedy's major discovery was that much of the evidence against Hauptmann was indeed fabricated. When arrested, he was asked to write out various sentences; the court was later told that Hauptmann's misspelling of various words had been exactly as in the ransom note. This was untrue; he had spelled correctly the first time, then been told to misspell various words—"singature'" for signature, "were" for where, "gut" for good. The court was also assured that handwriting experts had identified Hauptmann's writing as that of the ransom notes; Kennedy submitted the samples to two modern experts, who both said they were not written by the same man.

Kennedy's investigation also revealed that Millard Whited, the farmhand who identified Hauptmann as a man he had seen hanging around the Lindbergh property, had originally flatly denied seeing anyone suspicious; he was later offered generous "expenses," and changed his story.

As to Lindbergh himself, he had been invited to sit quietly in a corner of the room, in disguise, when Hauptmann was brought in for questioning; he therefore knew him well when he identified him in court as "John."

The Second Murder

The most serious piece of evidence against Hauptmann was, of course, the ladder. Hauptmann rightly pointed out in court that he was a skilled carpenter, and that the ladder was made by an amateur. If the jury registered this point, they may have felt that he had deliberately botched it to mislead investigators—for, after all, was there not the conclusive evidence of the sixteenth rung, whose wood was found in Hauptmann's attic?

But, as Ludovic Kennedy points out, this plank was only "found" when Mrs. Hauptmann had abandoned the house to the investigators. Was it likely that Hauptmann would go to the trouble of tearing up his attic floor, sawing out a piece of wood from the plank, then planing it down to size, when it would have been simpler to just get another piece of wood from his workshop? He was, after all, a professional carpenter. Kennedy quite clearly believed that the rung was concocted by Detective Bornmann or one of the other investigators.

Given the horror of the case, this faking of evidence may even seem understandable: the police really did firmly believe

Investigators at the Lindbergh's house in Hopewell, after the baby was discovered missing. The ladder left leaning near the bedroom window was a key factor in Hauptmann's conviction.

that Bruno Hauptmann was guilty—so they merely "strengthened" their case a little . . .

Unfortunately it seems that in doing so, they judicially murdered an innocent man and let the guilty go free.

The Ravine Murders

(September 14, 1935)

On a cool autumn day, September 29, 1935, a young woman walking the hills two miles north of the town of Moffat in Dumfriesshire, Scotland, looked down from a bridge over Gardenholme Linn, a stream running into the Annan River. She noticed a bundle jammed against a boulder in the ravine. Then she noticed that a human arm was sticking out of it.

After the police arrived and began scouring the bank, they soon made a gruesome discovery: two mutilated human heads, as well as four more grisly bundles. Each package proved to contain human remains—thighbones, lower legs, lumps of flesh, and an armless torso. One sheet of newspaper wrapped around two upper arms proved to be the *Sunday Graphic* for September 15, 1935.

Isabella Ruxton, 1935

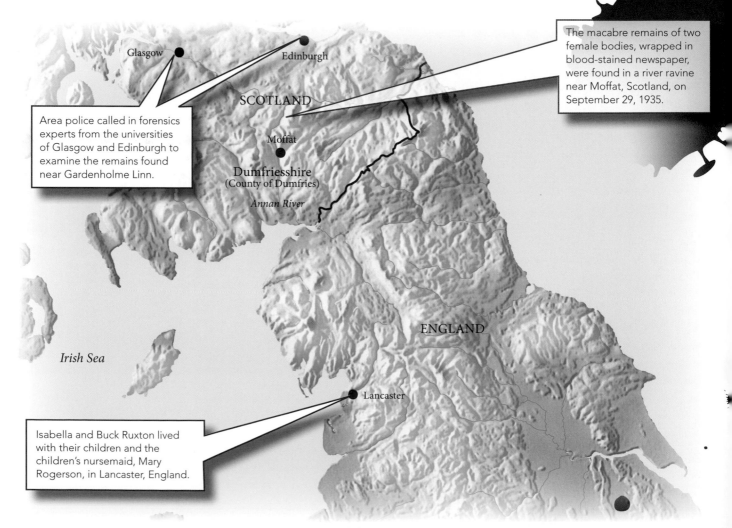

The macabre remains of two female bodies, wrapped in blood-stained newspaper, were found in a river ravine near Moffat, Scotland, on September 29, 1935.

Area police called in forensics experts from the universities of Glasgow and Edinburgh to examine the remains found near Gardenholme Linn.

Isabella and Buck Ruxton lived with their children and the children's nursemaid, Mary Rogerson, in Lancaster, England.

John Glaister Jr. (left) and two other men at Moffat during the search and recovery of the remains of Isabella Ruxton and Mary Rogerson.

Dr. Buck Ruxton, born Bukhtyar Rustomji in Bombay, India, moved to the United Kingdom five years before the murders. His patients in Lancaster, England, found him to be a caring, competent professional.

The Human Jigsaw Puzzle

The following day forensic pathologist John Glaister Jr. from the University of Glasgow and Dr. Gilbert Millar of the University of Edinburgh arrived to help the investigation. Professor Glaister quickly realized that this killing was not the work of some terrified amateur—the murderer had taken care to cover his tracks. He or she had not only skillfully dismembered the bodies but also removed the skin from the heads to make the faces unrecognizable, cut off the fingertips to make fingerprint identification impossible, and had pulled out the teeth to prevent dental identification.

Excitable Doctor

Meanwhile, the police were working on their own clues. The *Sunday Graphic* wrapping the bodies was a special local edition, printed only for the Morecambe and Lancaster, England, area. And the clothes in which some of the remains had been wrapped were also distinctive: the head of the younger woman had been wrapped in a blouse with a patch under the arm.

In Lancaster, Dr. Buck Ruxton, a diligent Indian-born GP, had already attracted the suspicions of the local police. Ten days after the remains were found in the Gardenholme Linn, Ruxton—a small, rather good-looking man with a wildly excitable manner—had called on the police to complain that people were saying that he had murdered his wife. The police must help him find her and prove that she was still alive . . .

Forensics Pioneers

The remains were taken to the anatomy department at the University of Edinburgh for extensive postmortem evaluation by a team of experts in the nascent science of forensic pathology. Professor Glaister sorted through the dismembered remains. When he was finally done, he found that he had one almost complete body, the taller one, and one body minus a trunk. The discovery that the assorted pieces of flesh included three breasts also made it clear that both bodies were those of women.

As to the cause of death, this was fairly clear. The taller woman suffered five stab wounds in the chest, several broken bones, and many bruises. The hyoid bone in the neck was broken, indicating strangulation before the other injuries had been inflicted. The swollen and bruised tongue confirmed this. Glaister reasoned that a murderer who strangled and beat his victim before stabbing her would probably be in the grip of jealous rage. As to the other body, the signs were that she had simply been battered to death with a blunt instrument.

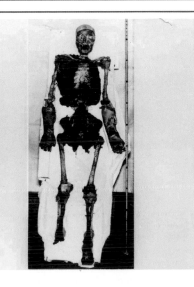

Strange Stains

Despite the doctor's apparent panic over the disappearance of his wife, Buck Ruxton was soon the investigation's chief suspect. The Scottish police had already visited the mother of the Ruxtons' nursemaid, Mary Rogerson, after she had reported her daughter missing. When Mrs. Rogerson saw the patched blouse used to wrap the severed head, she knew that her daughter was dead; Mary had bought it secondhand at a jumble sale and patched it under the arm.

The police also interviewed the Ruxtons' charlady, Mrs. Oxley. She told them that on the day Isabella Ruxton and Mary Rogerson had disappeared, Sunday, September, 15, 1935, the doctor had arrived early at her house and explained that it was unnecessary for her to come to work that day—he was taking the children to Morecambe, and his wife had gone to Edinburgh. The following morning, she found the Ruxtons' house—at 2 Dalton Square—in a state of chaos, with carpets removed and the bath full of reddish yellow stains.

On October 12 the police questioned Ruxton all night, and at 7:20 the next morning they charged him with the murder of Mary Rogerson and his wife, Isabella.

Mary Rogerson, shortly before her death

Cutting-Edge Evidence

Despite the killer's careful efforts to obscure the identity of the mutilated bodies found in Scotland, the forensics experts—Professor John Glaister Jr. and Dr. Gilbert Millar, along with Professor Sydney Smith, Dr. Arthur Hutchinson, and Professor J. C. Brash of the University of Edinburgh—made sense of the jumble of bones and body parts.

The forensics teams turned to innovative new techniques of photographic comparisons and reconstructions to assemble an impressive array of evidence that proved identity beyond a reasonable doubt.

For the photographic reconstructions and comparisons to work, the forensics team had to first find the scale. In the example at left, the team found the precise scale of a portrait of Isabella Ruxton wearing a dress and tiara, by staging a measured shot of the dress and tiara and then superimposing it on the portrait.

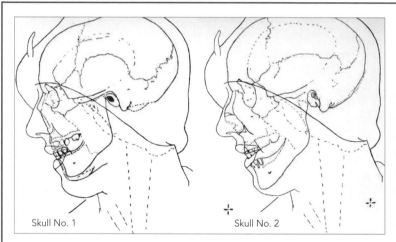

Skull No. 1   Skull No. 2

Above: The outlines of the two found skulls superimposed over the outlines of Isabella Ruxton's head and face. In the first, shown left, it is clear that the smaller skull, marked Skull No. 1, is not a match. The outlines of the larger one, marked Skull No. 2, superimposed on same outlines, show that this skull likely came from Isabella Ruxton.

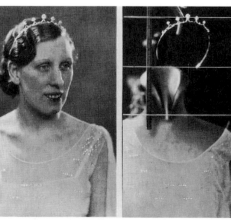

Insane Jealousy

The truth about the murders soon became plain. Ruxton was pathologically jealous, although there was no evidence that his wife—theirs was in fact a common-law marriage—had ever been unfaithful to him.

Isabella Ruxton had gone to spend the afternoon of Saturday, September 14, with two of her sisters in Blackpool. But convinced that she was actually in a hotel room with a man, Ruxton worked himself into a jealous frenzy. When she arrived back far later than expected from the trip, he began to beat her. He then throttled her unconscious and stabbed her to death. Mary Rogerson had probably heard the screams and come in to see what was happening; Ruxton beat her to death.

Crazed with the fear of discovery, Ruxton spent the next day dismembering the bodies and packing them in straw; that night, he made his trip north to dispose of them . . .

Red Stains on the Carpet

There was a children's playground song of the time of the Ruxton trial. It went (to the tune of "Red Sails in the Sunset"):

Red stains on the carpet,
Red stains on the knife,
Oh, Dr. Buck Ruxton,
You've cut up your wife.
The nursemaid, she saw you,
And threatened to tell,
So, Dr. Buck Ruxton,
You killed her as well.

The Trial

Dr. Ruxton's counsel, Norman Birkett, must have feared that his client did not stand a ghost of a chance. His only line of defense was that the bodies found in the Gardenholme Linn were not those of Isabella Ruxton and Mary Rogerson but of some other persons. But when the medical experts gave their evidence, it was obvious that the identity of the bodies had been established beyond all possible doubt. One particularly persuasive photograph presented in evidence superimposed the larger of the two skulls on a side-view photograph of Isabella Ruxton. She had a rather long, horsey face, and it was obvious that the two fitted together with gruesome exactitude.

And Dr. Ruxton's evidence was self-evidently a web of lies and evasions. The prosecution, however, presented convincing testimony against Ruxton, such as that of a cyclist in a town midway between Lancaster and Dumfriesshire. This man, though unhurt by the speeding car that knocked him from his bike, was fast-thinking enough to memorize the license plate number of the car that just sped on after the collision. The preponderance of incriminating evidence led to the jury declaring a unanimous verdict of guilty, arrived at in only one hour. The jealous doctor was hanged at Strangeways jail, Manchester, May 12, 1936.

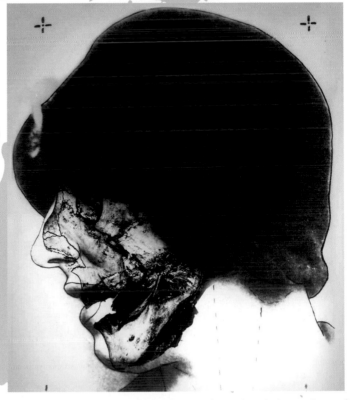

The forensics team presented evidence at the trial, including a photo of one of the found skulls superimposed over a photo of Isabella Ruxton.

The Lonely Hearts Killers
(1948-1949)

Raymond Fernandez and Martha Beck

Raymond Fernandez was a con man and a swindler of women. He was a Hawaiian-born Spanish American with gold teeth, and at the age of 31 he wore a wig to conceal his increasing baldness. He took advantage of the postwar man shortage in the United States (where, in 1947, there were one and a quarter million more women than men) to seduce lonely middle-aged women, making contact with them through "Lonely Hearts" clubs—clubs that, for a fee, would organize a meeting between lonely men and women.

Accidental Sex Maniac

Fernandez was a "sex maniac" but not by birth. The personality change came about in 1945, when the hatch of an oil tanker fell on his head while he was a seaman. The hatch knocked him unconscious, creating an indentation in his skull. After that he became sexually insatiable, happy to seduce any female between 17 and 70. He soon found that he could combine making love with making a living, by persuading the lady to hand over her savings.

Between 1945 and 1947 Raymond Fernandez seduced dozens of women, many of who gave him money voluntarily in return for the pleasure he gave them.

Enter Martha

In 1947 Fernandez met Martha Beck, an obese nurse who had been married three times and had been deprived of the custody of her children because she had been found unfit to take care of them. Fernandez's original intention was to separate her from her nest egg and flee, but when she fell fanatically in love with him, he found her frantic passion impossible to resist. Besides, like him, she was sexually insatiable.

Martha was only 26. As soon as Fernandez divulged the secret of how he made a living, she decided to join him in his self-chosen profession; she would pose as his sister and help him fleece middle-aged women—if necessary by "marrying" them.

The First Murder

In 1949 Martha added a refinement of her own—murder. When her lover was in bed with his latest conquest, 66-year-old Janet Fay, Martha was seized by frenzied jealousy and bashed Fay on the head with a hammer. Raymond finished the job by strangling her. They then dug a grave in the basement and covered the body in concrete.

On the day of Fay's murder, Raymond received a reply to one of his advertisements. It was from a widow named Delphine Dowling, 28, who lived in Grand Rapids, Michigan, with her 2-year-old daughter, Rainelle. In January 1949 the "brother and sister" moved in.

Film reenactment of Martha killing Janet Fay with a hammer

A Fitting Job

Martha had worked as a nurse, but found that the work would hire her was in a funeral home, where she spent her time surrounded by corpses.

Debacle

Five weeks later, on February 28, neighbors, who had not seen Rainelle and her mother in days, decided to call the police. Fernandez and Beck were at the cinema when they arrived and denied knowing where Mrs. Dowling had gone. They unwisely invited the police to search the house. In the cellar the police investigators noticed a spot of damp cement and soon unearthed the bodies of Mrs. Dowling and Rainelle.

Once arrested Fernandez and Beck talked freely. They admitted to murdering Mrs. Dowling by shooting her as she slept and then drowning the little girl two days later when she would not stop crying. Martha added that, in 1948, she had been so jealous of a widow, Myrtle Young, who had accompanied them to Chicago, that she had insisted on spoiling Raymond's fun by sharing a bed with her. They then poisoned Myrtle Young with barbiturates.

Trial

Because there was no death penalty in Michigan, the police decided to transfer the trial to New York. The killers naturally objected, but after a legal battle, the trial opened in New York on June 28, 1949. Fernandez and Beck were charged with the murder of Janet Fay. The details that emerged of Fernadez and Beck's sexual relationship were so indecent that they were never published. On August 22, 1949, the pair was sentenced to death.

In Sing Sing prison they still caused some commotion; they continued to declare their love for one another and to wave when they had a chance to catch a casual glimpse of one another across the exercise yard. Fernandez's boastfulness about his sex life with Beck led other prisoners to start a story that she was having an affair with someone in the women's wing, and Fernandez almost went insane with jealousy. Yet they were still declaring their undying love for one another when they were executed on March 7, 1951.

No full account of their murders has been published, since only the three murders to which they confessed were investigated. As many as 14 more were being considered.

Beck, second from left, and Fernandez, right, exchange smiles past the department of correction officer assigned to escort Fernandez as they wait in the court building of the Bronx Supreme Court in New York. During the trial the pair reached out to each other whenever possible.

Reggie Kray, left, and Ronnie Kray

London's East End Celebrity Mobsters

(1950s-1960s)

Ronald and Reginald Kray, identical twins, were born in 1933 in the East End of London, in what was then the slum district of Hoxton. Sons of a scrap gold dealer, Ronnie and Reggie were brought up rather better off than other East End boys, but they maintained their front as working-class criminal heroes throughout their gangster careers.

From Boxers to Brutes

Ironically, it was national service that pushed the Kray twins into careers as English Mafiosi. In their teens they had shown great promise as amateur boxers—neither of them ever lost a fight—and they were both preparing to go professional when, in 1952, they were called up. The twins joined the army, but they had no intention of serving out their full stint. They deserted together several times but were always recaptured. The third time, after assaulting the arresting officer, they were sent to await court-martial in the Tower of London (the Kray twins were among the last inmates of that historic prison).

While awaiting trial the pair discovered that they could bully the authorities. They threw tantrums, burned their beds, and emptied the toilet bucket over a guard. The army, seeing that at least one of them (Ronnie, as it turned out) was borderline insane, simply released them with dishonorable discharges.

But those discharges killed any chance for legitimate boxing careers, so the twins bought a snooker club in Bethnal Green. There they put their violent tendencies to work for them, setting up in the protection racket. By the late 1950s the Krays were the most feared gangsters in the city.

Pop Culture Heroes

The twins captured the imagination of writers, filmmakers, *[illegible]* and *[illegible]* designers. They *[illegible]* *[illegible]* in many songs, including *[illegible]* Davies, inspired *[illegible]* were the key *[illegible]* The hit British *[illegible]* features a crime *[illegible]*

Gentlemen Thugs

Even today there are those who believe that the Krays' mob, "the Firm," benefited the East End's poor. It is true that, as their empire of mob-funded nightclubs expanded across the city, they made a point of publicly handing out largesse and favors. But their protection rackets supplied most of the cash for such generosity. The loss of the money extorted from local businessmen helped keep the East End poor and crime-ridden, while the rest of London and Britain grew steadily more affluent. The Krays, for all their pretensions, were parasites first and foremost.

Their success was mostly due to a willingness to indulge in extreme violence. Although they murdered less often than their American mobster counterparts, they were always willing to use beatings and torture to cement their power base. Ronnie especially—a certified paranoid psychotic—could explode into violence on any pretext. He once slashed a friend's face so fiercely that he needed 70 stitches, all because the friend had made a playful remark about Ronnie putting on weight.

As well as the protection racket, the Firm committed arson for the insurance payouts, oversaw armed robberies, and hijacked lorries. The Krays also employed a little person to sneak up on enemies and slash their buttocks with a razor—a very painful and slow-healing wound that prevented the humiliated victims from sitting down for weeks.

Left: Celebrities of the 1960s, such as Frank Sinatra, Judy Garland, and Diana Dors (at left with actor Joe Robinson) were frequent—and pampered—guests at the Krays' nightclubs.

Right: The Blind Beggar, the Whitechapel pub where Ronnie killed a man in cold blood as pub patrons looked on

Friends of the Stars

Ronnie and Reggie carefully maintained a public image as nice, well-dressed, legitimate businessmen. Celebrities flocked to their nightclubs and reveled in the generous hospitality of the Krays. The twins wined and dined famous actors like George Raft, Frank Sinatra, Judy Garland, Diana Dors, and Barbara Windsor. They were photographed by top '60s photographer David Bailey. And many politicians also found the Kray charm irresistible, possibly including high-ranking Conservative peer Lord Boothby, who was rumored to have had a homosexual affair with Ronnie. When the *Sunday Mirror* alluded to the rumor, Boothby threatened to sue. The paper backed down and paid a staggering £40,000 to him in an out-of-court settlement. Whether the allegation was true or not, the British media got the message that the Krays were "friends of the Establishment" and backed off investigating their gangland activities.

But despite their (generally) acceptable public image, the Krays began to overreach themselves. In 1966 Ronnie openly shot rival gangster George Cornell dead in the Blind Beggar pub. Yet no witnesses came forward; the Krays' reign of fear was too strong, coupled with the traditional East End reluctance to "grass" (inform) to the police. Charges were dropped.

The Wall of Silence

Together in death: the shared grave of the Kray twins

In Loving Memory

RONALD KRAY
BORN 24th OCTOBER 1933
DIED 17th MARCH 1995

REGINALD KRAY
BORN 24th OCTOBER 1933
DIED 1st OCTOBER 2000

Grant them eternal rest, O Lord;
and let perpetual light shine on them

The Krays believed they were immune to the law, because nobody would dare give evidence against them. After an exhaustive investigation, Detective Superintendent "Nipper" Read of the Scotland Yard Murder Squad realized that nobody would snitch if the Firm was on the streets to enforce silence. So, risking his career, Read arrested the Krays and 16 of their gang, even though he had insufficient evidence to convict them on any major charge. But with the Firm off the streets, people felt safe to come forward. The Kray twins were tried and convicted on three counts of murder: Ronnie had killed Cornell; Reggie killed Firm member Jack "the Hat" McVitie, when McVitie failed to kill a gang enemy; and Ronnie broke Frank "Mad Axeman" Mitchell out of Dartmoor Prison only to kill him when he proved too insane to be kept safely in hiding.

The brothers were sentenced to life imprisonment in 1969. Ronnie was subsequently deemed criminally insane and died in the Broadmoor psychiatric hospital in 1995. Reggie was granted compassionate leave in August 2000, when he was diagnosed with colon cancer. He died 35 days later.

Public Enemy Number One

(1962-1979)

Jacques Mesrine

Jacques Mesrine was born in Clichy, Paris, in 1937. He was a poor student at school, but his charm made a strong impression on his contemporaries. At the age of 18 he married a beautiful girl from Martinique, but he soon found marriage boring. At 19 he was glad to be conscripted into the army and was sent to Algeria, where the French were trying to put down a Muslim revolt. Mesrine thoroughly enjoyed being in action and received the Military Cross for valor. On his return to civilian life he soon committed his first burglary. With two other men he broke into the flat of a wealthy financier and escaped with 25 million francs.

First Arrest

In spring 1962 Mesrine was arrested for burglary and sentenced to three years in prison. He was released on parole one year later. For a while he decided to "go straight." He married a second time, had a young daughter, and became an architect. But when, in late 1964, he was made redundant, he went back to crime.

In 1967 another attempt to go straight (this time as an innkeeper) failed—he found respectability too unexciting.

With a lover named Jeanne Schneider, Mesrine carried out a daring robbery at a hotel in Switzerland. In 1968, as one of the most wanted robbers in France, he decided to move to Canada.

He and Jeanne went to work for a Montreal millionaire, Otorges Deslauriers, as chauffeur and housekeeper, but when Deslauriers dismissed them, Mesrine responded by kidnapping him and holding him for a $200,000 ransom. Deslauriers managed to escape before this was paid.

Arrested by a border patrol when they crossed into the United States, Mesrine was given 10 years for the kidnapping of Deslauriers; Schneider received 5.

Escape

A year later Mesrine led a number of other prisoners in a spectacular escape from the "escape-proof" prison of Saint Vincent de Paul at Laval. Soon after, Mesrine and two accomplices were in the forests near Montreal where they were stopped by two forest rangers. One of the rangers recognized Mesrine and made the mistake of showing it. Both rangers were shot down, their bodies dumped in a nearby ditch and covered with branches.

There were more bank robberies. Then Mesrine met a beautiful 19-year-old, Jocelyne Deraiche, who became his mistress. With two accomplices Mesrine and Deraiche went south to Venezuela, where they were able to live quite comfortably on the profits of their bank robberies. When a police official told them that Interpol was on their trail, the couple flew quickly to Madrid.

The prison walls of Saint Vincent de Paul in Laval, Quebec, proved no match for Jacques Mesrine.

The venerable walls of La Santé Prison, above inset, also failed to contain Mesrine. Above, the lifeless body of France's Public Enemy No. 1 slumps in the BMW that failed to provide him with a fast getaway.

Achieving Fame

Mesrine now decided to become the best-known criminal in the world. In the remaining seven years of his life, he achieved that ambition.

Back in France, in 1973 Mesrine committed a dozen armed robberies, getting millions of francs. When police finally caught up with him on March 8, Mesrine staged a spectacular escape from the Palais de Justice in Compiegne, getting hold of a gun that an accomplice had left in a lavatory, then holding up the court and escaping with the judge as a human shield.

Not long after this a bank robbery went wrong, and Mesrine's accomplice was arrested. As a result, the police tracked down Mesrine to his flat and placed him under arrest.

Mesrine was sentenced to 20 years at La Santé, in Paris, another "escape-proof" prison. After a year there, he staged one of his most spectacular escapes. Using a cache of weapons a corrupt guard had smuggled into them, Mesrine and two other convicts held up their guards, stole their uniforms, and locked them in a cell. The convicts then found a group of workmen fitting new bars on the prison's windows and ordered them to move their ladder to an outside wall of the prison. Using a rope and grappling iron—also smuggled in for them—Mesrine and his fellows climbed to the top of the wall and then down the ladder. They flagged down a passing car and were gone.

He went to London and planned another astonishing crime—to kidnap the judge who had sentenced him to 20 years. He went to the judge's flat in Paris and held up his wife, daughter, and son-in-law. But the police were tipped off. When Mesrine saw the arrival of the police cars, he ran down the stairs and as he came face to face with several policemen, he pointed behind himself. "Quick, Mesrine's up there." And they went rushing past.

When the police finally located his hideout, in a flat in the Rue Belliard, they decided to take no chances. Mesrine had sworn never to be taken alive. On November 2, 1979, Mesrine came out of the building with his girlfriend, Sylvie Jeanjacquot, and walked toward his BMW, parked nearby. At a road junction, a blue truck signaled that he wanted to cut across Mesrine's vehicle and turn right. Mesrine waved him on. The truck stopped in front of the car, and another truck drew up behind. Four policemen climbed out and within seconds, 21 bullets had shattered the windshield. Mesrine was killed immediately.

Pablo Escobar

The Most Successful Drug in the World

(1980s-1993)

It is now not uncommon to hear of self-made multibillionaires, like Bill Gates and Ingvar Kamprad. But it is sobering to think that one of the first such billionaires was the ruthless criminal Pablo Escobar of Colombia.

Rising from humble beginnings—stealing and reselling gravestones as a schoolboy—Escobar became the world's most visible drug lord, indirectly taking on numerous Western governments in their "War on Drugs."

The People's Drug Dealer

Born in the poor Colombian town of Medellin in 1949, Pablo Escobar clawed his way up the spine of the criminal underworld: from stealing gravestones he moved on to fencing cars, then he got into the drug trade and ruthlessly killed his way to the top.

By the late 1970s Escobar was indisputably the most powerful cocaine dealer in the world. The drug was grown in Peru and Bolivia, processed in Columbia, and smuggled to North America, Europe, and as far away as East Asia.

His power also stretched to the public arena: in 1982 Escobar was even elected to the Colombian Chamber of Representatives. He did not fix this election; the people of Medellin—especially the poor—loved him because he built them churches, housing projects, and sports facilities out of his own pocket.

Escobar could easily afford such generosity. In 1989 *Forbes Magazine* published its list of the richest people in the world: Pablo Escobar was listed as number seven, with an estimated fortune of $25 billion.

The Price of Success

Pablo Escobar's power and wealth came at some cost . . . to others. It is believed that he ordered the murder of 30 judges and 457 policemen during the course of his career. His attitude to authority figures was summed up by his policy of "*plata o plomo*" (translation: "money or lead").

As to the number of competitors and employees he had killed, nobody can accurately guess. At one point he was killing around 20 people a day for a period of two months. Police once tapped a telephone conversation in which Escobar apologized to the caller for all the noise; his men were torturing someone to death in the same room. He is thought to have been directly responsible for the deaths of at least 4,000 people.

Some law enforcement officials were beyond the reach of both Escobar's bribes and bullets: he evidently lived in fear of being extradited to a foreign country, like the United States. In 1985 the Colombian Supreme Court was considering an extradition treaty with the United States. These considerations were terminated when left-wing guerrillas of the M-19 movement, under the instruction of Escobar, stormed the Supreme Court, and murdered half of the judges.

Influencing the Election

Resistance to the seemingly untouchable power of the drug lords in Colombia came to a head during the run-up to the 1990 general election. Several of the candidates for the presidency ran on an anticorruption ticket and seemed serious enough to disturb men like Escobar. He reacted more savagely than anyone could have guessed.

On August 18 the leading contender in the presidential race, former political journalist Luis Carlos Galán, was shot to death. A leading issue of his campaign had been to approve the extradition treaty with the United States.

On November 27 Avianca Airlines Flight 203 was blown to smithereens by a bomb while in flight. All 107 people on the plane died. Escobar's Medellin Cartel openly admitted that they had planted the bomb—mistakenly believing that presidential contender César Augusto Gaviria Trujillo would be on the aircraft. Trujillo was another candidate who backed the breaking of the cocaine cartels.

Admitting to the Flight 203 bombing was an act of stunning arrogance by Escobar: he was effectively saying that he was willing to hold the whole of Colombia under the gun. He underlined this message by bombing the Administrative Department of Security (DAS) headquarters on December 6, 1989, killing 52 people and injuring more than 1,000 more.

Luis Carlos Galán lost not only his bid for the Colombian presidency but also his life to the ruthless tactics of Escobar.

The government expropriated the Hacienda Napoles ranch, once Escobar's estate, in La Dorada, Colombia. It served as housing for low-income families before it was converted into a theme park.

A Nice, Comfortable Cell

Then Pablo Escobar did a genuinely surprising thing: he gave himself up and went to jail. But his idea of prison—dutifully provided by the Colombian authorities—was something like a private luxury hotel in which he could effortlessly continue his "business." He even had two brothers, accused of stealing from his cartel, brought into the prison and shot dead by his henchmen.

When news of this double killing surfaced, the embarrassed government threatened to allow his extradition to the United States. So he escaped his "prison" and went on the run in July 1992.

A man with as many enemies as Escobar should have realized that they would be after him at the first sign of weakness. A group calling themselves *Los Perseguidos por Pablo Escobar* (People Persecuted by Pablo Escobar) formed and hunted down and killed more than 300 members of the Medellin Cartel.

Escobar himself was trapped by Colombian police on December 2, 1993, and he was killed in the resulting gunfight.

The Beltway Snipers

(2002-2003)

The classic 1971 cop movie *Dirty Harry* was largely based on the real-life "Zodiac" murders that took place in the San Francisco Bay area in the late 1960s. The scriptwriters made one significant change to the *modus operandi* of their fictional serial killer: he used a sniper rifle to kill from a distance.

Fortunately criminal history has shown this to be a flight of fantasy, not something that a real serial killer would do. Serial killers are typically hands-on sadists, men who like to get close to their victims to more intensely enjoy the sense of power they get from ending innocent lives. No serial killer has been known to use a sniper rifle as his main method of killing . . . until the turn of the twenty-first century, that is.

John Allen Muhammad

A Bullet Out of the Blue

On October 2, 2002, James D. Spring, a program analyst at the National Oceanic and Atmospheric Administration, was crossing a car park in the Wheaton district of Washington, D.C. A gunshot cracked, and Spring dropped to the ground; he was dead, shot by a single, high-velocity rifle bullet.

It was immediately plain to investigators that this was no ordinary murder—even in crime-riddled D.C., police don't see murders by sniper fire. The high-velocity rifle is a specialist's weapon demanding specialist skills; it's not the sort of gun used in street gang drive-by shootings. Moreover, whoever had killed James Spring had done so expertly with a single shot, suggesting either military or paramilitary training. Given the events of September 11, just over a year before, some officers feared that the murder had been a terrorist incident.

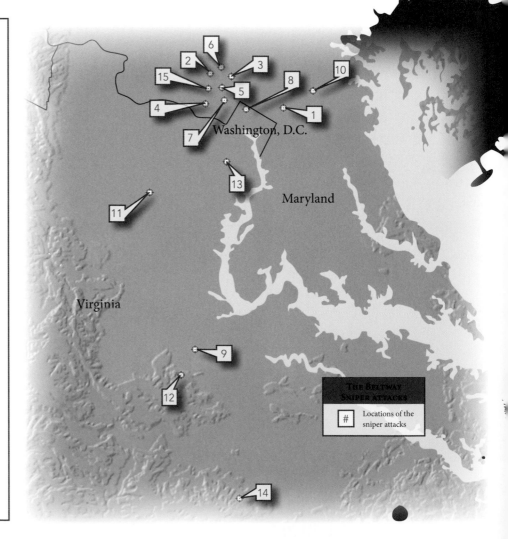

Washington, D.C.

Maryland

Virginia

The Beltway
Sniper attacks

| Locations of the sniper attacks

Spree Killer or Serial Murderer?

The difference between a spree killer and a serial murderer is not just one of time but of motive. Serial killers are cold and ruthless hunters, taking a lone victim at a time—cautiously—usually over a period of weeks, months, years, and even decades. Spree killers, on the other hand, murder lots of people at once. After a few hours they generally turn the gun on themselves.

What evidence we have (because such murderers are almost never taken alive to give confessions) is that spree killers egotistically decide to sacrifice others before they kill themselves as a bloody and final act of defiance to the world that they are rejecting. Serial killers are essentially homicidal sadists (disinclined to risk their liberty, let alone physically endanger themselves), while spree killers are usually social misfits who become homicidally violent after suffering a massive mental breakdown. Leaving aside the actual killing, the difference in motivation between a serial killer and a spree killer is as wide as the difference between that of a rapist and a suicide bomber.

Busy Day

Over the next 24 hours—between October 3 and 4—long-range sniper shots killed five more D.C. area residents. James Buchanan, 39, was cutting the grass at a car dealership in the White Flint area when a bullet hit him. Another bullet found Prenkumar Walekar, a 54-year-old taxi driver, as he filled up at a gas station in Aspen Hill. Sarah Ramos, a 34-year-old mother, was reading a magazine on a bench outside a post office in the Silver Spring district. Lori Ann Lewis-Rivera, 25, was vacuuming her van at a gas station in Kensington district.

The last fatality that grim day was a retired 72-year-old carpenter, Pascal Charlot, who was killed while standing at a bus stop in the inner city. But he was not the last victim. A 43-year-old woman was also shot while crossing a parking lot in Fredericksburg—a town 40 miles south of Washington—but she survived.

The murderer clearly liked to move about and had wasted no time. One police officer grimly commented that his annual county homicide rate "just went up 25 percent today."

This concentration of murders in such a short period suggested either a terrorist operation or a so-called spree killer. At this stage few police officers thought it likely that they had a serial killer on their hands.

At left, map plotting the locations of the Beltway Sniper attacks

A reflection pool and a stone memorial, shown above, were built at Brookside Gardens in Wheaton, Maryland, to pay respect to the lives lost during the Beltway Sniper killing spree.

"I Am God"

Panic spread across Washington, D.C., as soon as the story hit the news: a sniper was stalking the capital and nobody was safe. Some people refused to leave their homes, and many didn't dare use self-service gas stations because these seemed one of the killer's favorite hunting areas.

After a few days' pause, the killing began again. A 13-year-old boy was shot in the stomach as he got off his school bus in the Maryland suburbs of Washington, D.C. Surgeons struggled to save his life, but he died of massive internal injuries. The following day the killer returned to the scene of the boy's murder and left a tarot card with the words "Dear Mr. Policeman. I am God" written on it.

On October 9 the sniper once again moved away from the Washington suburbs, killing civil engineer Dean Harold Meyers, 53, at a gas station in the Virginia town of Manassas. Two days later Kenneth H. Bridges, also 53, was shot dead at a gas station near the town of Fredericksburg. On October 14 the sniper killed Linda Franklin, 47, while she and her husband loaded their car outside a shop at the Seven Corners Shopping Center on one of northern Virginia's busiest intersections. Coincidentally Linda Franklin was an FBI analyst.

Citizen crime control groups like the Guardian Angels tried to allay the fears of area residents.

God Wants Money

On October 19 a 37-year-old man was shot once in the stomach as he left a restaurant in the town of Ashland, 70 miles south of Washington. He suffered severe damage to his internal organs, but survived. He was to be the sniper's last victim.

The bizarre tarot card note had partly alleviated suspicion that the sniper might be an Islamic terrorist; no radical Muslim would claim to be God—not even in jest. More evidence to this effect came in the form of a letter found at the Ashland crime scene. The writer again referred to himself as God and accused the police of incompetence—adding that it was their fault that five people had had to die. Presumably this indicated that he had expected to be caught after the first two days of his killing spree. The letter demanded $10 million dollars to stop the killings and added chillingly, "Your children are not safe anywhere or at anytime." So the sniper was apparently a murderous extortionist—like the 1960s Zodiac serial killer—not an Islamic terrorist.

A deputy from Hanover County, left, and an Ashland city police officer stand guard at the crime scene at a Ponderosa restaurant after a man was shot and wounded.

The Ducks Are Noosed

Then, on October 24, the police caught him . . . or rather, them. There turned out to be two perpetrators working together: John Allen Muhammad, 41, and John Lee Malvo, 17, the older African American, the younger African Jamaican.

A member of the public had noticed a car parked for a long time in a road stop on Virginia Interstate Route 70 and had become suspicious. The police were informed and investigated as a matter of routine—with no notion that they were about to catch the Washington Sniper. Muhammad and Malvo were found fast asleep in the car, but fortunately the officers did not simply move them on. Closer inspection of the vehicle showed that it had been modified to allow a man to lie inside it and aim a rifle while remaining unseen.

Muhammad, who seems to have done the actual killing, turned out to have been an ex-U.S. Army soldier who had served in the 1992 Gulf War and had subsequently converted to Islam. Lee Malvo was a Jamaican who lived with Muhammad and evidently regarded the older man as a father figure. Both were convicted of murder, extortion, and terrorism charges in 2003. Muhammad was sentenced to death and Malvo to life imprisonment without chance of parole.

Montgomery County Police Chief Charles Moose holds two composite images of the type of van that was seen at the Spotsylvania County, Virginia, shooting.

Social Activist or Serial Killer?

Malvo originally claimed to have been the sole killer—called the "triggerman" in Virginia state law—but later retracted this confession, admitting that he had only made it to move the potential death sentence onto his own shoulders. This was rather less heroic than it at first sounds because, being a minor at the time of the killings, he was much less likely to be actually executed.

Malvo also claimed that Muhammad was a convert to the Nation of Islam—an Islamic black separatist movement—and had told Malvo that the killings were solely to extort money from the white-dominated U.S. government. This money, he went on, would be used to fund a separate nation that could be populated solely by young black people.

The fact that such a goal was patently impossible—given international law, the certain tracing of the extortion money, and numerous laws that protect young people of all races—suggests that Muhammad was spinning a tale to his young friend to justify his urge to kill.

It seems certain that Muhammad was simply a serial killer—a man addicted to murder. Support for this explanation came when it was suggested that the Washington, D.C., killings had not been his first. Investigating police believed that Muhammad was responsible for several unsolved murders.

Sniper shooting suspect John Lee Malvo is escorted from court after his preliminary hearing in Fairfax, Virginia. Only 17 at the time of the shootings, Malvo was not eligible for the death penalty in Maryland.

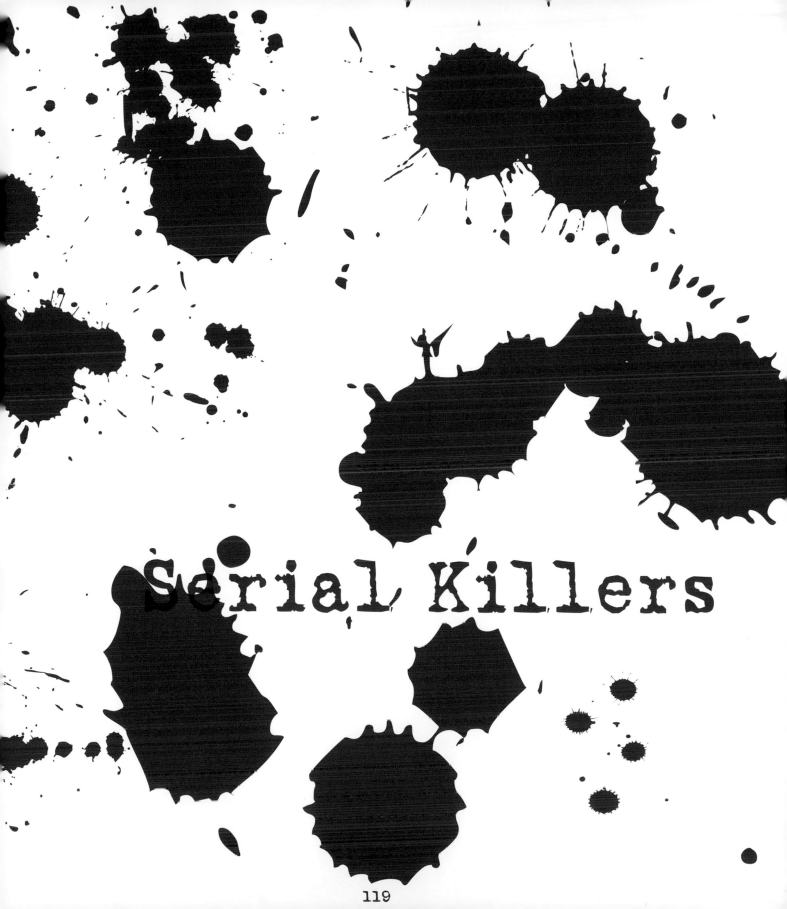

Serial Killers

Pee Wee Gaskins

(1953–1982)

Pee Wee Gaskins

Donald Henry "Pee Wee" Gaskins Jr. has a strong claim on being the worst serial killer in modern times. A harmless-looking little man with a high voice, Gaskins enjoyed torturing his victims, mostly hitchhikers, to death—and his victim total is well over 100.

Wilton Earle, a writer, found Gaskins particularly interesting. Gaskins was in prison awaiting execution for killing a number of "business associates," people involved with him in his car-theft racket. Earle wrote to ask him if he would like to collaborate on his autobiography. Gaskins invited Earle to visit him in prison, and in unsupervised conversations revealed that he was a sadistic killer who had often cooked and eaten part of his victims—sometimes while they were still alive.

Development of a Sadist

Born in the backwoods of South Carolina in 1933, Gaskins was sent to reform school for burglary when he was a teenager. There 20 youths gang-raped him. Later, after another prison sentence for raping an underage girl, he resolved to kill any woman he raped. The first time he did this he was so carried away by the sensation of power that he began doing it regularly.

When Gaskins was arrested on November 14, 1975—charged with contributing to the delinquency of a minor—it was for suspected involvement in the disappearance and murder of 13-year-old Kim Ghelkins.

On May 24, 1976, Gaskins went on trial in the Florence County Courthouse, was found guilty, and was sentenced to die in the electric chair. Successful plea-bargaining commuted this to a life sentence.

After his capture Pee Wee Gaskins agreed to show the law where he'd buried some of the bodies. At right, Gaskins, in handcuffs, directs officers to a spot in Florence County near Johnsonville, South Carolina.

Murder in a Prison Cell

In late 1980 prison contacts of a man named Tony Cimo approached Gaskins, asking him if he would murder a fellow prisoner, Rudolph Tyner. Tyner, a 24-year-old drug-addict, had killed an old couple in the course of robbery. Cimo was their son. Bored and frustrated, Gaskins rose to the challenge of committing a murder under the nose of the prison guards.

The plan was brilliant in its ingenuity. Gaskins suggested that he and Tyner install a homemade telephone between their cells, running it through a heating duct. Tyner's phone contained plastic explosives. When, at a prearranged time, Tyner said "Over to you," Gaskins plugged his end of the wire into an electric socket, and the explosion rocked the whole cell block. It blew Tyner to pieces.

Soon Tony Cimo was arrested, and he confessed everything. He and Gaskins stood trial for the murder of Rudolph Tyner. Cimo received eight years. Gaskins was sentenced to the electric chair.

Most of Gaskins's victims were hitchhikers who were unlucky enough to accept a ride with the ruthless killer.

Final Truth

When Wilton Earle, who felt that Gaskins's story might be worth telling, approached him in 1990, Gaskins cautiously agreed. Gaskins agreed to tell Earle what he called "the final truth." Earle did not realize that he was about to hear the most appalling and terrifying story of serial murder in the history of twentieth-century crime.

Having served two terms for rape, Gaskins had vowed it would never happen again. His solution was simple: to kill his victims. Having raped and killed his first female hitchhiker with a knife, he discovered that torture and murder were becoming such an addiction that after a while, it made no difference whether the victim was male or female; it was the torture—and the sense of power—that gave the pleasure. In effect, he became a character out of one of the Marquis de Sade's novels.

Gaskins estimated that in the six years between September 1969 and his arrest in November 1975, he committed between 80 and 90 "coastal kills," an average of 14 a year. He distinguished these murders of hitchhikers picked up on the coast road from his "serious murders," those committed for business or personal motives like revenge.

A crowd gathered outside the prison to celebrate Gaskin's execution.

The End

Hours before his execution on September 6, 1991, Gaskins tried to commit suicide with a razor blade that he had swallowed the previous week, then regurgitated. He was found in time, and given 20 stitches. Soon after midnight, he walked into the execution chamber without help and sat in the chair. After his wrist and ankles had been strapped, a metal headpiece was placed on his skull, with a wet sponge inside it. Before the black hood was placed over his head, he gave a thumbs-up salute to his lawyer. Three men then pressed three buttons—so that none of them would be sure who had been responsible for the execution.

The lifeless body of Pee Wee Gaskins was handed over to his daughter, and was later cremated.

Melvin Rees

Melvin Rees

(1957-1959)

On Sunday, January 11, 1959, an old blue Chevrolet forced another car off a lonely country road in Virginia. A tall, thin young man stepped out of the Chevy, waving a revolver. He ordered the occupants of the other car—Carroll and Mildred Jackson and their two children, Susan, age 5, and Janet, 18 months old—into the trunk of his car, got back into the driver's seat, and sped off.

A search for the Jacksons brought no result. Then another couple came forward to say that an old blue Chevrolet had also forced them off the road. A man had walked back toward their car, but they had quickly reversed and sped away.

Cruel Death

Two months after the Jacksons went missing, two men driving near Fredericksburg, Virginia, got stuck in the mud. Wanting to get some traction under the tires, they went in search of some dry sticks and brush. What they found was the decomposing body of a man laying in a ditch, a necktie binding his hands in front of him. Wasting no time the men got the car out of the mud and headed for a police station.

When police detectives inspected the body, which had a bullet wound in the head, they made another, grimmer discovery. A female baby lay beneath the man—with no apparent injuries. The pathologist who performed the postmortem determined that she had been tossed into the makeshift grave first and left to suffocate beneath the man. The bodies were those of Carroll and Janet Jackson.

Two months later, the bodies of Mildred and Susan Jackson were uncovered in Maryland. Mildred had been strangled with a stocking and Susan had been battered to death.

Anonymous Tip-Off

Five months after the murders of the Jackson family, in May 1959, the police received an anonymous tip-off that the murderer was a jazz musician named Melvin Rees, but police were unable to trace him. Early the following year a salesman named Glenn Moser went to the police, acknowledged that he was the author of the anonymous tip-off, and told them that he now had the suspect's address: Melvin Rees was working in a music shop in Memphis, Arkansas.

Rees was arrested there, and soon after the army sergeant identified him as Margaret Harold's shooter. A search of the home of Rees's parents uncovered the revolver with which Carroll Jackson had been shot and a diary describing the abduction of the Jacksons and their murders. "Caught on a lonely road. . . . Drove to a select area and killed the husband and baby. Now the mother and daughter were all mine." He described forcing Mildred Jackson to perform oral sex and then raping her repeatedly; the child was apparently also raped. (Full details have never been released.) He concluded: "I was her master."

The diary also described the sex murders of four more girls in Maryland: Mary Shomette, 16; Ann Ryan, 14; Mary Fellers, 18; and Shelby Venables, 16. The first two were found near the University of Maryland during the time that Rees had attended classes there. The other two were removed from rivers in the area. Rees would later confirm killing Fellers and Venables.

Blood Music

A song composer, Grant S. McWilliams, wrote "Crimson Concerto," based on his "favorite serial killer," Melvin Rees.

Earlier Victim

Two years earlier, in June 1957, a man had approached a courting couple in a car near Annapolis, Maryland—an army sergeant and his girlfriend, Margaret Harold—and asked for a lift. During the ride the man pulled out a gun and demanded money; when Harold said: "Don't give it to him," the man shot her in the back of the head. The sergeant flung open the door and ran. When police found the car, they also found Harold's body lying across the front seat without her dress; a police spokesperson described the killer as "a sexual degenerate." Near the scene of the crime, the police discovered a deserted shack full of pornographic pictures.

Rees was tried for the murder of the Jackson family in the Spotsylvania County Courthouse, shown above.

Reprieve

Rees was tried and found guilty of the murder of Margaret Harold in Baltimore in February 1961. In September of that year he again faced a jury, this time in Spotsylvania, Virginia, for the murder of the Jackson family. He escaped the death penalty, however. He was still appealing when, in 1972, the U.S. Supreme Court suspended the death penalty.

A Benzedrine inhaler. Rees had used the stimulant Benzadrine the night before killing the Jackson family. Benzadrine, a potent amphetamine that has a euphoric stimulant effect, was once sold over the counter in inhaler form. In the 1940s and 1950s, many people abused the drug, cracking open the inhalers and swallowing the Benzadrine-soaked strip inside. In 1959 the FDA made Benzadrine a prescription drug in the United States.

Philosophy of Murder

On the night before the Jackson killings, Rees had been on a Benzedrine kick and in the course of a rambling argument had told Glenn Moser: "You can't say it's wrong to kill. Only individual standards make it right or wrong." He had also explained that he wanted to experience everything: love, hate, life, death . . . When, after the murders, Moser asked him outright whether he was the killer, Rees disdained to lie; he simply refused to answer, leaving Moser to draw the self-evident conclusion.

There is not much known about Rees's background, or what turned him into a serial killer. Yet based on other cases, we can state with a fair degree of confidence that parental affection was lacking in childhood, and that he was a lonely, introverted child who was not much liked by his classmates. It is difficult, if not impossible, to find a case of a serial killer of whom this is not true.

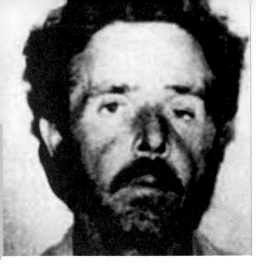

Henry Lee Lucas

Henry Lee Lucas
(1960-1983)

Henry Lee Lucas was thought, for a number of years, to be the most prolific known serial killer on the planet. He was eventually believed to have been at least on a par with Pedro Lopez—the "Monster of the Andes," who claimed to have killed 360 small girls. Yet subsequent evidence brought to light something perhaps even more shocking: that Lucas's lies coupled with the incompetence of the Texas police had effectively allowed many other killers to escape justice.

Bad Start

Born in 1937 in Blacksburg, Virginia, Lucas was the son of a prostitute and a railway worker who had lost both legs in an accident. His mother seems to have detested the child and treated him with sadistic cruelty, once causing brain damage when she struck him on the head with a piece of wood. His teacher, who charitably gave him hot meals, described him as one of the most impoverished and desperate hill children she had ever met. An accident led to the loss of one eye, so that he had to have it replaced with a glass one.

By the age of 15 Lucas was a juvenile delinquent, and was sent to a reformatory for breaking and entering. "I started stealing as soon as I could run fast," he later bragged. He had also by this time committed his first murder: he attempted to rape a 17-year-old girl at a bus stop, then strangled her when she resisted. He escaped arrest.

Free-Range Victims

In January 1960 he killed his mother during the course of a quarrel. He told arresting police officers that he was innocent of her death, putting her sudden collapse down to a heart attack. In fact she had been slashed to death with a knife—a fact Lucas could

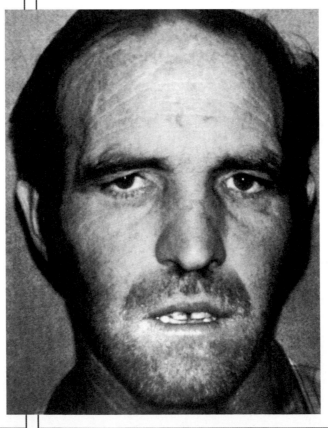

Ottis Toole. Toole and Lucas met at a soup kitchen in Jacksonville, Florida. In 2008 police announced that they had identified Toole as the likely murderer of 6-year-old Adam Walsh. Adam's abduction inspired his father, John Walsh, to become an advocate for victims of violent crime and the host of the TV show *America's Most Wanted*.

hardly have forgotten, and one that he must have known the police already knew. But automatic lying was also a habit with him.

He was sentenced to 40 years in prison, where he made several suicide attempts. He was recommended for parole after 10 years. In fact he seemed to have felt secure in prison and wanted to stay there; when paroled, he told the board that he would kill again.

After an unsuccessful marriage, he drifted through the South. In 1978 he met another drifter, Ottis Toole, a homosexual who fantasized about cannibalism. The two teamed up and set off on a murder spree with cavalier abandon. They kept the head of one murder victim in the trunk of their car for two days. "Killing someone is just like walking outdoors," Lucas once mused. "If I wanted a victim I'd just go to get one."

Enter Becky

Ottis Toole's sister liked Lucas enough to appoint him the guardian of her two youngest children, Frieda Powell, 9, and her younger brother Frank.

A year or two later, Frieda—who hated her name and insisted on being called "Becky"—left her Florida home with Lucas and her uncle Ottis. Lucas then began having sex with the still-underage girl. Becky was present during a number of killings, although it seems unlikely that she actually participated directly. But she did apparently help bury the bodies.

When Becky was 13 she was caught and sent to a juvenile detention center in Florida; with the help of Lucas and Toole she escaped, and the three of them went on another killing spree.

Police composite sketch of the woman known only as "Orange Socks"

One Murder Too Many

In 1982 Lucas was paid to look after 88-year-old Kate "Granny" Rich. Around this time Lucas and Becky had become members of a fundamentalist sect called House of Prayer in Stoneberg, Texas, and lived and worked there for several weeks. Under the influence of the religious teaching, Becky decided that she wanted to go back to Florida and finish her sentence in the reformatory. Lucas wanted her to stay but finally agreed to let her go. On the way to Florida they stopped to have sex in a field. Then they quarrelled, and when Becky suddenly slapped his face, Lucas stabbed her to death. He then dismembered her body and buried it.

It might seem surprising that for a man who had by that time killed dozens (by his own claim, hundreds) of people, this one extra betrayal and murder would have a shattering effect. But that is not to take into account the fragile humanity and emotional stability that seems to lurk in even the most monstrous serial killer.

Lucas deliberately had no feelings, other than negative and sexual, for most of his victims. He blanked any natural empathy for them, much as a diner makes a point of not regretting the premature death of the chicken he is eating. But Lucas had actually loved Becky, and her death struck him under his emotional armor. As far as Lucas was concerned, the murder of his lover was the beginning of the end.

Smug Confession

Back in Texas at the House of Prayer, he took Granny Rich for a long drive and both drank cans of beer. Lucas became angry at her questions about Becky—so he stabbed her to death, raped her corpse, and hid it in a culvert.

Lucas was the chief suspect in Rich's disappearance, but there was no evidence against him. In June 1983 Reuben Moore, head of the House of Prayer, reported to the police that Lucas owned a gun, a felony for an ex-convict. Lucas was arrested and in prison underwent a religious conversion that led him to confess to murdering Becky and Granny Rich. He then also confessed to a total of 360 murders.

Naturally the police used every available lead to confirm Lucas's claims, and soon found convincing evidence that he had committed a number of his professed kills. These included the rape and murder of a woman in Jackson, Michigan; a West Virginia police officer; and of an unknown female hitchhiker known simply as "Orange Socks" because that was all she was wearing when police found her body and because that was all Lucas could remember about her (apart from relished details of her murder).

Since the legal definition of a serial killer is one who kills at least three persons over a protracted period of time with no direct reason to do so, Lucas was officially designated a serial killer. He was eventually sentenced to death for eleven murders; his accomplice Ottis Toole also received a death sentence.

A History of Sex, Violence, and Lies

From the first murder, at the age of 15, Lucas killed anyone who resisted him. He was a high-dominance, highly sexed male, with an extremely low rage point.

"Sex is one of my downfalls. I get sex any way I can get it. If I have to force somebody to do it, I do. If I don't, I don't. I rape them; I've done that. I've killed animals to have sex with them." He also admitted that he had skinned animals alive during his teens; torturing animals is a classic sign of a budding serial killer. The murder of Becky Powell seems to have been a watershed for Lucas. It is obvious—from his confession—that he loved her in a way he had never loved anyone else, She was at once his wife, mistress, and daughter, the only person who had ever accepted him without criticism, who regarded him as a kind of god. Yet because of his fatal tendency to explode under pressure, he killed her.

After that he was not only on his own but also deprived of his main reason for living. The murder of Granny Rich—one of the few people who had ever treated him with any kindness at all—may have been a masochistic gesture of defiance and despair, as if impotently shaking his fist at the sky.

Lucas stands with state and local law enforcement officers at the site of a double homicide in San Luis Obispo County during a 4,000-mile tour of California. Lucas claimed that he and Ottis Toole abducted two little girls and murdered them under this bridge, located seven miles north of San Miguel.

V.I.P.: Very Important Prisoner

Sheriff Jim Boutwell of Williamson County, Texas, who came to know Lucas well in prison, noted in 1985: "Henry Lee Lucas is helping write a new chapter in the history of law enforcement. . . . Henry's confessions, and the subsequent investigations, have exposed the mobility of crime in the United States." In fact it was the Lucas case more than any other that made America aware of the existence of the "free-ranging" serial killer.

Asked about the problems of interrogating Lucas, Boutwell replied: "You don't interrogate him. . . . you talk with him just as a conversation. If at any time you indicate you disbelieve him

. . . you'll ruin your credibility with him." Boutwell described a case in which a police officer had driven three thousand miles to interview Lucas and, even though he had been warned against it, called Lucas a liar within the first two minutes. The officer's journey was wasted; Lucas immediately refused to hold any further "conversation" with him.

Lucas was allowed all kinds of privileges—as much coffee as he liked (he was a caffeine addict) and endless cigarettes. Asked whether this was not "babying" him, Boutwell again emphasized that this was the only way to get Lucas to cooperate—make sure he never felt like an "ordinary" prisoner.

Jogging His Memory

The Texas authorities quickly set up a Lucas Task Force and flew the killer from state to state to meet with local law enforcement officials who had unsolved murders on their books. Again and again Lucas gave convincing details of cases, and eventually the Lucas Task Force claimed to have "cleared up" 213 previously unsolved murders. It is for this reason that some crime books still list Lucas as the most prolific serial killer on record. Unfortunately, those books are wrong.

It seems now that Lucas made up many—some say most—of his confessions. The Texas authorities would give him details of a case before he met local law officers. This was doubtless done with the best of intentions—they believed that he had killed several hundred people and therefore was unlikely to remember key details of each murder. So they gave Lucas the files on each case to "jog his memory."

If, in fact, Lucas had had nothing to do with the murder case he was being shown, he would nevertheless concoct a story, based on the file he had just perused. Since local police were not told that he had read their own files on the case, they would usually be convinced that he had knowledge that only the killer could have known. And thus yet another murder would have been "cleared up" and added to the Lucas roster.

Philosophy of Murder

But then Lucas later retracted most of his "confessions." His reasons for originally giving them seem to have been three-fold. First, Lucas was given special privileges because the authorities so valued his stream of confessions. Second, Lucas took a malicious pleasure in misleading everyone. And third, he had the typical antisocial serial killer egotism that made him want to be known as "the most prolific murderer in the world."

Subsequent investigation of Lucas's movements over the years of his killing spree has shown conclusively that he could not have committed a large number of the murders originally ascribed to him. The fact is that nobody can be sure just who, or how many murders Henry Lee Lucas, Becky Powell, and Ottis Toole were involved in. And neither Toole or Lucas can help either. Ottis Toole died in prison of cirrhosis of the liver in 1996. Lucas escaped execution when George W. Bush, then governor of Texas, surprised just about everyone by commuting his death sentence to life imprisonment. But then Henry Lee Lucas died of heart failure in 2001—almost certainly brought on by all the extra coffee and cigarettes he had been given by the authorities over the years.

Estimates of the number killed by Lucas and Toole are now comparatively "low." Indeed Texas Ranger Phil Ryan—who was involved in the investigation—gave 15 as the highest count for the three of them. That would mean that at least 198 of the cases "cleared up" by the Lucas Task Force were actually closed prematurely. And because the authorities indulged in this bogus clearing up of unsolved cases, many murder investigations were closed down, leaving the real killers free.

A small crowd watches as the casket of Henry Lee Lucas is lowered into his grave Thursday, March 15, 2001, in Huntsville, Texas. Rather than death by execution, Lucas died of heart failure while still in prison.

Gerard Schaefer

The Killer in a Cop's Uniform

(1960s-1970s)

John Gerard Schaefer qualifies as one of the worst serial killers of the twentieth century. Although he was only convicted of killing two young women, crimes he committed while he still served as a deputy sheriff in Florida, he may have killed as many 30—or even more. In prison he turned his experience as a killer into horrific short stories that featured, in savage, sickening detail, the rape, torture, and murder of young women.

Teaching Them a Lesson

Criminologist Sondra London has described how, in 1964, when she was 17 and Schaefer 18, he became her first lover. When he confessed to her that he daydreamed of hanging women dressed only in their underwear, she broke off their engagement.

Later Schaefer developed a taste for abducting two girls together, so one could watch in terror as he killed the other. This is undoubtedly what he had in mind on July 22, 1972, when he drove two teenagers, Nancy Trotter, 17, and Paula Sue Wells, 18, to Hutchinson Island, south of Orlando, Florida. The girls had met Schaefer, a deputy sheriff in Broward County, the day before while they were hitchhiking, and he had offered to drive them to the beach.

Instead he took them into the woods and handcuffed them both. He forced Paula to stand on the giant roots of a cypress, where he tied her and made Nancy stand on the roots of another cypress, with a noose around her neck.

While Schaefer was terrorizing Paula, a call came in on his police radio. He had to leave but kept the girls tied to the trees. He intended to return. Luckily for Nancy and Paula they worked free of their bonds and ran from the woods—and straight to a police station to report the tale. When Schaefer arrived back at the woods to continue his torture, he found the girls gone. His plan had failed. He went home and rang the sheriff—his boss—and confessed. His intention, he explained, was to frighten the girls and make them realize that hitchhiking was dangerous.

The sheriff found his story suspicious and immediately dismissed Schaefer from the police force. The sheriff also charged him with assault and imprisonment. Schaefer was released on $15,000 bail, and ordered to appear for trial in November 1972.

Nancy Trotter and Paula Sue Wells thought they were in safe hands when the "nice" deputy sheriff offered them a ride. Instead of a day at the beach on Hutchinson Island, Deputy Sheriff Schaefer took them into the woods and tied them to huge cypress trees, intending to torture them.

More Victims

Two months later Schaefer introduced himself to Susan Place, 18, and her friend Georgia Jessup, 17. He went to Susan's home with the girls and told her parents that they were going to the beach to "play some guitar." Mrs. Place was suspicious of the guy—he was at least 10 years older than the girls—and noted down the license plate number of his blue Datsun. When neither girl returned home, Mrs. Place notified the police. The license plate had apparently been lifted from another car.

A month later, on October 23, 1972, two more teenaged girls vanished. Elsie Farmer and Mary Briscolini had set out to hitchhike and were never again seen alive. In January 1973 their skeletons were found in undergrowth near Fort Lauderdale.

Trapped by a License Plate

In November 1972 Schaefer was sentenced to six months for kidnapping Paula and Nancy. While he was in jail, his luck ran out. As Susan Place's mother was driving through Martin County, she noticed that all car license plates began with 42. The license number of the blue Datsun had started with a 4, and she wondered if she had the number wrong. When further research revealed that the owner of a blue Datsun, Gerard Schaefer, was in jail for assaulting two teenaged girls, she knew Schaefer had to be the abductor of Susan and Georgia.

From 1938 to 1980 Florida license plates bore a prefix number that indicated the county of origin. Although the initial trace of the blue Datsun that Susan Place's mother had seen the girls go off in came up empty, when Mrs. Place realized that she had written down the wrong prefix, the police were able to firmly identify the car as Schaefer's.

Killer Fiction

A search of Schaefer's home—where he lived with his mother—revealed various items that belonged to missing women and some extremely explicit pornography, written and illustrated by Schaefer himself, describing murder, rape, and acts of necrophilia.

Schaefer was sentenced to two life terms for the murders of Susan Place and Georgia Jessup. The items found in Schaefer's room convinced the police that he had killed at least 20 young women, as well as a child of 9. Later evidence suggested that even this could be less than half the total murders.

In February 1989 Sondra London addressed a letter to Schaefer in Florida State Prison. He replied effusively and soon had agreed to allow her to work on a book about him. She asked him if he still wrote pornographic stories, and he forwarded her some of his more recent efforts. Most of the stories have the same plot: he picks up a girl, they have sex, and he kills her sadistically, strangling, shooting, or disemboweling her. "She stared in wide-eyed fascination as the ropy coils of her own intestines slid out of her belly," one of them recounts.

Sondra London wrote: "What is scary is the idea of the hideously deformed, shadowy monster lurking behind this nice, normal guy." She decided to publish Schaefer's "killer fiction" herself, deciding, "You do not have to like something to learn from it." It appeared as a 70-page paperback.

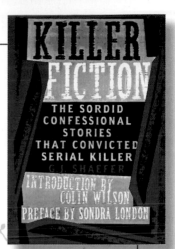

Killer Fiction contained the sick fantasies of Gerard Schaefer.

Death Inside

Gerard Schaefer was murdered in his cell on December 3, 1995, stabbed by a fellow inmate.

SUNSHINE STATE '72
42-0-28
FLORIDA

Fred and Rosemary West

(1960s-1990s)

Fred West

In the summer of 1993, Fred and Rosemary West—a builder and his wife living in Gloucester, England—were accused of sexually assaulting a young woman. The charges were eventually dropped after the accuser refused to give evidence, but in the meantime the West's children had been taken into foster care.

The children's caregivers overheard them talking about their older sister, Heather, being "under the patio." Questioned about this ominous phrase, the kids said that they had been told that Heather had been working in the midlands for the past five years, but that their parents would still occasionally threaten them with being "put under the patio with Heather . . ."

One Leg Bone Too Many

When the police checked Heather West's National Insurance number, they found that she had never claimed any state benefits or National Health care, despite supposedly leaving home at the tender age of 16. They applied for a warrant and entered 25 Cromwell Street to dig up the patio. When they found the dismembered skeleton of a young girl, they arrested Fred West.

Fred admitted to killing Heather in 1987, but insisted that his wife knew nothing about it. He admitted nothing else.

The investigation might have rested there, but then the scene-of-crime officers unearthed a third femur: there was more than one body under the patio. Confronted with this fresh evidence, Fred confessed to two more killings. He failed to mention the six other bodies—buried beneath his cellar and bathroom—in part because he didn't want his beloved home damaged by more digging. Later, however, under the pressure of intense questioning, he admitted to these killings, plus an additional three victims buried in the countryside.

A crowd gathers to watch as workers prepare to demolish the house owned by Fred and Rosemary West at 25 Cromwell Street.

Common Bond

When Rose's father once tried to persuade her to leave Fred, he noticed that a seemingly innocuous phrase from Fred clearly upset Rose terribly. Fred had implored Rose to stay with the words, "Come on, Rose, you know what we've got between us . . ."

Ending Unwanted Relationships

In custody Fred told the police that he didn't know the identity of each victim. The first three had been girlfriends. Then he killed his first wife and, later, her daughter by another man—then, of course, there was Heather. Several other victims had been lodgers at 25 Cromwell Street, but the others he had picked up hitchhiking or had simply abducted. Painstaking police investigation filled in the gaps in Fred's confession, but it is by no means certain that he told the whole truth as to the number of his victims.

Fred's first known victim was his girlfriend Anna McFall in 1967—he likely killed her because she was pregnant and pressuring him to marry her. He carefully dismembered her body and buried it and the fetus near the caravan they had been living in. He did not bury her fingers or toes, however, keeping them as keepsakes.

In summer 1971, Fred and his new girlfriend had Anne-Marie, his daughter with his first wife, Rena, and Rena's 8-year-old daughter, Charmaine, living with them. It took a few months for Rena to ask where her eldest child was. When it became obvious she might go to the authorities, Fred got Rena drunk, strangled her, dismembered her, and buried her under his house.

Fred Goes Hunting

Fred's live-in mistress was Rosemary Letts, soon to become Mrs. Rose West. By the time Rose moved in with him, Fred had developed the habit of raping, torturing, and killing strangers, but he never harmed her. Monster that he was, he genuinely loved his new wife.

In 1972 he killed Linda Gough and Lucy Partington, both 21—burying them beneath his new home at 25 Cromwell Street. Throughout the decade he continued killing: schoolgirl Carol Cooper in '73; Juanita Mottand and Shirley Hubbard in '75; Therese Siegenthaler—a Swiss hitchhiker he called "Tulip" because he thought she was Dutch—and Alison Chambers in '77. In '78 he killed 18-year-old Shirley Robinson, a lodger and lover heavily pregnant with his baby. He claimed to have given up murder until May 1987, when he killed Heather during a row.

The happy couple: Fred and Rose

Fred West hanged himself in his cell on New Year's Day 1995, before he could be tried, but the horror was not yet over. As the police investigation continued, it became obvious that his insistence that Rose knew nothing about the murders was a lie.

The Loving Accomplice

Testimony given by the six surviving West children and by friends and acquaintances clearly indicated that Rose West was fully involved in Fred's sexual predations. Further evidence came from Caroline Raine, who reported being abducted and sexually assaulted by *both* Fred and Rose.

Then there was the circumstantial, yet damning fact that Charmaine had died while Fred was in prison for petty crimes. The most likely candidate for that murder? The then 17-year-old lover, Rose.

At the trial, held in October 1995, the prosecution claimed that Rose had helped in all 10 of the killings that had taken place since 1972. The jury agreed (although there remains some doubt as to whether Rose actually helped kill her own daughter Heather). She was sentenced to 10 life terms in jail.

A court artist's sketch of defense barrister Richard Ferguson questioning his client, Rosemary West, during her trial

The Michigan Murders

(1967-1969)

John Norman Collins

On the evening of July 29, 1969, Michigan state trooper David Leik returned from a 12-day holiday to his home in Ypsilanti, Michigan, with his wife, Sandra, and their three young sons. The following morning Mrs. Leik carried a basket of clothes down to the washing machine in the basement and was mildly annoyed when she noticed a splotch of black paint on the concrete floor. Then she saw that a can of black spray paint had disappeared, along with some laundry detergent and a bottle of ammonia. Her husband remarked that only one person could have taken them: her nephew, John Norman Collins, a 22-year-old student at the University of Michigan, who had kept an eye on the house and fed the dog while they were away.

Hiding the Evidence

The telephone rang. It was a police station on Michigan Avenue. A Sergeant Walters asked if Leik could get over there immediately. The sergeant lost no time in explaining why he needed to see Leik so urgently.

"That nephew of yours, John Collins. He's the prime suspect in these coed murders."

Leik was incredulous; Collins was like a younger brother. Yet when Walters had outlined the strength of the evidence and mentioned that Collins had backed down from a lie detector test, the shaken Leik had to acknowledge that there was powerful evidence against his nephew. Collins really might be "the coed killer," suspected of killing seven female students in the area over the past two years.

That night Leik went down to the basement and scraped off some of the black paint with a knife. Underneath was a stain that looked ominously like blood.

A Frenzied Killer

The first victim, 19-year-old Mary Fleszar, had been found near a deserted farmhouse in Ypsilanti on August 11, 1967. Her killer had stabbed her 30 times, obviously in a sadistic frenzy, and then hacked off her hands and feet. Fleszar had gone out for an evening walk on July 18 and never returned home. A neighbor had seen a well-built, good-looking young man driving an old blue-gray Chevrolet, trying to pick her up.

Joan Schell, 20, disappeared almost a year later. She had gone out to spend the night with a boyfriend in Ann Arbor but never arrived. Her body was found among weeds outside Ann Arbor and, like the other, had been stabbed repeatedly. This time two students thought they had seen her walking with John Norman Collins. Collins flatly denied this, insisting that he had been at home in Detroit that weekend.

Four days later, on March 25, the body of 16-year-old Maralynn Skelton was found in Ann Arbor, lying facedown among weeds with a branch jammed into her vagina. She had been brutally beaten to death. She had apparently been hitchhiking.

The youngest victim, 13-year-old Dawn Basom, was found on April 16, 1969, strangled with an electrical cord, her breasts slashed repeatedly. She was a junior high school student. She had also been found near a deserted farm near Ypsilanti.

On June 9, 1969, searchers found another body on a deserted farm, this time in Ann Arbor. Alice Elizabeth Kalom, a student from Kalamazoo, had been stabbed repeatedly and her throat cut. She had also been shot in the back of the head.

On July 27, 1969, a doctor and his wife found a naked young woman's body in a wooded gully in Ann Arbor. It was Karen Sue Beineman, and she had been last seen alive four days earlier when, outside a wig maker's shop, she had accepted a lift on a motorcycle from a good-looking young man. She had been brutally beaten, raped, and strangled. Her panties, stuffed into her vagina, contained human hair clippings.

At least the manager of the wig shop had gotten a good look at the guy on the bike.

The Vital Clue

When David Leik found a dark stain underneath the black spray paint, he thought someone had tried to cover up a bloodstain. When technicians examined the stain, it was not blood, however, but varnish, which Leik had used to refinish his basement. Collins had mistaken it for blood, though, and sprayed over it.

The basement was also used for cutting the children's hair, and the hair clippings were identical to those in the panties stuffed in Beineman's vagina. The case against Collins was watertight. Collins sobbed when he learned of his mistake.

Michigan State and Salinas, California, city officers investigate a house trailer found in Salinas, which Collins towed west and lived in for a while. It was located in an alley behind the home of the parents of his Michigan roommate, Andrew Manuel.

Reflection of the landmark water tower in the window of an Eastern Michigan University campus building. The killer was called both the Ypsilanti Killer and the Coed Killer because several of his victims were students at EMU in Ypsilanti. A couple of the other victims were students at the University of Michigan in Ann Arbor.

Trial

The trial of John Collins for the murder of Karen Sue Beineman opened on June 22, 1970, and the hair evidence was crucial. He was found guilty and sentenced to life, meaning a minimum of 20 years. He is still in prison in Marquette, Michigan. To this day Collins maintains that he did not kill Beineman.

Attorney Hale Saph, front left, escorts members of Collins's family to his pre-trial hearing on August 7, 1969, in Ypsilanti.

Muddying the Waters

The 1969 murder of 23-year-old University of Michigan law student Jane Mixer, originally attributed to Collins, was reopened as "cold case" in 2004, on the basis of DNA evidence from perspiration found on Mixer's pantyhose. The DNA pointed to a man called Gary Leiterman. There was also evidence that Leiterman had given Mixer a lift on the evening of her murder. In 2005 a jury found Leiterman guilty, and he is at present serving life — while continuing to strongly protest his innocence.

The Houston Mass Murders

(1970-1973)

Dean Corll

At 8:24 AM on August 8, 1973, the voice of a young man came over the telephone at the Pasadena Police Department, just south of Houston, Texas: "I just killed a man . . ." The caller identified himself as Elmer Wayne Henley and said he was at 2020 Lamar Street.

A patrolman who went to the address found three frightened teenagers—two boys and a girl—outside; one of them identified himself as 17-year-old Wayne Henley and produced the .22-caliber pistol with which, he said, he had killed his friend Dean Corll. In the hallway of the house the body of a heavily built man lay face down with six bullet holes in the shoulder and back.

Henley Tells His Tale

Henley's story was that he and two friends, Rhonda Williams, 15, and Timothy Kerley, 16, had arrived at Corll's house at three in the morning for a glue-sniffing party. Corll, who was homosexual, had been furious that Henley had brought a girl. "You spoiled everything," he complained. The teenagers sniffed acrylic paint from a paper bag, and an hour later all three were unconscious on the floor. When Henley woke up, he was tied and handcuffed, and the angry Corll was threatening to kill him.

Wayne Henley, shown below, during a phone interview in 2008. He remains in prison for his role of accomplice to sadistic killer Dean Corll.

Corll finally agreed to let Henley go—on the condition that Henley rape and kill the girl, while Corll did the same to the boy. Henley accepted the terms. Back in the other room, Corll stripped the unconscious Timothy and handcuffed him, face down, to a plywood board, He then took off his own clothes. Henley said he tried to rape Rhonda, but he just couldn't bring himself to do it. Instead he grabbed the gun and went in to the other room, shouting, "Back off! Stop it!" Corll jumped up and taunted Henley, "Go on, kill me." Henley fired repeatedly until Corll collapsed on the floor. He then released his semiconscious friends, who were unaware of what had been going on.

Wall-to-Wall Bodies

Under interrogation Henley told the police that he procured boys for Corll. He also reported Corll as saying he'd already killed a few boys and buried them in the boat shed.

Later Henley took the police to Southwest Boat Storage south of Houston. Two detectives began digging in Number 11—Corll's stall. Six inches below the surface, they encountered something in clear plastic and found themselves looking into the face of a young boy, a rope embedded in his throat.

It was the first of 17 corpses to be uncovered in the shed. One detective described the boat shed as having "wall to wall bodies."

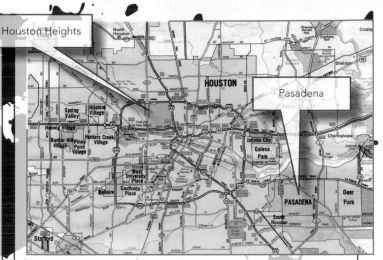

Houston Heights, shown above shaded in green-blue, is known simply as "The Heights." This neighborhood supplied Corll with most of his victims. Corll had a house in the suburb of Pasadena.

Ten More

Henley led detectives to a site near Lake Sam Rayburn, and they located four more bodies. Finally they went to the beach on High Island and dug up another six. The final total was 31.

Henley implicated another teen, David Owen Brooks, who had introduced him to Corll two years previously. Brooks explained that he had met Corll while he was in school. Corll had paid him $10 a time to allow him to commit "oral sodomy." In 1970 he had walked into Corll's apartment and found Corll naked, and two naked boys strapped to a board.

What gradually began to emerge was that both Henley and Brooks had been actively involved in the murders. Corll had offered to pay $200 each for the boys. Brooks or Henley would take boys along to Corll's house, where they would be invited to join in drinking and glue sniffing until they were unconscious. Then Corll tied or handcuffed them to specially constructed wooden boards and sodomized them. Henley explained that Corll often kept them there for several days.

Asked if Corll had tortured the victims, Henley said, "It wasn't really what you would call torture." But he declined to describe what one would call it.

Workers take on the grim task of digging for bodies in Dean Corll's rented boat shed.

The Heights

A majority of the victims came from a rundown part of the Heights area of Houston; two of them had been neighbors of Wayne Henley and had been taken by him to Corll's house.

The first killing, according to Brooks, had taken place in 1970 when Corll was living in the area of Yorktown; it was probably a hitchhiking University of Houston student, Jeffrey Konen. Corll's victims were almost exclusively between the ages of 13 to 17. On several occasions he killed two at a time, murdering James Glass and Danny Yates, in December 1970; two brothers, Donald and Jerry Waldrop, in January 1971; and Wally Simineaux and Richard Embree, in October 1972. The youngest victim was a 9-year-old boy who had lived opposite Corll's apartment.

At the trial, which began in July 1974, Henley and Brooks were both sentenced to life imprisonment for their parts in the murders.

Pedro López

The Monster of the Andes

(1970s-1980s)

In April 1980 the rain-swollen river flowing through the Ecuadorian town of Ambato overflowed its banks and revealed the partially buried bodies of four missing prepubescent girls. Three days later the man now known as "the Monster of the Andes" tried to lure away the 11-year-old daughter of Carlina Poveda. The frantic mother caught up with her daughter, walking hand in hand with her abductor. She summoned some men to come and help her; they held López down until the police arrived.

The prisoner, 31-year-old Pedro Alonzo López, denied that he had anything to do with the murders. But a priest who posed as a fellow prisoner finally talked him into bragging about his crimes. Confronted with his own words, López decided to open the floodgates: he told police that over the past decade he had raped and killed about 360 little girls.

If true that makes López the most prolific living serial killer on record.

Seventh Son

López was the seventh son of a prostitute in Tolima, Colombia. At 8 years old he was thrown out of his house for fondling his sister. His mother took him on a bus to another town and left him there. That night a man found the crying child and promised to be a father to him; he took Pedro to an empty building and raped him.

The boy drifted to Bogotá, where he begged in the streets for 10 years. At 18 he was sent to prison for stealing a car. Four of his fellow inmates grabbed him and raped him. It took López two weeks to manufacture a knife; then he lured the rapists, one by one, into a dark cell and killed three of them. The fourth stumbled onto the bodies and fled, screaming. Just two years were added to López's prison sentence, because the murders were an act of "self-defense."

Saved by a Missionary

Once out of prison he began abducting and raping young girls, preferably under the age of 12. He would then strangle them and bury the bodies. They were mostly South American Indians, because the authorities would not pay much attention to their disappearances.

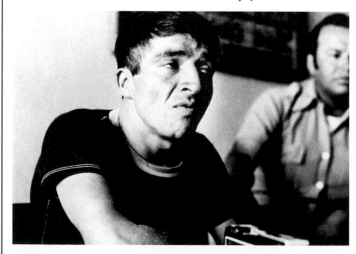

López, in custody in Ecuador, confessed to raping and murdering more than 300 young girls in Peru, Colombia, and Ecuador.

He was caught abducting a 9-year-old girl, and his captors, after torturing him, prepared to bury him alive. An American missionary intervened and took the bound rapist in her jeep to the nearest Peruvian police outpost. The police weren't interested and sent him back across the border into Colombia, where he continued to murder children.

A Look of Innocence and Beauty

López's method was always the same—to walk around markets until he saw a girl with "a certain look of innocence and beauty." He would follow the girl, for days if necessary, until her mother left her alone. Then he would approach her and tell her that he had a present for her mother. He would lead her by the hand to the outskirts of the town.

If night fell while he did this, he would forcibly keep the child with him, trying to soothe her with promises and gentle words. He would wait for sunrise and then rape and simultaneously strangle her. He would only kill the children in daylight because he wanted to see the life drain from their eyes.

The Man of the Century

While López was explaining his life to American journalist Ron Laytner, he declared: 'I cannot see the sky. This is wrong, for I am the Man of the Century. I will be famous in history."

The Monster Set Free

López later lowered his claimed number of murders to 140. It is not known if this modest reappraisal contributed to the prison authorities' decision to free him, on grounds of good behavior, in early 1999. His model behavior in prison did not, however, prevent the Ecuadorian government from immediately deporting him to Colombia.

Political relations between Ecuador and Columbia had been very bad for a number of years. Instead of handing López over to the Colombian authorities to stand trial for his crimes in that country, the Ecuadorians are said to have simply taken López, at night, over the Colombian border and released him.

López is on record as saying that, if freed, he would return to his "mission" of raping and killing little girls. Victor Lascano, the governor of the Ambato Prison that held López for 20 years, is quoted as saying of the release: "God save the children. He is unreformed and totally remorseless. This whole nightmare may start again."

Pedro López's present whereabouts are unknown.

Snow-capped Andean peaks can be seen from Tolima, Colombia, hometown of the man known as the Monster of the Andes.

The BTK Killer

(1970s-2000s)

Dennis Rader

On January 15, 1974, 15-year-old Charles Otero, finished with school for the day, walked into his house in a peaceful suburb of Wichita, Kansas. Although nothing seemed odd at first, he felt his heart race. Something was very wrong. He headed to his parents' bedroom—and was met with the horrific and heartbreaking sight of his parents, their wrists and ankles bound, sprawled dead in their bedroom. He raced to the neighbors, who rang the police. They found Charles's 9-year-old brother, Joe, wearing a hood, dead in his bedroom. His 11-year-old sister, Josephine, was hanging from a pipe in the basement, wearing only a shirt and socks. The two other Otero children—teenagers Danny and Carmen—had fortunately been at school during the killing spree.

Possessed by a Monster

In spite of semen traces, there had been no rape. It looked as if the killer was a sadist who gained pleasure from the act of strangulation. The killer had probably entered the Wichita, Kansas, home when Charlie's father, the 38-year-old Joseph Otero, was taking the teenagers to school. The killer had tied up Julie, 34, and her two children, then waited for the father to return.

The police had no leads. But nine months later a tip to look in a certain book in the Wichita Public Library revealed a letter from the killer. In it he described in detail how he had killed the Otero family—and he promised more murders. He declared, "I find it hard to control myself," and said he felt possessed by a monster. He called himself BTK—short for "blind, torture, kill."

Three months later, 20-year-old Kathryn Bright and her 19-year-old brother Kevin came home soon after midday to find an intruder with a gun. He told them that he needed money to escape from the police. He tied up Kathryn, then took Kevin into the bedroom and tried to strangle him. When Kevin resisted, the assailant shot him in the head. Even though he was badly wounded, when Kevin heard sounds of distress from his sister, he dragged himself to her—only to take another bullet. Still, he managed to escape and went for help. Nevertheless Kathryn died at the hospital, from stab wounds in the stomach.

Members of the Otero family do their best to contain their emotions at the BTK trial.

Final Victim

The BTK killer gained entry to the house of his 11th and final victim, Delores Davis, 62, on January 19, 1991, by hurling a concrete block through her plate-glass window. He then told her that he was on the run and needed food and money. He hand-cuffed her, pretended he was leaving, and then returned and strangled her. He loaded her body into the trunk of her own car and then dumped it under a bridge.

For 13 years nothing further was heard from the killer. But on March 19, 2004, the newsroom of the *Wichita Eagle* received another letter from the man calling himself BTK, who claimed responsibility for the death of Vicki Wegerle. He enclosed a photograph of her driver's license and photographs of her body.

Miscalculation

After 11 subsequent communications, BTK made his mistake; he asked the police if he could send a message on a floppy disk, and on being assured (via a newspaper advertisement) that it would be acceptable, he sent one to a television station. Electronic traces on the disk indicated that it was last used in the Christ Lutheran Church in Wichita by someone named Dennis. Police kept a man named Dennis Rader, 60, president of the church council, under observation and approached his daughter about giving a blood sample. The DNA proved to be the same as in the semen left at crime scenes, and on February 25, 2005, Rader was arrested and charged. He quickly confessed, reveling that women like Marine Hedge, who he'd killed in 1985, were his "projects." He observed and stalked them for days or weeks before he struck.

The trial, from June 27 to August 19, 2005, ended with the expected guilty verdict, and Rader received 10 life sentences, which would last 175 years. He is serving them at the El Dorado Correctional Facility, Kansas.

Unaware that electronic traces left on a floppy disk are traceable, Dennis Rader used one to send a message to the police.

Detective Tim Relph of the Wichita Police gives testimony during Dennis Rader's sentencing hearing. Wearing gloves, he holds up the nightgown worn by Nancy Fox the night she was killed.

Stop-and-Start Killing Sprees

The BTK slayings ceased for three years. The next victim was a 26-year-old mother of three, Shirley Vian, found strangled on her bed on March 17, 1977. Her three children, locked in the bathroom, had escaped through a tiny window—the killer later admitted that he had intended to kill them too.

Nine months later, on December 8, 1977, the BTK killer called the police and told them that a girl named Nancy Fox was dead. The police traced the call, but when they went to the location they found only a dangling public phone.

The next victim, 53-year-old widow Marine Hedge, disappeared from her home nearly eight years later, on April 27, 1985. After manually strangling her, the killer put her in the trunk of her car, took photographs of the body in various types of bondage, and then drove her to a ditch. Her disappearance was not at first attributed to the same killer. This was also true of his next victim, 28-year-old Vicki Wegerle. Claiming to be a telephone repairman, he gained entry to her house on September 16, 1986. He strangled her after holding her at gunpoint. Then he snapped photos of her.

Herb Mullin

(1972-1973)

Herb Mullin

The psychotic serial killer is a favorite monster of Hollywood slasher movies, but fortunately such people are in fact very rare. The violently mentally ill are usually more of a threat to themselves than to others . . . Herb Mullin was an exception to this rule.

Herbert Mullin was born on April 18, 1947, in Salinas, California. His mother was a devout Roman Catholic, and Mullin's upbringing was oppressively religious. Otherwise he seems to have been a completely normal boy, and his high school class even voted him "most likely to succeed." By 17 he had a girlfriend and a close male friend named Dean. Dean's death in a motor accident in July 1965 seems to have marked the beginning of the schizophrenia that led Mullin to commit 13 murders.

Falling into Madness

By October 1969 Mullin was suffering from full-blown paranoid schizophrenia, hearing voices that told him to shave his head and burn his penis with a lighted cigarette. He had been smoking marijuana and taking LSD for a number of years, and this undoubtedly contributed to his mental derangement. Placed in an institution, he wrote dozens of letters to people he had never met, signing himself "a human sacrifice, Herb Mullin." But, thanks largely to mental healthcare budget cuts, he was simply given antipsychotic drugs and discharged after one month.

In June 1971 he moved to San Francisco and lived in cheap hotels; when evicted from his hotel in September 1972, he returned home—still highly disturbed. He had begun receiving what he believed were telepathic messages, ordering him to kill.

Preventable Deaths

The foreman of the jury that eventually convicted Mullin was convinced that the California government's closing of mental hospitals during the Reagan years directly resulted in the 13 murders. "I hold the state executive and the state legislative officers as responsible for those 10 lives as I do the defendant himself," said the foreman.

Turning to God

On October 13, 1972, Mullin was driving along a deserted stretch of highway in the Santa Cruz Mountains when he saw an old man walking along. He stopped the car and asked the man to take a look at the engine. As the tramp bent over the car, Mullin hit him with a baseball bat, killing him. He left the body—later identified as Lawrence White—by the roadside and drove off.

On October 24 Herb picked up a Cabrillo College student Mary Guilfoyle. As they drove toward downtown Santa Cruz, he stabbed her in the heart with a hunting knife, killing her instantly. Then he took her to a deserted road and began cutting open the body with the knife, pulling out her internal organs. He left her to the vultures and drove off—her skeleton was found four months later. On November 2 he entered the confessional of Saint Mary's Church, Los Gatos, and stabbed Father Henri Tomei to death. Herb had originally entered the church in the hope that religion would somehow prevent him from killing again, but he didn't even get to confess before he killed the priest.

Satan Makes People Do . . . Things

Now the voices in Mullin's head seemed to come from potential victims, begging him to kill them. In December 1972 he bought a gun. On January 25, 1973, he drove out to Branciforte Drive, looking for Jim Gianera, the man who, years before, had introduced him to marijuana. He now believed Gianera had deliberately set out to destroy his mind. He went to Gianera's cabin, but 29-year-old Kathy Francis, the current resident, told him that Gianera no longer lived there. She gave him Gianera's address in Santa Cruz. Mullin drove there and shot Gianera dead; then, as the dying man's wife bent over him, he stabbed her in the back, then shot her with the gun.

He then returned to the cabin and killed Kathy Francis and her two sons, who were sleeping in the same bed.

On January 30 Mullin went to discuss his problems with a Lutheran minister in Santa Cruz, explaining obsessively, "Satan gets into people and makes them do things they don't want to."

On February 6 he was hiking aimlessly in the state park in Santa Cruz when he saw a makeshift tent. Mullin pulled out his revolver and shot the four teenage boys inside the tent in rapid succession. Their deaths brought the number of his victims up to 12.

One of Mullin's victims was targeted because he had been the first to supply Mullin with marijuana and LSD. One of the medical experts at the trial contended that it was probably LSD that precipitated the murders.

Killing to Save Lives

A few days later, on February 13, Mullin was preparing to deliver firewood to his parents' house when the internal voices told him he had to kill someone. He stopped his station wagon, went up to an old man, Fred Perez, who was working in the garden, and shot him. A neighbor looking out of her window saw the station wagon driving away and Fred Perez lying face down. She called the police, and within minutes Mullin was under arrest.

At his trial Mullin explained his reasons for killing. He was convinced that he was averting natural disasters—like another San Francisco earthquake—and had saved thousands of lives. Murder, he said, decreases natural disasters.

The court found Mullin to be legally sane and guilty. He will become eligible for parole in the year 2020.

Mullin argued that his murders were necessary to save the world from catastrophes like the 1906 San Francisco earthquake, shown at left. He told a psychiatrist, "if [you] would prepare a chronology of the world's wars and famines and compare it with a list of major earthquakes throughout history, [you] would see that when the death rate goes up, the number of earthquakes goes down."

Killer Clown

(1972-1978)

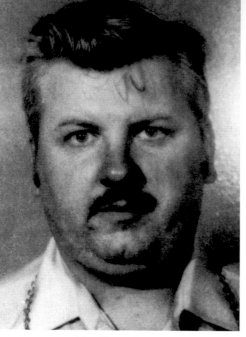

John Wayne Gacy Jr.

On March 21, 1978, a 27-year-old Chicagoan, Jeffrey Rignall, got into a conversation with a fat man who drove a sleek Oldsmobile and accepted an invitation to smoke a joint in his car. The man clapped a chloroform-soaked rag over Rignall's face, drove him to a house, and spent several hours raping him and flogging him with whips. Rignall woke up at dawn by the lake in Lincoln Park. In the hospital doctors discovered that he was bleeding from the rectum and that the chloroform had permanently damaged his liver.

The police were slow to investigate the crime, so Rignall hired a car and spent days sitting near motorway entrances looking for the black Oldsmobile. Eventually his patience paid off; he saw the car, and noted the number.

A Well-Respected Man

The black Oldsmobile proved to belong to businessman John Wayne Gacy Jr. But it was mid-July before the police, more or less accidentally, arrested Gacy on an unconnected misdemeanor charge. The Rignall abduction case was not pursued very rigorously, but even a cursory check of Gacy's police records would have shown the police that he had previously been sentenced to 10 years in prison for sodomy. But Mr. Gacy, who denied everything, was a respected member of the community—the police did not want to believe that he might be an abductor and rapist.

In fact he *was* both those things—and a sadistic serial killer.

Gacy often subdued his victims with chloroform, rendering them unconscious before he raped and killed them.

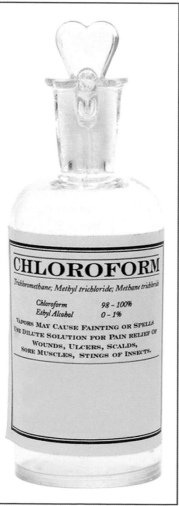

CHLOROFORM

Trichloromethane; Methyl trichloride; Methane trichloride

Chloroform   98 – 100%
Ethyl Alcohol   0 – 1%

VAPORS MAY CAUSE FAINTING OR SPELLS
USE DILUTE SOLUTION FOR PAIN RELIEF OF
WOUNDS, ULCERS, SCALDS,
SORE MUSCLES, STINGS OF INSECTS.

A Good Job Offer

On December 11, 1978, Elizabeth Piest drove to the Nisson Pharmacy in Des Plaines, Illinois, to pick up her 15-year-old son, Robert; it was her birthday and she intended to have a party. She arrived at nine in the evening, and the boy asked her to wait a few minutes while he went to see a man about a summer job. Robert did not return. Elizabeth drove home to tell her husband, and they called the police to report his disappearance. The police investigated at the drugstore and noticed that the inside had been renovated recently. They inquired about the contractor, were told that his name was Gacy and that he could have been the man who had offered Robert Piest the job.

Eventually the police went to Gacy's house at 8213 West Summerdale Avenue, Des Plaines, and questioned him further about Piest. They noticed an odd, unpleasant odor in the house. Finally, tracking the smell, they raised a trapdoor leading to a crawl space under the house. There was a heavy odor of decaying flesh, and they found rotting bodies and human bones.

Ran Out of Storage Space

At the police station, Gacy admitted that he had killed 32 male teenagers—in the course of raping them—and said that 27 of them had been buried or disposed of in or around his house; the remaining five—including Robert Piest—had been disposed of in other ways (Piest had been dumped in the Des Plaines River).

Seven bodies and various parts of others were found in the crawl space. Eight more were quickly unearthed. Gacy's house was demolished in search of more corpses; eventually, the remains of 28 were discovered—Gacy had lost count by one.

Evidence technicians remove the remains of a body from Gacy's house.

Keen to Succeed

John Wayne Gacy had been born on March 17, 1942, in Chicago. He went to business school, became a shoe salesman, and married a coworker whose parents owned a fried chicken business in Waterloo, Iowa. Gacy became a member of the Junior Chamber of Commerce. He was known as an affable man who badly wanted to be liked. What no one realized was that he had a secret gay sex life in which he was becoming increasingly predatory.

His married life ended with his imprisonment for attempted homosexual rape; his wife divorced him. In prison Gacy worked hard, avoided other gay prisoners, and obtained parole. In 1972 he married a second time and started in business as a building contractor. His wife found his violent temper a strain. His sexual performance was also infrequent. And then there was the peculiar odor that hung about the house . . .

In 1976 they divorced.

Tasteless to the End

Gacy tried to plead insanity when he was tried for the murders, but this plea was rejected as ridiculous. During the trial Gacy callously joked that all he was really guilty of was "running a cemetery without a license."

A Bachelor Life

Gacy continued indefatigably to try to rise in the world and to impress people: when he became involved with the local Democrats, he had faux cards printed identifying himself as a precinct police captain.

He used the building business to contact young males. One of these was John Butkovich, who vanished on August 1, 1975—he may have been the first victim. He had quarreled with Gacy about pay.

Once Gacy was separated from his wife, there was nothing to stop him inviting young men to his house. Some of these—like a young male prostitute named Jaimie— he handcuffed and violently sodomized, but he allowed them to go—with payment. The boys who resisted—at least 33 of them, one as young as 9 years old—he murdered.

In 1980 John Wayne Gacy was sentenced to death and was executed in May 1994.

Gacy became notorious as the "Killer Clown" because he threw block parties for his friends and neighbors, and donning makeup and a clown suit, he entertained the children as "Pogo."

Ted Bundy

(1973–1978)

Ted Bundy

On January 31, 1974, a student at the University of Washington, in Seattle, Lynda Ann Healy, vanished from her room; her bed sheets were ominously bloodstained, suggesting that she had been struck violently on the head. There was an extensive search, but there was no sign of her.

In the following March, April, and May, three more female students vanished; in June, two more. On July 14 two young women vanished on the same day. It happened at a popular picnic spot, Lake Sammanish. A number of people saw a good-looking young man, with his arm in a sling, approach a girl named Janice Ott and ask her to help him lift a boat onto the roof of his car. She walked away with him and never returned. Later the same young man approached Denise Naslund; she also vanished. Witnesses overheard him introduce himself as "Ted."

Gone to Utah

In October 1974 the abductions (and presumed killings) shifted to Salt Lake City; three young women disappeared. In November the police had their first break in the case: a young man claiming to be a detective stopped 18-year-old Carol DaRonch in a shopping center. The "office" told DaRonch that there had been an attempt to break into her car; she agreed to accompany him to headquarters to view a suspect. In his car he snapped a handcuff on her wrist and pointed a gun at her head; she fought and screamed, pulled her hand out of the cuff, and managed to jump from the car. She described her abductor to the police.

That evening 17-year-old Debra Kent vanished on her way to meet her brother. Investigators found a handcuff key near the place from which she had evidently been taken.

In January, March, April, July, and August 1975, five more girls vanished in Colorado, Idaho, and Utah. On August 15, 1975, as a police car cruised along a dark Salt Lake City street, a parked Volkswagen Bug launched into motion; the cruiser motioned for it to pull over, but the VW accelerated. The police caught up with the car at a service station. In the vehicle with the driver, 29-year-old Ted Bundy, were a pantyhose mask, a crowbar, an ice pick, and various other tools; there was also a pair of handcuffs. It did not take long to link Bundy to the Utah disappearances. But, without any bodies, no murder charges could be brought against him.

When found guilty of kidnapping, Bundy sobbed and pleaded not to be sent to prison. The judge gave him 1 to 15 years.

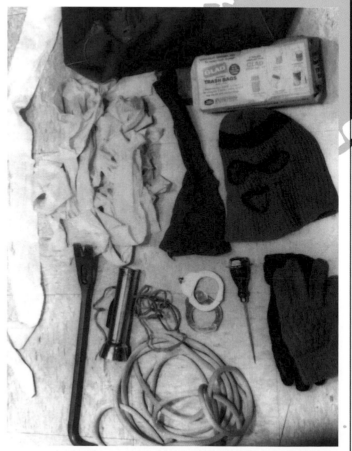

Police photo of items found in Bundy's VW, including an ice pick, crowbar, ski mask, handcuffs, and an assortment of binding materials

Escaped!

The Colorado authorities next charged Bundy with the murder of Caryn Campbell, who had been abducted from a ski resort in which a witness had spotted Bundy. But on December 30, 1977, Bundy escaped from custody, using a hacksaw blade to cut through an imperfectly welded steel plate above the light fixture in his holding cell.

On January 15, 1978, a man broke into the Chi Omega sorority house of the Florida State University in Tallahassee and attacked four girls with a club, knocking all of them unconscious. He raped Lisa Levy and strangled her with her pantyhose; Margaret Bowman died on her way to the hospital. One of Levy's nipples was nearly bitten off, and she had a bite mark on her left buttock. An hour and a half later, a student woke up in another sorority house when she heard banging next door and a girl whimpering. She dialed the number of the room, and as the telephone rang, someone could be heard running out. Cheryl Thomas was found lying in bed, her skull fractured. But she was still alive.

Above, a young woman peers through the drapes of a second-story window of the Chi Omega sorority house just hours after the press learned of the campus attacks. The inset above shows the two murdered women, Lisa Levy, left, and Margaret Bowman, right.

The Last Victim

On February 7, 1978, 12-year-old Kimberley Leach walked out of her classroom in Lake City, Florida, and vanished.

At 4:00 AM on February 15 a police patrolman noticed an orange VW driving suspiciously slowly and radioed for a check on its plate number; the license plate proved to be stolen from Tallahassee. After a struggle and a chase, during which Bundy tried to kill the policeman, the officer recaptured Bundy.

A jury convicted Bundy of the Chi Omega sorority house killings, and the judge sentenced him to die. After a decade of appeals, the courts turned down the last one, and the date of execution was fixed. Bundy then made one more last-minute attempt to save his life by offering to bargain murder confessions for a reprieve. In fact Bundy went on to confess to eight Washington murders and then to a dozen others. Finally, when it was clear that there was no chance of further delay, he confessed to the Chi Omega killings, admitting that he had been peeping through the window at girls undressing, until he was carried away by desire, entered the building, and attacked them.

Carol DaRonch of Utah lived to testify against Bundy. At right, she is shown at a presentencing hearing in Miami, Florida, after Bundy's conviction in the murder of Lisa Levy and Margaret Bowman at the Chi Omega sorority.

Fried

At 7:00 AM on January 24, 1989, Bundy was led into the execution chamber at Starke State prison, Florida; behind Plexiglas, an invited audience of 48 people sat waiting. As two guards attached his hands to the arms of the electric chair, Bundy recognized his attorney among the crowd; he smiled and nodded. Then straps were placed around his chest and over his mouth; the metal cap with electrodes was fastened onto his head with screws and his face was covered with a black hood.

At 7:07 AM the executioner threw the switch. Bundy's body went stiff and rose fractionally from the chair. One minute later, as the power was switched off, the body fell back into the chair. A doctor felt his pulse and pronounced him dead. Outside the prison, a mob carrying FRY BUNDY! banners cheered as the execution was announced.

Nobody knows how many women Bundy killed. Estimates range from his confessed 30 victims to nearly 100.

The World's Worst Serial Killer

(1975-1998)

Dr. Harold Shipman

In September 1998, police arrested Manchester GP Harold Frederick Shipman on suspicion of murder. At the time, even investigators found it hard to believe that this pleasant-mannered man, with a practice of more than 3,000 patients, could be a killer. But as the evidence mounted, they began to suspect that he was actually the most ruthless killer in British history.

Born in Nottingham in 1946, Shipman had struggled out of his dull, working-class background to get into Leeds University Medical School. Sadly he was a less than brilliant student. Throughout most of his time at medical school he remained a loner, without close friends and without even one girlfriend. Unfortunately, despite these inadequacies, he also had an extraordinarily high —some might say delusional—opinion of his abilities. He seems to have had dreams of being a famous physician, and each social and academic failure was like salt in the wound of his blocked ambition.

The Respected Senior GP

His first professional appointment as a general practitioner came in March 1974, in the small town of Todmorden, in the Pennines. It was here that Harold Shipman turned into a serial killer. At least one man in Todmorden, the husband of Eva Lyons—who was dying of cancer —believed that Shipman injected his elderly wife with an overdose of morphine as a "mercy killing." Soon thereafter eight more elderly patients were found dead after Shipman had been to see them.

Dr. Shipman's above-average patient death rate was eventually noted by one of his colleagues, Dr. Linda Reynolds. By 1997 she had realized that Shipman seemed to have been present at the deaths of an unusually high number of patients—three times as many as might have been expected—and reported her suspicions to the local coroner. But her report came to nothing.

Shipman first came under real suspicion after the sudden death of an elderly patient named Kathleen Grundy, on June 24, 1998. Mrs. Grundy had left a will in which her considerable fortune—over £300,000—was left to her doctor, Harold Shipman. The will was carelessly typed, and the two witnesses who had signed it would later explain that they had done so as a favor to Dr. Shipman.

Digging Up the Past

It was not until autumn 1998, when Mrs. Grundy's body was exhumed, that the authorities felt there was enough evidence to finally act against Dr. Shipman: the postmortem clearly showed that Mrs. Grundy had died of an overdose of injected morphine. After that another 14 exhumations of Shipman's patients revealed the same thing. Moreover it was clear that these 15 were only a small proportion of those he had murdered.

When he was questioned on suspicion of 15 murders, Shipman angrily denied any wrongdoing. He was sure that he had covered his trail so carefully that he was safe, but the investigators soon discovered that he had made extensive changes to his patients' records, after their deaths, to make them seem more ill than they actually had been. He was almost certainly unaware that

Sisters Sal Freeman, right, and Jude Lang hold photos of their mother Margaret Waldron, who died two days after visiting Dr. Shipman's office.

Too Many to Count

Convicted, he was given 15 life sentences for murdering 15 of his elderly patients by injecting them with lethal doses of diamorphine (medical heroine). Yet a government report later concluded he possibly murdered between 215 and 260 people over the 23-year period of his general practice.

Shipman was found hanged in his cell on the morning of January 13, 2004. He never admitted to any of the murders. Since disinterment and effective forensic autopsies on as many as 260 bodies is practically impossible, there will never be an accurate account of his murders.

Why Harold Shipman became a murderer is difficult to comprehend. Unlike most serial killers, there seems to have been no sexual or sadistic element to Shipman's murders. He killed most of his victims in their own homes, convincing them that he was giving them a normal, harmless drug injection; soothing them before administering the fatal dose. But these were definitely not mercy killings: although all his known victims were elderly, few were actually seriously ill or even in particular discomfort.

Given his character, it seems likely that Shipman simply enjoyed the God-like power of handing out death. His victims, like everyone else in his life, lived and died for the sole purpose of feeding his bloated ego.

the computer automatically registered the date and time of every one of the changes.

On October 7, 1998, Shipman was full of self-confidence when he was interviewed by the police and confronted with evidence of his crimes. But when a detective constable began to question him about changes he had made in the patients' records, pointing out that many of them had been made within minutes of the death of the patient, he began to falter and flounder.

Yet there was no confession. From that moment onward, he simply refused to cooperate during interviews.

A court artist's sketch of the trial of Dr. Harold Shipman, left, shows him standing before the presiding Judge Thayne Forbes, foreground.

Composite sketch of the Hillside Strangler

The Hillside Stranglers
(1977-1979)

In January 1979 two female students—Karen Mandic and Diane Wilder—disappeared from the small house they shared in Bellingham, Washington. The following day their bodies were found in the back of Karen's car. Karen had confided to a friend that she had been offered some kind of "detective" job by a security guard named Kenneth Bianchi, who had recently moved to Bellingham from the Los Angeles area. In that area, between October 1977 and February 1978, a man who became known as the Hillside Strangler had raped and murdered 10 young women.

The Victims

The first victim was Yolanda Washington, a Hollywood prostitute. Her naked corpse was found October 18, 1977, in the Forest Lawn Cemetery near the Ventura Freeway; she had been raped and then strangled with a piece of cloth. Two weeks later, on November 1, 1977, police found the body of 15-year-old Judy Miller, a runaway, in the Eagle Rock section of Los Angles. She had been raped vaginally and anally and then strangled. By the last weeks of November, around Thanksgiving, Los Angeles area police departments realized that they had an epidemic of sex murders on their hands; seven more strangled corpses were found, tossed casually on hillsides or by the road, as if thrown from a car. The youngest victims were 12- and 14-year-old schoolgirls; the oldest was a 28-year-old actress and scientology student Jane King. The last victim of the Thanksgiving "spree" was 18-year-old Lauren Wagner. Burn marks on her palms suggested that she had been tortured before death.

Twelve of the victims of the Hillside Stranglers. Top, from left: Yolanda Washington, Judith Ann Miller, Lissa Teresa Kastin, Jill Barcomb, Kathleen Robinson, and Kristina Weckler. Bottom, from left: Kimberly Diane Martin, Cynthia Lee Hudspeth, Jane King, Sonja Johnson, Lauren Rae Wagner, and Dollie Cepeda.

Panic

Los Angeles suffers about seven murders a day, but this series of sex murders between 1977 and 1978 had been something of a record. Los Angeles was in a state of panic.

The police had one important clue. Lauren Wagner had been abducted as she climbed out of her car in front of her parents' home. A neighbor had looked out of her window and had heard Lauren shout: "You won't get away with this." She had then seen two men force the girl into a big, dark sedan with a white top and drive away. The woman had seen the men clearly; the older of the two had bushy hair and was "Latin-looking," while the younger one was taller and had acne scars on his neck.

Two Stranglers

The clues led investigator to Kenneth Bianchi and his cousin Angelo Buono, who had been involved in procuring prostitutes. In court Bianchi confessed to murdering the two Bellingham girls, and admitted to five of the Hillside Strangler murders.

In later confessions Bianchi stated that his cousin Angelo had also been involved in the murders. He also succeeded in convincing a psychiatrist that he had a dual personality, whose "other self" killed the girls. The jury remained unconvinced, and he was sentenced to six life terms in prison at his trial in October 1979.

Kenneth Bianchi testifies before the court.

Murderous Duo

When Sergeant Frank Salerno, a detective on the Hillside Strangler task force, heard of Bianchi's arrest, he hurried to Bellingham. Bianchi sounded like the tall, acne-scarred young man seen outside Lauren Wagner's home, and his cousin Angelo Buono, who lived in Glendale, Los Angeles, sounded exactly like the other—the bushy-haired, "Latin-looking" man. Buono was a highly unsavory character. He had been married four times, but all his wives had left him because of his brutality—when one of them had refused him sex, he had sodomized her in front of

Angelo Buono in court

their children. He had also been a pimp, forcing girls into sexual slavery—and Bianchi had been his partner.

The trial of Buono, which began in November 1981 and ended in November 1983, was the longest murder trial in U.S. history. When it came Bianchi's turn to testify, it was obvious that he had no intention of standing by his plea-bargaining agreement; he was vague and contradictory. When Judge George pointed out that he could be returned to Washington's Walla Walla—a notoriously tough jail—he became suddenly more cooperative. Bianchi spent five months on the stand, and the murders were described in appalling detail. Buono was finally found guilty of seven of them. Buono received a life sentence with no possibility of parole. Bianchi was returned to Walla Walla to serve out his sentence.

Buono died of a heart attack on September 21, 2002.

Murder by Proxy

In 1980 a crime writer named Veronica Compton volunteered to get Bianchi out of jail. She planned to stage a series of copycat murders made to look like they were committed by the Hillside Strangler. She would leave semen (as yet untraceable by DNA analysis)—provided by Bianchi in a condom—inside the victim. The first murder attempt went wrong when the victim fought back, and Compton landed in jail—for life.

The Bodies in the Drains

(1978-1983)

Dennis Nilsen

On the evening of February 8, 1983, a drain maintenance engineer named Michael Cattran was asked to call at 23 Cranley Gardens, in Muswell Hill, North London, to find out why tenants had been unable to flush their toilets. It was a shoddy house, divided into flats. A tenant showed Cattran the manhole cover that led to the drainage system. When he removed it, he staggered back at the smell of decaying flesh. Closer inspection revealed a mass of whitish rotting meat . . . and some bones that resembled human fingers.

"Altogether"

Detective Chief Inspector Peter Jay, of Hornsey CID, was waiting in the hallway of the house when Dennis Nilsen walked in from his day at the office. Nilsen invited the policeman into his flat, and Jay's face wrinkled at the stink of decaying flesh. He told Nilsen that they had found human remains in the drain and asked what had happened to the rest of the body.

"It's in there, in two plastic bags," said Nilsen, pointing to a wardrobe.

In the police car, the chief inspector asked Nilsen whether the remains came from one body or two. Nilsen said calmly, "There have been 15 or 16 altogether."

At the police station, Nilsen—a tall man with metal-rimmed glasses—seemed eager to talk. He told police that he had murdered three men in the Cranley Gardens house—into which he moved in autumn 1981—and 12 or 13 at his previous address, 195 Melrose Avenue, Cricklewood.

The plastic bags from the Muswell Hill flat contained two severed heads and a skull from which the flesh had been stripped. The bathroom contained the whole lower half of a torso. The rest was in bags in the wardrobe and in a tea chest. Digging at Melrose Avenue revealed several human bones.

Lonely Guy

Dennis Nilsen later insisted that all the murders had been without sexual motivation—he just wanted the men to not leave him—a statement that led criminologist Brian Masters to entitle his book on the case *Killing for Company*.

Britain's Biggest Mass Murderer

The self-confessed serial killer—he seemed to take a certain pride in being "Britain's biggest mass murderer"—was Scottish, born in Fraserburgh on November 23, 1945. In the early 1970s he moved to London and became a job interviewer for the Manpower Services Commission. In November 1975 Nilsen began to share a North London flat—on Melrose Avenue—with a young man named David Gallichan. Then, in May 1977, Gallichan decided he could bear London no longer and accepted a job in the country. Nilsen was furious; he felt rejected and deserted. Gallichan's departure triggered the homicidal violence that would claim 15 lives.

Stealing is Dishonest

The killings began in December 1978. Nilsen picked up a young Irishman, Stephen Holmes, in Cricklewood Arms. They went back to his flat to continue drinking. Nilsen wanted him to stay over, but Holmes had other plans.

Nilsen took a necktie and strangled Holmes in his sleep. Then he undressed the body and carefully washed it, a ritual he observed in all his killings. He kept the body stuffed under the floorboards for nearly eight months. He then burned it in a bonfire at the bottom of the garden, burning some rubber at the same time to cover the stench.

The next murder victim was a 23-year-old Canadian called Kenneth James Ockendon, who had got into a conversation with Nilsen at a bar on December 3, 1979. They went back to Nilsen's flat and listened to rock music on Nilsen's hi fi system. While Ockendon sat listening to music wearing earphones, Nilsen strangled him. Later, he dissected the body. Ockendon had a great deal of money in his clip, but Nilsen tore it up. His Scottish upbringing would not allow him to steal.

Stephen Holmes

Cricklewood

Dennis Nilsen's accounts of the murders are excruciatingly repetitive; he was certainly a mechanical madman.

The third victim, killed in May 1980, was a 16-year-old butcher, Martyn Duffey. Nilsen strangled him and placed him under the floorboards. Number four was a 16-year-old, Billy Sutherland— killed the same way as Duffey. Number five was an unnamed Mexican. Number six was an Irish building worker. Victim number seven was an undernourished vagrant picked up in a doorway. The next five victims, all unnamed, were killed equally casually between late 1980 and late 1981.

Muswell Hill

In October 1981 Nilsen moved into an upstairs flat in Cranley Gardens, Muswell Hill.

The next victim was John Howlett. He woke up as Nilsen tried to strangle him and fought back hard; Nilsen had to bang Howlett's head against the headboard of the bed to subdue him. Then Nilsen drowned him in the bath. He hacked up the body and then boiled chunks in a large pot to make them easier to dispose of.

The last two victims were both unnamed; one was a drunk and the other a drug addict. Both were dissected, boiled, and flushed down the toilet. It was after the 15th murder that the tenants complained about blocked drains, and Nilsen was arrested.

The trial began on October 24, 1983. The jury found Nilsen guilty of multiple murders. He was sentenced to life imprisonment.

Nilsen proved to be an extremely cooperative prisoner once the police had discovered his crimes. In 2006 he even helped identify his earliest victim, whose family had never given up hope of finding.

Andrei Chikatilo

The Rostov Ripper
(1978-1990)

On December 24, 1978, the mutilated body of 9-year-old Lena Zakotnova was found in the Grushevka River, where it flows through the Russian mining city of Shakhty, near Rostov-on-Don. The corpse had been tied in a sack and dumped in the water some 48 hours before its discovery. Lena had been sexually assaulted and partially throttled, but multiple knife wounds to her lower torso had caused death. Lena had last been seen after leaving school on the afternoon of her death. A woman reported seeing a girl of Lena's description talking to a middle-aged man at a nearby tram stop, and then they had walked away together.

The Shakhty police soon arrested a suspect. Aleksandr Kravchenko had been in prison for a similar murder in the Crimea. He was found guilty of Lena's death and executed by a single shot in the back of the head in 1984. By that time, the *real* killer of Lena Zakotnova had murdered at least 16 other women and children.

Raised in Hell

Born on October 6, 1936, in the Ukrainian farm village of Yablochnoye Andrei Romanovich Chikatilo was soon well acquainted with death. Joseph Stalin, in his drive to harden the peasantry, reduced Ukraine to chaos, starvation, and fear. Then the Nazis invaded and public executions became a regular event.

When he was 5 years old, Chikatilo's mother told him about the disappearance of one of his cousins, seven years earlier. She believed he had been stolen in the woods, butchered, and eaten. The gruesome story made a deep impression on the boy.

As an adult Chikatilo became a teacher. He married, but he found it difficult to perform sexually with his wife, partly because he was developing pedophiliac tendencies. He was shuffled from one Soviet school to another, always because he had been caught sexually abusing children. But the authorities, afraid of scandal, never fired him; they just moved him on with no warning to his new school.

In 1978 the Chikatilos and their two children were living in the town of Shakhty. Chikatilo bought an old shack in the slum end of town and began to invite down-and-out young women over, offering them food and vodka. There he would request them to perform sexual acts—usually fellatio—yet his real interest remained prepubescent children.

On December 22, 1978, he persuaded Lena Zakotnova to follow him to his shack. As he abused her he ruptured her hymen, and the sight of her blood threw him into a sexual frenzy. He pulled out a knife . . .

Shakhty, a mining town north of Rostov-on-Don, Russia, was home to Andrei Chikatilo and the site of many of his murders. He would lure victims from crowded places, such as train stations and bus depots.

A Political Embarrassment

By summer 1983 the Rostov police department realized that they had a serial killer on their hands, but they couldn't admit the fact: serial killers, every good Soviet citizen knew, were a side effect of decadent capitalist society. Such deviants were therefore impossible in the worker's paradise of the USSR.

But more than a dozen murdered young victims had been found in woods and isolated stretches of parkland. Each had been killed with the same method: a slashing knife attack to the face and genitals. There was no sign of actual rape, but semen was found splattered on or near the bodies. There were also teeth marks, indicating attempts at cannibalism.

Eventually, in September 1983, a police team arrived from Moscow. It concluded that a single serial killer was indeed on the prowl and made suggestions on how best to reform the local investigation. Yet neither the Moscow police nor the local authorities took the key measure of informing the public. It was unthinkable that the Soviet Union admit that a serial killer was loose.

Unaware of the danger in their midst, both male and female children and teenagers around Rostov continued to be beguiled into following the nice, bespectacled, middle-aged man into secluded woodland . . . and he continued to brutally butcher them.

The Soviet's reluctance to admit that they had a serial killer in their midst, meant that authorities did not distribute or post sketches such as the one shown above, drawn up from witness descriptions, of the man known as the Rostov Ripper. Warnings to the public might have saved innocent lives.

Rare Secretions

The relentless horror continued until 1990. Chikatilo would have been arrested earlier if not for one striking fact: the blood type secreted in his semen was different from that in his veins. It was only when Japanese scientists discovered that this was possible—in very rare cases—that investigators put him back on their shortlist of suspects.

He was identified acting strangely near the scene of a murder and arrested. Under intense questioning, he admitted to total of 53 murders. He then confirmed his confession by leading investigators to a number of undiscovered bodies.

In 1992 he was put on trial, remaining in a specially constructed steel cage to protect him from attacks by the public. Aware that he was facing a death sentence if convicted, Chikatilo tried to secure an insanity plea by raving throughout the proceedings.

On October 14, as Chikatilo received individual death sentences for 52 murders, he filled the court with shrieks that often drowned the judge's voice. But at one point Judge Akubzhanov showed unexpected agreement with one of Chikatilo's arguments: he accepted that it was the Soviet Union's refusal to acknowledge the high national level of crime that had contributed to Chikatilo's long freedom from arrest.

Sixteen months later, on February 14, 1994, Andrei Chikatilo was executed by a single shot in the back of the neck.

Chikatilo, shown above, maintained that he was insane, and during the trial he would constantly disrupt the proceedings by ranting and raving, sometimes to the point of nearly drowning out testimony.

Mike DeBardeleben

Mall Passer Murderer

(1980s)

When the Secret Service arrested rapist and killer Mike DeBardeleben on May 25, 1983, it was not for murder or rape but for passing counterfeit bills.

In 1980 a counterfeiter dubbed the "Mall Passer" was regularly unloading fake $20 bills in shopping malls all over the United States. He had an ingenious method, handing them over in exchange for small items, like cigarettes and men's socks, and taking the change. He drove far and wide; in one year, he traveled to 38 states and unloaded as much as $30,000 in fake bills.

Hunt for the Mall Passer

Police artists drew up sketches of the Mall Passer based on descriptions by store workers. On May 25, 1983, a bookstore clerk in West Knoxville, Tennessee, recognized the culprit and called the police. The man the clerk had fingered realized that he was being tailed and broke into a run. Soon he found himself cornered by two policemen, who had been summoned by radio.

Fingerprint identification revealed him to be James Mitchell DeBardeleben II. Police records showed that Mike, as he was known, had already spent two years in jail for passing dud $100 bills.

In DeBardeleben's apartment, investigators discovered a Yellow Pages directory with a tiny slip of paper in the pages listing storage facilities. A visit to the facility nearest his home uncovered a great deal of pornography, including dozens of photographs of women in various stages of undress, many looking terrified and battered. A bag containing bloodied panties, a chain, handcuffs, a dildo, and lubricant suggested why the women looked so terrified—they had been tortured. Videotapes proved it.

DeBardeleben enjoyed having women at his mercy— he forced them to say that they enjoyed the pain he was inflicting on them.

For years Mike DeBardeleben made a success out of passing counterfeit bills in shopping malls all over the United States.

Pain and Power

In his study of DeBardeleben, *Lethal Shadow*, Stephen Michaud remarks that investigators concluded that he was "the most dangerous felon ever at large in America," and added, "for Mike DeBardeleben, possession meant a live victim, suffering under his control."

DeBardeleben himself once wrote, "There is no greater power over another person than that of inflicting pain on her."

The reason for DeBardeleben's misogyny emerged when investigators spoke to his previous wives. Apparently his relationship with his mother, Mary Lou (whom he called Moe), damaged the young DeBardeleben irreparably. Theirs was a twisted variation of the classic Freudian relationship. Mary Lou's loveless childhood led to her cantankerous demeanor. She became an alcoholic, and was, partly, responsible for turning her son into a sociopath.

Rape

In the early hours of Sunday, September 4, 1978, DeBardeleben passed a 19-year-old nurse who was walking home. He snapped handcuffs on her wrists, gagged her, and blindfolded her with adhesive tape. Two hours later they stopped at a house and he took her indoors. He undressed her, leaving the blindfold in place, and then raped her for an hour without climaxing. He then sodomized her, ordering her to call him "Daddy." After a nap, he drank root beer, smoked a cigarette, and forced her to fellate him.

Finally, he allowed her to dress, drove her to an isolated area, and released her.

DeBardeleben liked to handcuff his victims so that he could easily subdue them.

Downfall

Incredibly, after his capture, it looked as if the authorities might be willing to forget all his criminal activities except the counterfeiting. Researching his criminal career, it was clear, would be a lengthy and costly exercise. Moreover the Secret Service's responsibilities began and ended with the counterfeiting case. Agent Jane Vezeris, in charge of the investigation, was outraged by the idea, and went to see her boss, Acting Assistant Director Joe Carlos. She took with her a videotape in which DeBardeleben could be heard making various sadistic demands, while his victim screamed in anguish.

By chance, the director of the Secret Service, John R. Simpson, dropped in during the meeting and heard the tape. When it was over Simpson told Carlos: "Give them whatever they want."

DeBardeleben was a narcissistic egomaniac, and his decision to act as his own defender at his trial directly led to his conviction. DeBardeleben's major mistake came when he was cross-examining Lori Jensen, one of his victims.

"There were no overhead interior lights, were there?"
"No."
"The only lights they had there were these little small ones next to the door at the bottom of the door, right?"
"Correct."

Prosecutor Miliette would point out to the jury that DeBardeleben's question revealed knowledge of the car that indicated ownership. The panel required just 38 minutes to convict.

This was his sixth and final trial, for the abduction and rape of Lori Jensen. In all he was sentenced to serve 375 years.

Sadist DeBardeleben could not resist videotaping his victims' agony. His decision to hoard tapes and "souvenirs" ultimately led Secret Service investigators to realize that they had captured a criminal far more dangerous than a currency counterfeiter.

The Night Stalker

(1984-1985)

The Night Stalker was the nickname given to a serial killing burglar and rapist who terrorized Los Angeles in the mid-1980s. He would break into family homes, shoot the man of the house in the head with a .22-caliber pistol, and then rape and beat the wife or girlfriend. If he had time, the Night Stalker would also steal any valuable items he could find.

Throughout the spring and summer of that year there were multiple attacks traceable to the same sadistic murderer. Surviving victims gave consistent descriptions—tall, greasy-haired Hispanic man in his 20s, with bad teeth and terrible breath.

Richard Ramirez

Crime Wave

The first victim, 79-year-old Jennie Vincow, was sexually assaulted and stabbed to death in her bed on June 28, 1984. Then on March 17, 1985, the killer approached Maria Hernandez, 22, as she parked her car outside her student condo. He fired a pistol into her face, but she raised her hand at the last moment and the bullet ricocheted off the keys in her palm. She survived, but her roommate, Dayle Okazaki, 34, was killed and her body sexually molested.

The killings then followed in fast order. On March 21 the Night Stalker carjacked and shot dead Tsia-Lian Yu. On March 27 he burgled the house of Vincent and Maxine Zazzara. Both were shot dead, but Maxine's corpse was then hideously mutilated. On April 15 he struck again, this time shooting William Doi fatally and raping his wife, Lillian.

Between May and August the homicidal burglar attacked seven more times, killing six people and raping or severely beating others.

Love for Satan

By now the whole of Los Angeles was terrified by the Night Stalker's one-man crime wave.

August of 1985 was the peak of the terror. It was clear that the killer was reaching a frenzy—as sometimes happens with serial killers. In that month he attacked four more homes, killing three people, attempting to kill six more, and raping two women.

The final victims were William Carnes and his fiancée. On August 24 the killer broke into their house and shot Carnes as he slept. He then dragged the terrified woman from the bed and bound her with neckties. He became so furious that he could find nothing worth stealing that he raped her twice, and then insisted that she swear her "love for Satan." He made her repeat the ridiculous oath several times and then forced her to perform oral sex on him. He then laughed savagely and made his getaway. Luckily the woman managed to free herself and call an ambulance in time to save her fiancé's life.

Violent Roots

Ramirez's cousin Mike was a Vietnam War veteran who bragged to Richard about raping, torturing, and killing Vietnamese women—and he had photos to prove his claims. Mike eventually shot his wife in the face, killing her. The 14-year-old Richard witnessed the murder, standing close enough to be splashed with her blood.

Ramirez displays a pentagram symbol on his hand during his trial. He left satanic symbols at some of the murder scenes and forced several of his victims to "swear to Satan."

Ramirez was sentenced to die, but appeals have kept him alive on death row in San Quentin, shown above.

"Evil"

Fortunately during an attack on August 21, a local youth managed to note the licence plate of the killer's getaway car. This stolen vehicle was found and recovered fingerprints allowed the police to match an identity: the Night Stalker's actual name was Ricardo Leyva Muñoz Ramírez.

The 25-year-old Ramirez, known as Richard, was out of town when his name and photograph were printed on every newspaper front page in Los Angeles. As a result he blithely wandered into a liquor store on his return . . . and was recognized. Members of the public chased Ramirez before he could find a policeman, into whose protection he sobbingly surrendered himself.

Richard Ramirez was found guilty of 13 murders, as well as 30 other major crimes, such as rape and attempted murder. Asked by reporters about how he felt after the verdict, Ramirez replied, "Evil."

After the death sentence was passed, the Night Stalker commented laconically: "Big deal. Death always went with the territory. I'll see you in Disneyland."

Decades of Waiting to Go to "Disneyland"

Since his conviction Ramirez has received fan mail from dozens of women, many enclosing sexual photographs of themselves. Most of these "followers" are probably like children who lean over the edge of a bear pit at a zoo—he's caged, so they can play at titillating him. None, however, should have any illusions about what he would have done to them if it had been their house he broke into during his 1985 rampage.

Yet Ramirez gained at least one devoted and genuine friend—his wife. In October 1996 he married Doreen Lioy—a 41-year-old free-lance magazine editor—in a secular ceremony in the San Quentin prison.

Afterwards Doreen said: "The facts of his case ultimately will confirm that Richard is a wrongly convicted man, and I believe fervently that his innocence will be proven to the world." She is reputed to have sworn to kill herself on the day that Ramirez long-delayed execution is finally carried out.

Ramirez and Lioy pose for their wedding portrait.

Joel Rifkin

(1989-1993)

Joel Rifkin

In the gray light just after dawn on a morning in late June 1993, two New York State troopers patrolling Long Island's Southern State Parkway noticed that a station wagon ahead of them lacked a license plate. They signaled it to stop, but instead it swerved off the freeway into the streets of Wantaugh. The troopers switched on their sirens and set off in pursuit in what turned into a high-speed chase. Five additional police cars joined the chase before the station wagon veered out of control and crashed into a telephone pole. The driver was the bespectacled 34-year-old Joel Rifkin. He claimed to have no explanation for his wild flight, but when the troopers noticed a foul order emanating from the car, they checked the back of the wagon. There, wrapped in tarpaulin, was the naked, decomposing corpse of a woman.

Dumping the Bodies

The woman turned out to be a 22-year-old prostitute named Tiffany Bresciani, who had vanished three days earlier. Rifkin confessed to strangling her as they had intercourse. He then took the body home with him to East Meadow, Long Island, where he lived with his mother and sister.

In the summer heat, the corpse quickly began to decompose, so Rifkin decided to dump it among some bushes on rough ground near the local airport. Once he had confessed to the Bresciani murder, he decided to tell all. He in fact made a habit of picking up prostitutes and strangling them—17 in all. (The police calculated the number as 18; they assumed that Rifkin had simply lost count.)

Inadequate

Rifkin was an unemployed landscape gardener, and he had been picking up prostitutes on an average of three times a week since he was 18. In his bedroom, police found plenty of "souvenirs" from the victims: ID cards, drivers' licenses, credit cards, and piles of panties, bras, and stockings. In the garage, which reeked of decaying flesh, they found the panties of his last victim, Tiffany Bresciani.

The more investigators found out about Rifkin the more it became clear that—as with so many serial killers—he was basically an inadequate. An illegitimate child, he had been adopted a few weeks after his birth in January 1959 by a Jewish couple, Ben and Jeanne Rifkin, who also adopted a girl. Joel was backward at school; he mumbled, walked with hunched shoulders, and was dyslexic. His schoolfellows called him "turtle" and made fun of him. When he left home he tried various jobs, on one occasion working in a record store, but he was usually late, and would turn up with rumpled clothes and dirty fingernails.

Rifkin's dream was to become a famous writer, and it could be argued that he had the right kind of preparation—a certain amount of childhood and adolescent frustration often seems to be good for writers. He holed up in his bedroom writing poetry, but a few half-hearted attempts at further education fell through. He simply had no ability to concentrate. A job as a landscape gardener was lackluster—he was so inefficient that he usually lost his customers within days.

After his arrest Rifkin told police investigators where to find more bodies. Above, they examine the remains of a body found near JFK Airport.

Liar

He was already in his late 20s when his stepfather was diagnosed with prostate cancer and committed suicide because he could not bear the pain. A shattered Jeanne Rifkin fell into a depression.

Not long after, Rifkin met an attractive blonde in a coffee shop; he was scribbling, and they began a casual conversation. She impressed him by telling him she was writing a film script. He told her—untruthfully—that he was a university student also writing a film script. When she took a small apartment, she even invited him to move in, to help her with her script. Rifkin saw this as the beginning of a love affair; she refused even to let him kiss her. A few weeks later, tired of his laziness and untidiness, she threw him out. After Rifkin's arrest it was reported that she had worked as a streetwalker and was suffering from AIDS, although it is not clear whether he was aware of either of those facts.

Asking for Trouble

What is certain is that Rifkin began to kill prostitutes in 1989, picking them up on Manhattan's Lower East Side. One hooker with whom he had sex on two occasions said he seemed perfectly ordinary and normal and made no odd sexual demands. But many others turned him down—he looked and smelled peculiar. One of them refused when he asked for oral sex.

His habit of murder continued for almost five years. Many of the 18 dead women had been drug addicts. He may well have had sex with the corpses; he often took them home and kept them for days before he disposed of them. One body, tossed on landfill near John F. Kennedy Airport, was where he'd dumped it more than a year later, under a mattress. Other bodies were stuffed into metal drums and tossed in the East River.

Rifkin's motivation has never been adequately explained. What is clear is that he was, like so many serial killers, an inept under-achiever, a person who found life too much for him. As one of his schoolmates told a reporter, he was a lifelong loser. We can only assume that he killed because violence satisfied some long-held fantasy, and because it gave him a bizarre sense of achievement, a feeling that, in spite of a habit of failure, he was a "somebody," a multiple killer, a man to be reckoned with.

Yet soon after his arrest, one of the policemen involved in the chase commented that he had probably wanted to get caught, because driving with a corpse in a car without license plates seems to be asking for trouble.

On May 9, 1994, Joel Rifkin was sentenced to 203 years.

Ivan Milat

Backpacker Murders

(1989-1994)

On October 5, 1993, skeletons of two missing hitchhikers, James Gibson and Deborah Evrist, were found in the Belanglo State Forest, near Melbourne, Australia; they were both 19 and had vanished on December 30, 1989, after setting out from Melbourne.

Soon after the discovery police dogs found the decomposed body of Simone Schmidl, 20, a German woman who had vanished on January 20, 1991. Three days later the dogs found the bodies of two more German backpackers, Gabor Neugebauer, 21, and his traveling companion, Anja Habscheid, 20, who had vanished on December 26, 1991. Anja's body had been decapitated, and the angle of the blow made it clear that she had been forced to kneel while the killer cut off her head.

Like a Loaf of Bread

Six months later, a suspect emerged, when a coworker of a man named Ivan Milat reported that Milat had been heard saying "killing a woman was like cutting a loaf of bread." On May 22, 1994, police arrested the 50-year-old Milat in Eaglevale, a Sydney suburb.

In Milat's garage, police found a bloodstained rope, a sleeping bag that proved to belong to Deborah Evrist, and a camera owned by another victim, Caroline Clarke, 22, who had vanished with her friend Joanne Walters in April 1992. Joanne had been stabbed 14 times in the chest and neck; the fact that she had not been shot suggested that there had been two murderers. Both girls had been raped.

German tourist Anja Habschied, 20, was backpacking through Australia with her boyfriend, 21-year-old Gabor Neugebauer. Nearly two years after they went missing their bodies were uncovered in shallow graves. Like other victims of Milat, each of them had been shot and strangled.

Escape from Bill

The New South Wales Police Department finally received the tip that they had been hoping for. A young Englishman from Birmingham, Paul Onions, called a police hotline after seeing a news report about the murders. Onions recounted that while he'd had been on holiday in Australia, a man matching Milat's description had attacked him near the Belanglo State Forest. Onions had been hitchhiking from Sydney on January 25, 1990, when he had encountered a short, stocky man with a drooping moustache. The man asked the backpacker where he was heading and then offered him a lift in the direction of Melbourne.

The stranger introduced himself as Bill and said that he was Yugoslavian. As they passed Bowral, "Bill" slowed down. Asked why, he explained that he was trying to find a place where he could take an audiocassette player out of the trunk.

Some instinct told Onions to get out of the car at the same time as "Bill," and this seemed to annoy his companion. "What are you doing out of the car?" he asked. Then suddenly "Bill" produced a black revolver, and the friendly manner vanished.

"You know what this is—a robbery." The man

Ivan the Terrible

Cooperating with the Australian authorities, the Birmingham police lost no time in flying Onions to Sydney. There he identified Milat as the man who had fired his revolver at him.

Milat had a long police record. In 1971 he had picked up two female hitchhikers. He had suddenly turned off the highway, produced a knife, and announced that if they didn't have sex with him, he would kill them both. One of the girls was 18, and she allowed him to have sex with her on the front seat.

In 1979 he again gave a lift to two women near the Belanglo State Forest and suddenly pulled off the road. Upon realizing his intentions, the women managed to jump out of the car and hid in a ditch until he gave up his pursuit of them.

Milat's trial began in the New South Wales Supreme Court in Sydney on March 25, 1996. The press dubbed him "Ivan the Terrible."

Investigations exposed Milat as a control freak, whose chief pleasure came from seeing his victims terrified and helpless. It also became apparent that as he killed more and more victims, he also became more sadistic and enjoyed taking his time. At one murder site half a dozen cigarette butts were found. He paralyzed some of his female victims by stabbing them in the spine, so that he could sexually attack them at his leisure.

Milat was found guilty on July 27, 1996, and sentenced to life imprisonment on seven counts of murder.

Onions on his way into court to testify for the prosecution. The British backpacker was lucky enough to get away from the murderous Milat.

then reached into the back seat and took out a bag containing lengths of rope. "That was enough," said Onions later. "I decided to leg it." He started running.

A bullet whizzed past his head. Milat caught up with Onions, and they began to wrestle at the side of the highway. Onions broke free and ran over the top of the hill. A Toyota was heading toward him, and Onions flung himself on the ground to force it to halt. He shouted, "Give me a lift, he's got a gun." The driver let him clamber into the back and drove him to the Bowral Police Station. Incredibly the Bowral police succeeded in losing the report.

WELCOME TO
BELANGLO
STATE FOREST

PLEASE BE CAREFUL

In September 1992 a group of orienteers discovered a decaying corpse in the Belanglo State Forest in New South Wales. The sign at the entrance of the forest cautions visitors to "please be careful."

Anatoly Onoprienko

The Beast of Ukraine
(1989-1996)

For the people of Ukraine, the mass murders began on Christmas Eve 1995, in a small village called Garmarnia in central Ukraine. The killer entered the home of a forester, and killed the man, his wife, and their two sons with a sawed-off double-barreled hunting rifle. He stole a few items of jewelry and a bundle of clothes, then set the house on fire.

The murderer was labeled "the Terminator" (after the Arnold Schwarzenegger movie), and made a habit of killing whole families, including children. By the time of his arrest in April 1996, the Terminator had killed 40 people. Later he would confess to another 12 murders in an orgy of killing in 1989.

Anatoly Onoprienko's killing spree lasted for nearly seven years and ranged across Ukraine before Onoprienko was finally apprehended in Zhytomyr in 1996.

Death in the Ukraine

Five nights after the murders in Garmarnia, the Terminator headed to Bratkovychi, where he slaughtered another family of four—a young man, his wife, and her twin sisters. Again he stole a few items—gold jewelry and an old jacket—and set fire to the house.

During the next three months there were eight similar attacks in two villages; 28 people died and one woman was raped. In Enerhodar 7 people were killed. The killer returned to Bratkovychi on January 17, 1996, to kill a family of five. In Fastov, near Kiev, he murdered a family of four. In Olevsk, four women died. His usual method was to shoot the men, knife the women, and bludgeon the children to death.

Onoprienko, photographed in his prison cell on the day of his guilty verdict, raises his hands as he counts off the number of his victims.

The Arrest

There was panic, and an army division began to patrol the villages. Police mounted an intensive manhunt. Finally, in April 1996, the police received a tip-off about a man who visited the region to see a girlfriend, a woman with two children, who lived in Zhytomyr. More than 20 patrolmen and detectives assembled for the raid on the woman's apartment.

The police who burst into the apartment on April 14 found a small, bald-headed man with piercing blue eyes. He made a grab for his case, but one of the policemen knocked him to the floor with the butt of his gun. In the case, police found the double-barreled sawed-off rifle.

The man was Anatoly Onoprienko, a 36-year-old former psychiatric patient, and he soon confessed to a total of 52 murders.

Onoprienko insisted that he felt nothing during the murders. "For me killing people is like ripping up a duvet," he told British journalist Mark Franchetti, in his tiny prison cell in Zhytomyr, where his trial had been held. He told Franchetti that he had committed his first act of violence in his 20s, shooting a deer in the woods. He felt sorry and upset to see the dead animal but noted, "I never had that feeling again."

The act of killing, he insisted, gave him no pleasure. On the contrary, he felt oddly detached from it. "I watched all this as an animal would stare at a sheep," he told police in a 1997 videotaped confession. "I perceived it all as a kind of experiment. There can be no answer in this experiment to what you're trying to learn." He said he felt like both perpetrator and spectator.

Waiting for Orders

The administration building in Zhytomyr. Onoprienko's trial was held in this Ukraine city.

Onoprienko claimed some unknown force drove him, and voices ordered him to kill. "I'm not a maniac," he told Franchetti. "I have been taken over by a higher force, something telepathic or cosmic." But he had to wait for this force to give him orders. "For example, I wanted to kill my brother's first wife, because I hated her. I really wanted to kill her, but I couldn't, because I had to receive the order first. I waited for it, but it did not come.

"I am like a rabbit in a laboratory, a part of an experiment to prove that man is capable of murdering and learning to live with his crimes. It is to show that I can cope, that I can stand anything, forget anything."

His trial began in Zhytomyr in late November 1998. At first the authorities could not afford to try him because of the expense of prosecuting such a vast range of crimes. The trial was delayed. Eventually, after two years, his judges went on television to appeal for funds, and the Ukrainian government contributed the necessary £30,000 for the trial.

The Man in the Cage

The Beast of Ukraine was kept in a metal cage in the courtroom. Investigators uncovered the fact Onoprienko had spent three months in a Kiev psychiatric hospital, where he had been diagnosed as schizophrenic. It was after his release that he had started his killing spree.

The trial ended four months later, on March 31, 1999, when Onoprienko was found guilty and sentenced to death. Because Ukraine is being considered for membership in the European Union, Onoprienko's sentence has since been commuted to life imprisonment.

The Versace Killer

(1997)

Andrew Cunanan

It all started when a 28-year-old gay prostitute Andrew Cunanan began to suspect that he had contracted AIDS. He went for a blood test in early 1997 but could not bring himself to collect the results. After that date his friends began to notice that the usually humorous and effervescent Cunanan seemed increasingly depressed—perhaps because he assumed—incorrectly as it turned out—that he indeed had the fatal disease.

Another cause of depression was his jealous fear that two of his former boy-friends, Jeffrey Trail (a former Navy officer) and David Madson (a Minneapolis architect) were seeing each other behind his back. In an attempt to soothe his ex-lover's suspicions, Madson invited Cunanan to fly from his home in San Diego to Minneapolis to meet with himself and Trail to talk matters over.

Target for Torture

The meeting, on April 27, 1997, in Madson's apartment, proved stormy and ended with Cunanan grabbing a meat mallet from a kitchen drawer and beating in Jeff Trail's skull.

It is a mystery just why David Madson—a respected and successful professional—helped Cunanan to roll Trail's corpse in a rug and then go on the run with the killer, but he did. The mystery will remain forever unsolved because Cunanan shot Madson dead and left him in a roadside ditch several days later. Ironically Cunanan shot Madson with Trail's revolver.

At this point Cunanan seems to have decided to live the life of a reckless outlaw and never made any particular effort to cover his tracks—even leaving photographs of himself in Madson's Cherokee Jeep when he abandoned it in Danville, Illinois, a week after Trail's murder.

He left no diaries or similar indication to his mental workings, so it is a matter of conjecture why Cunanan became a serial killer. His next killing, however, almost certainly stemmed from a sick urge to reenact a scene from one of the sadomasochistic porno-graphic videos he loved to watch (and had at least once "acted" in).

After abandoning Madson's Jeep, he walked a few blocks and approached 72-year-old Chicago-based property developer Lee Miglin. Drawing his revolver, Cunanan forced Miglin into the garage of Miglin's home and bound and gagged him with duct tape. Then, apparently re-creating a scene from a video called *Target for Torture*, he beat and kicked Miglin, stabbed him several times in the chest with a pair of pruning shears, and then slowly sawed the old man's throat open with a hack saw. Cunanan then crushed the corpse to a pulp with Miglin's own car—driving over it backward and forward several times. Then, after stealing some ornamental gold coins from the house, he simply drove off.

Killing a Good Samaritan

The Miglin murder, taking place as it did in a separate state from the first two killings, allowed the FBI to become involved in the case. They realized that they had a very unstable serial killer on the loose (Cunanan had killed the requisite three people to earn this categorization). The FBI issued a nationwide police alert, placing

Celebrity Target

It seems certain that Cunanan preplanned his next killing, that of the high-flying fashion designer Gianni Versace. At 50 Versace was at the top of his profession and counted international idols like Princess Diana among his closest friends.

For two months Cunanan wandered about Miami quite openly, keeping an eye on Versace's favorite clubs and restaurants. The fact that the Miami police failed to pick Cunanan up in this time is a matter of considerable embarrassment to the department. As soon as Reese's abandoned Chevy was found, it should have been clear that the killer might be at large in the city.

On the morning of July 15, 1997, Cunanan finally caught sight of Versace outside his Miami mansion. As the designer went to open the gate, Cunanan stepped up behind him and shot him twice in the head, killing him instantly. This was Cunanan's last murder.

He went into hiding as hundreds of law officers and FBI agents flooded the city to hunt for him. Eight days after the Versace killing, he was discovered hiding in a luxury houseboat in Miami Beach by the boat's caretaker. Before the police could capture him, however, Cunanan shot himself in the temple with Jeff Trail's revolver.

EMTs remove Cunanan's covered body from the houseboat in which he killed himself.

From left, Gianni Versace, David Madson, Lee Miglin, William Reese, and Jeffrey Trail, all victims of Andrew Cunanan's murder spree

Why Did He Do It?

Some investigators believed that Cunanan went on his killing spree because he thought he was dying of AIDS. While it remains uncertain just what it takes to turn a person into a serial killer, it is clear that fear of retribution is the main break that stops many borderline sadists from becoming habitual killers. Perhaps, with that break removed—thinking he had nothing left to lose—Cunanan gave into his dark temptations. He might never have become a serial killer if he had had the courage to collect the results of his blood test earlier in the year.

Cunanan at the top of the 10 Most Wanted list. Yet he avoided all attempts to catch him, either through incredible luck or, more likely, grotesque police bungling. Cunanan certainly wasn't making much effort to avoid detection; he drove Miglin's stolen, blood-spattered Lexus all the way to New Jersey before dumping it to steal a new vehicle.

To do this he murdered 45-year-old William Reese—a groundskeeper at the Finn's Point Cemetery, near Pennsville, New Jersey. Cunanan arrived at the cemetery, abandoned the Lexus, approached Reese, and asked for an aspirin and a glass of water (both were found spilled next to the body). Following him into the groundskeeper's lodge, Cunanan shot Reese dead and stole his Chevy pickup truck. Then he drove to Florida.

Inciting to Kill?

Can horror movies like *Target for Torture* turn people into serial killers? No. The sort of person who will eventually become a serial killer is highly likely to want to watch sadomasochistic movies, but a sadist with no access to such material may still become a serial killer—so blaming movies for inspiring serial crime is oversimplistic.

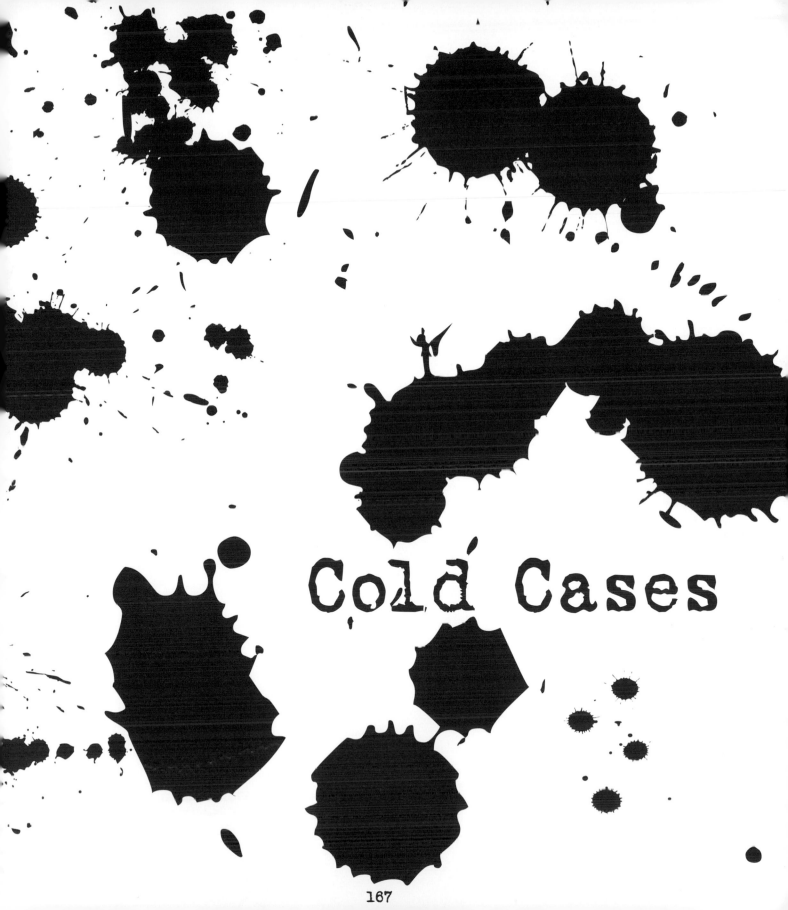

Cold Cases

The Poisoning of James Maybrick

(May 11, 1889)

Florence Maybrick

James Maybrick was a rich, self-made Liverpudlian businessman, who fell in love with 18-year-old Florence Chandler, from Alabama, on a ship crossing the Atlantic to Liverpool in 1881. Maybrick was then 41. Ignoring their 23-year age difference, they married. The couple became the toast of the town—Alabama girls being a considerable rarity in Liverpool. The Maybricks attended all the best social gatherings and seemed to everyone to be a picture of marital happiness. But things started to go wrong in their relationship. Florence found out that Maybrick not only kept several mistresses before they had married, but that he was still continuing to see one of them. James explained that he could hardly stop visiting this lady, as she had born him five illegitimate children . . .

Death of a Wife Beater

When she found out about James's mistress, Florence naturally felt that she had been betrayed and deceived, but she could do nothing publicly: divorce was unthinkable, both because of the attendant scandal and the near certainty that the court would award sole custody of their children to James. So she denied Maybrick her bed and began a series of flirtations. Her "flirtation" with a man called Alfred Brierly resulted in three nights spent together in a London hotel. Maybrick, finding out, became insanely—and some would say hypocritically—jealous.

The Maybricks quarrelled violently about her relationship with Alfred Brierly after returning from the Grand National Horse Races on March 29, 1889. The argument ended with James beating Florence and shouting that he wanted a divorce. It was this, the prosecution later argued, that drove Florence to murder her husband: the assault and his mistress were one thing, but if Florence were divorced for committing adultery, she would be a "ruined woman" in Victorian society—a social outcast and, quite possibly, destitute.

A month later, on April 27, James fell ill with diarrhea and vomiting. After days of agony he died on May 11. At the autopsy doctors found small traces of arsenic poisoning, and questioning of the Maybrick servants turned up the fact that Florence had been seen soaking arsenic-based flypapers in water in her bedroom shortly before James became ill. She insisted that she was simply using it for a beauty preparation. Still she was charged with her husband's murder. The jury found her guilty.

After their marriage the Maybricks settled into Battlecrease House in Aigburth, a suburb of Liverpool. It was there that James died after a short, violent illness.

Addicted to Poison

Florence Maybrick's trial was a travesty of justice: the jury was not told an essential fact that would otherwise have certainly caused them to acquit her.

James Maybrick had been a drug addict, and—strangely enough—the drug to which he was addicted was arsenic. This is, in fact, a powerful stimulant—if taken in nonlethal doses—and doctors in the nineteenth century often prescribed it as both a painkiller and as a pick-me-up.

Sooner or later James would have died of arsenic poisoning—for years he'd been ingesting doses that were large enough to kill anyone who had not built up a phenomenal resistance. But James was aging, and his system couldn't have taken the punishment indefinitely. If Florence's jury knew that James was an arsenic addict who would have inevitably dosed himself to death, it would almost certainly acquitted Florence on the strength of "reasonable doubt."

The judge, Fitzjames Stephen, seemed to be of that opinion; during the first day of his summation, he all but told the jury to acquit Florence. Then something odd happened: that evening Florence asked to speak to the judge in private, which he allowed. The next day Stephen had changed his tack, and all but told the jury to convict. The jury complied, and Stephen sentenced Florence to death by hanging.

Florence Maybrick in court before Judge Stephen

Arsenical Fantasy

A single fact seems to prove the "Maybrick-Ripper diary" a fake: Florence's affair with Brierly apparently took place around Christmas 1888—months too late to have inspired the Ripper murders. Yet it is possible that the arsenic-mad Maybrick might have fantasized that he was the killer, and he may have "confessed" as much to his hated wife.

Mrs. Jack the Ripper

What did Florence tell the judge to make him violently—some might say homicidally—against her, when he had been previously on her side? The matter remained a mystery until 1992, when a document was discovered that purported itself to be the secret diary of James Maybrick. It did indeed contain details of murder, but not those of James himself. In the diary, James gave a detailed confession to being Jack the Ripper.

The Jack the Ripper murders took place in autumn 1888—more than eight months before James's death. In the diary James claimed that jealousy over his wife's adultery and his addiction to arsenic had driven him to murder prostitutes in London. Each killing, he wrote, was a proxy for the wished-for murder of his wife.

The "Maybrick diary" remains a highly controversial document. Both the ink and paper appear to be old enough to be genuine, and it contains accurate details about the murders that were not generally known. Yet many believe it is a forgery. It seems just too perfect that one of the nineteenth century's most famous murder victims was himself the Victorian period's most infamous murderer.

In the light of the diary, it's tempting to speculate that James made a deathbed confession that he was Jack the Ripper, and Florence then passed this on to the judge in the hopes of some leniency. Instead Judge Stephen may have decided Florence was an outrageous liar and turned against her. He sentenced her to death, but judgment was later commuted to life imprisonment. Florence was released in 1904, having spent 14 years in prison.

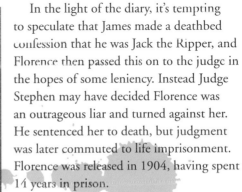

The death of James Maybrick, left, raises a few questions. Was he a murder victim? Or an accidental overdose? And, was Maybrick also an infamous murderer himself?

Jack the Ripper

(1888)

Jack the Ripper, the mysterious murderer, who terrorized Victorian London, is perhaps the most iconic serial killer in the public mind. When asked to name famous serial killers most people will mention him, even though nobody knows his real name or even very much about him. Some believe (incorrectly) that "Jack" was the first known serial killer. Others suppose that the Ripper crimes took place over many years and that his victims ran into the dozens. In actual fact, the murders took place over just a few months in 1888, and the victims were possibly no more than five in number.

Jack the Ripper: identity unknown

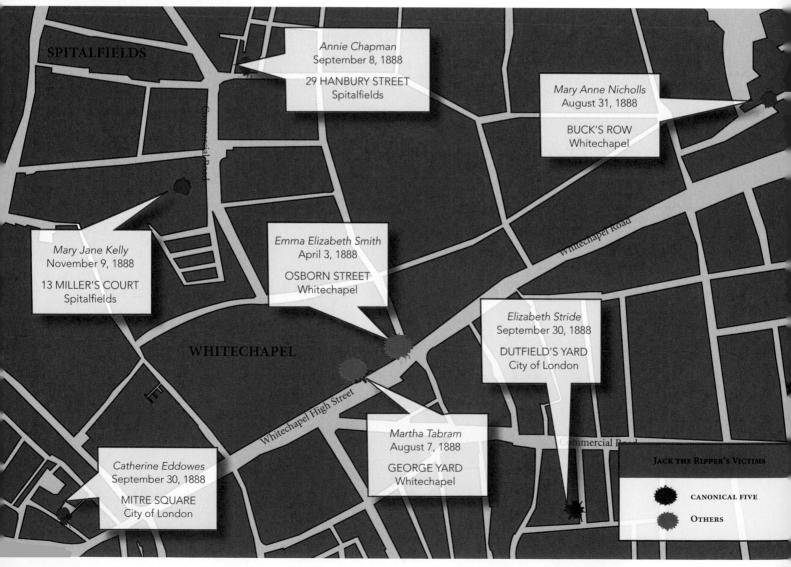

SPITALFIELDS

Annie Chapman
September 8, 1888

29 HANBURY STREET
Spitalfields

Mary Anne Nicholls
August 31, 1888

BUCK'S ROW
Whitechapel

Mary Jane Kelly
November 9, 1888

13 MILLER'S COURT
Spitalfields

Emma Elizabeth Smith
April 3, 1888

OSBORN STREET
Whitechapel

Whitechapel Road

WHITECHAPEL

Elizabeth Stride
September 30, 1888

DUTFIELD'S YARD
City of London

Whitechapel High Street

Martha Tabram
August 7, 1888

GEORGE YARD
Whitechapel

Commercial Road

Catherine Eddowes
September 30, 1888

MITRE SQUARE
City of London

JACK THE RIPPER'S VICTIMS

● CANONICAL FIVE

● OTHERS

The "Canonical" Five

Just who was a Ripper victim? Experts agree on five names—these are often referred to as the canonical five: Nicholls, Chapman, Stride, Eddowes, and Kelly. Two others, Emma Elizabeth Smith and Martha Tabram, are also strong contenders, and there may be as many as five others.

Polly Nicholls's Bad Luck

At 2:30 AM on Friday, August 31, a fellow prostitute saw Mary Anne "Polly" Nicholls on Osborn Street in the seedy Whitechapel district of London's East End. Three-quarters of an hour later, her body was found by a cart driver named Cross on Bucks Row (now called Durward Street), lying in the entrance to the Old Stable Yard at the west end of the street. In the mortuary of the Old Montague Street Workhouse it was discovered that she had been disemboweled. Death was due to severing of the windpipe. A bruise on her face indicated that the murderer clamped his hand over her mouth before cutting her throat. A woman sleeping in a bedroom only a few yards from the murder had heard no sound.

"I shant quit ripping them . . ."

On September 28 the Central News Agency received a letter threatening more murders: "I am down on whores and shant quit ripping them till I do get buckled." It was signed "Jack the Ripper."

The murders caused a mass panic. Meetings were held in the streets, criticizing the police and the home secretary. Bloodhounds were suggested, but when used they promptly lost themselves in the borough of Tooting. The newspapers of the time gave extremely full, lurid reports of the murders and inquests and tirelessly offered theories.

Someone who saw Annie Chapman talking to a man outside 29 Hanbury Street mentioned that the possible murderer sported a large moustache and was of a "foreign appearance." Newspapers and broadsheets widely circulated this description and unfortunately played directly to Londoners' bigotry; many would have liked to believe that only a foreigner was capable of such monstrous crimes.

Coins Laid at Annie's Feet

The next Ripper murder took place on September 8. Annie Chapman, aged 47, was turned away from a lodging house in Dorset Street, having no money to pay for a bed. It seems probable that the murderer picked her up outside the yard where the murder took place, 29 Hanbury Street in the Spitalfields district just north of Whitechapel. She accompanied him down a passageway at the side of the house some time after 5:00 AM. The body was found shortly after 6:00 AM. The head had been almost severed from the body. The body was cut open, as in the case of Mary Anne Nicholls, and the kidneys and ovaries had been removed. Two front teeth were missing (repeating a curious feature of the Nicholls murder), and two brass rings and some copper pennies were laid neatly at her feet.

Annie Chapman's mortuary photo

Again the murderer had carried out the crime with extreme coolness and had made no sound. There were 16 people living at 29 Hanbury Street, and a scream would have quickly brought help to the victim.

Mr. Deimschutz Almost Catches Jack Red Handed

On the morning of September 30, two murders were committed in Whitechapel. The first was of a Swedish woman called Elizabeth Stride. A hawker named Louis Deimschutz drove his horse and cart into the backyard of the International Workers Educational Club in Berner Street. (A school now stands on the site.) He saw a woman's body on the ground and rushed into the club to raise the alarm. Stride's throat had been cut very recently—so recently that it is likely that Jack the Ripper had been interrupted and hid in the shadows of the yard. He then made his escape, as Deimschutz ran past him into the club to get help. This was at 1:00 AM.

Jack Takes Some Souvenirs

At around 1:00 AM on September 30, Catherine Eddowes, a 43-year-old prostitute, was released from Bishopsgate Police Station, where she had been held for drunkenness. The Ripper picked her up and took her into a narrow alleyway that extends between Mitre Square and Duke Street, known as Church Passage (now St. James's Passage). Police Constable Watkins passed through the passage on his beat at 1:30 AM. A quarter of an hour later he again passed through the square and found Eddowes's body in the corner of the square near Church Passage. Her face had been badly mutilated—perhaps to delay identification—and the body cut open in the usual way: the left kidney and some of her entrails had been removed and taken away. It was some time before she was identified, and, in the meantime, one of the newspapers published a report that she was thought to be a certain "Mary Anne Kelly." This is a remarkable coincidence, since the name of the final victim was Mary Jane Kelly.

A householder who lived in nearby Bemer Street testified that she saw a young man carrying a shiny black bag walking away from the scene of the crime.

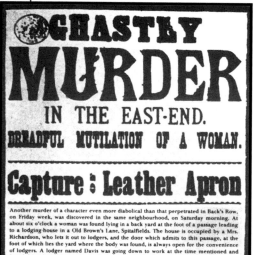

GHASTLY MURDER IN THE EAST-END. DREADFUL MUTILATION OF A WOMAN. Capture: Leather Apron

Another murder of a character even more diabolical than that perpetrated in Back's Row, on Friday week, was discovered in the same neighbourhood, on Saturday morning. At about six o'clock a woman was found lying in a back yard at the foot of a passage leading to a lodging house in a Old Brown's Lane, Spitalfields. The house is occupied by a Mrs. Richardson, who lets it out to lodgers, and the door which admits to this passage, at the foot of which lies the yard where the body was found, is always open for the convenience of lodgers. A lodger named Davis was going down to work at the time mentioned and found the woman lying on her back close to the flight of steps leading into the yard. Her throat was cut in a fearful manner. The woman's body had been completely ripped open and the heart and other organs laying about the place, and portions of the entrails round the victim's neck. An excited crowd gathered in front of Mrs. Richardson's house and also round the mortuary in old Montague Street, whither the body was quickly conveyed. As the body lies in the rough coffin in which it has been placed in the mortuary - the same coffin in which the unfortunate Mrs. Nicholls was first placed - it presents a fearful sight. The body is that of a woman about 45 years of age. The height is exactly five feet. The complexion is fair, with wavy brown hair; the eyes are blue, and two lower teeth have been knocked out. The nose is rather large and prominent.

A wanted poster from 1888 calls the killer "Leather Apron." He was called several names before giving himself the name Jack the Ripper in a letter to a news agency.

Jack or Jill?

One early theory was that Jack was actually a Jill—that is, a woman. Some Ripper theorists posit that she might have been a mad midwife (thus the basic medical knowledge suggested by the killings and the lack of rape in the attacks). But the Ripper must have been very strong to kill so quickly, and cases of female serial killers are rare.

Jack's letter "from hell"

Jack Writes in Red

After these murders the Central News Agency received another letter signed "Jack the Ripper," in which he expressed regret that he had been interrupted while with his victims and had not been able to send the ears to the police. (There had been an attempt to cut off the ear of Catherine Eddowes, although this fact had not been made public at that time.) He also mentioned that "number one squealed a bit," which is borne out by a witness in Berner Street who heard a cry. Jack himself most likely wrote the letter, which he posted only a few hours after the murders and wrote in blood red ink.

Bands of vigilantes patrolled the streets of Whitechapel at night, but as weeks passed without further crimes, the panic died down. Then, on November 9, the last of the murders took place at a house in Miller's Court, which ran off Dorset Street (now Duval Street). Mary Jane Kelly was younger than any of the other victims. She was 24.

Mary's Room

On the morning of November 9, at 10:45, a man knocked on the door of Mary Jane Kelly's one-room, ground-floor flat to collect the rent. Getting no reply, he peered in through the dirty, broken window. Jack had evidently spent a long time in there. The walls of the room were spattered with blood, and what remained of Kelly lay on the bed. Her throat had been slashed so deeply that her head had been almost severed from her body. Her lower face was slashed to ribbons. Her heart had been cut out and placed on the bed pillow. Her belly had been torn open and her entrails pulled out and draped over a picture frame. One of the thighs of her spread-eagled legs had been filleted to the bone.

As usual with the Ripper, he had swiftly killed his victim, then mutilated her corpse. He had apparently worked by the light of a lit pile of rags, the ashes of which were lying burned out in the grate. The probable time of the killing was set by neighbors' reports of hearing a cry of "Murder!" at about

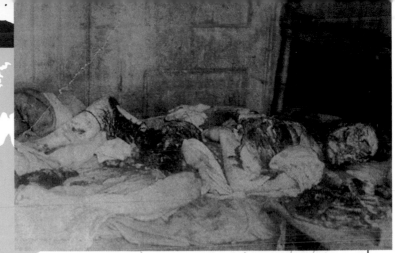

The mutilated corpse of Mary Kelly

3:30 AM. It goes some way to show just how frightened the people of the East End were by the Ripper murders that none of the dozen or so inhabitants of Miller's Court investigated the cry. The inquest revealed that no parts of Kelly's body had been taken away this time.

Why Did Jack Stop?

We have no certain idea who Jack the Ripper was, so we cannot be certain just why he apparently ceased killing in November 1888. But, given the frequency of the murders and the savagery of the attack on Mary Kelly, it seems likely that Jack was rapidly getting out of control.

It is possible that he moved to another country—where at the time savage murders were easier to conceal than in England—but this does not seem likely. He was evidently an "antisocial" serial killer; these prefer to leave their victims to be found—thus horrifying and terrifying the public. Totally hiding his activities would not fit his psychological needs.

It is also possible that he simply got tired of killing, but this is almost unknown among serial killers. A more likely reason that the killings stopped was that "Jack" was either locked in a mental asylum, had committed suicide (although this is also almost unknown among serial killers), or he had died, possibly killed by a potential victim who fought back.

The Metropolitan Police Service, charged with solving the Whitechapel murders, received a great deal of criticism for its inability to identify the elusive Jack the Ripper. Newspapers and magazines began to satire their ineffectual efforts, such as this cartoon that shows a blindfolded policeman wandering through the East End.

Lizzie Borden
(August 4, 1892)

Lizzie Borden

Lizzie Borden is remembered as one if the most infamous murderers of the nineteenth century. There is even a jump-rope song—still chanted in school playgrounds of today by happily ghoulish children—that gives the details of the gruesome case:

> *Lizzie Borden took an axe*
> *And gave her mother 40 whacks.*
> *And when she saw what she had done,*
> *She gave her father 41.*

What is less well known, however, is the fact that Lizzie Borden was acquitted of the brutal murder of her father and stepmother.

The Double Murder

In 1892 Lizzie Borden, aged 32, lived with her father, her stepmother, and her older sister at 92 Second Street—an unfashionable address in the city of Fall River, Massachusetts. Nonetheless Andrew Borden, a bank director, was one of the richest men in town. He was known, however, as something of a miser.

At 11:10 AM on August 4, housemaid Bridget Sullivan heard Lizzie screaming: "Come down quick! Father's dead! Somebody's come in and killed him!"

Bridget found the 72-year-old Andrew lying sprawled on his back on the couch in his study. He was quite dead, and his head was a shattered, red mess. Upstairs they found Abby, Lizzie's 64-year-old stepmother, lying on the guest bedroom floor with her head also smashed in, this time from behind.

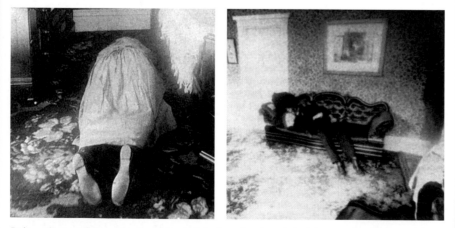

Police photos of Abby Borden, left, and Andrew Borden, right. The murder of the couple was excessively violent, which suggests that the culprit was very angry or upset.

Whodunit?

It was a fairly short list of suspects in the double murder. The only people in the house at the time of the killings, other than the victims, were Lizzie and Bridget. The evidence ruled out any possibility that either Andrew or Abby killed the other and then his- or herself. One of the two women or some undetected interloper had to have done it.

Medical examination showed that an axe or a hatchet had felled both victims. Contrary to the 40 or so "whacks" listed in the playground rhyme, Abby had taken only 18 blows to the back of the head and Andrew 11 blows to the front. But the amount of "overkill" in each murder—just 2 or 3 blows would have been deadly—suggested a frenzy or fury.

A key factor in the investigation was blood spatter. Lizzie had raised the alarm only minutes after the murders, but neither she nor Bridget bore bloodstains when the neighbors arrived. And neither apparently had time to wash and change into clean clothes. The police nevertheless charged Lizzie with double homicide.

Motives

The Borden household had been an unhappy one for some time. Lizzie and her sister, Emma, were in their 30s and, by Victorian standards, considered "old maids." Their main hope—if they indeed wanted to marry—was their father's fortune: once the old man died they would both be rich spinsters and thus prime targets in the local marriage market.

Andrew's marriage to Abby Durfree Gray—his second wife—had damaged these prospects. Not only would she inherit the lion's share of his money, but she was also pressuring him to lend money to her relatives.

The Borden daughters were habitually frosty with their rather meek stepmother and even took over the front half of the house as their private preserve. They'd often row with their father and stepmother and refused to call Abby anything but the coldly formal "Mrs. Borden." Emma, though, was not a suspect; she'd been away at the time of the murders. But it turned out that both she and Lizzie had had a blazing argument about money with Andrew shortly before *both* of them had stormed off on holiday. Lizzie, however, had unexpectedly returned home . . . just before the killings.

The Borden house in Fall River, Massachusetts, still stands. It is now open as the Lizzie Borden Bed and Breakfast / Museum.

The Trial

The tension in the Borden household did give Lizzie some motive for the crime, but there was no confirming physical or witness evidence. The prosecution claimed that a broken hatchet found in the cellar had been the murder weapon and that Lizzie had cleaned its blade and then broken off the bloodstained wood handle. But the missing handle had then shown up in the cellar—quite unstained.

The prosecution offered only one bit of strong evidence: a few days after the murders, Lizzie was seen burning a dress. She maintained that it had been ruined by wet paint, but the prosecution argued that it was the bloodstained garment that she wore during the murders. But no nineteenth-century jury was going to hang a rich woman on the grounds of a single piece of circumstantial evidence.

Lady Killer

Domestic murders were quite common in late-nineteenth-century America, as was death by extreme violence (such as axe blows). It was the titillating thought that a genteel lady might have swung the hatchet that created the persistent interest in the case.

The jury found her not guilty, yet until her death in 1927, Lizzie (still a spinster) was dogged by the rumor that she had committed bloody murder. Various theories have been presented to explain the mystery. Some have suggested that the maid, Bridget, had done the gruesome deed. Alfred Hitchcock proposed that the supposedly absent Emma killed Andrew and Abby but admitted that this was just speculation. In the end, Lizzie is still the most likely candidate, but like the jury we still must admit that there is no conclusive evidence against her.

A newspaper illustration of Lizzie Borden during her trial in June 1893. Although she gave incriminating testimony at the inquest, enough for the police to charge her with murder, none of it was allowed in the actual trial, which made it far easier for the 12 jurors to acquit her.

Monster of Cinkota

(1910s)

Bela Kiss

In 1900 a handsome, blond young man named Bela Kiss went to live at 9 Kossuth Street in the Hungarian village of Cinkota, just outside Budapest, accompanied by his wife, Maria, aged 25. Maria Kiss acquired a lover, Paul Bihari, and eventually Kiss lamented to the inhabitants of Cinkota that Maria and Paul had run away together.

In 1912 the forsaken spouse hired an elderly widow, Mrs. Jakubec, as house-keeper. Mrs. Jakubec regarded the frequent arrival of women at first with surprise, then understanding tolerance. Kiss then started collecting enormous metal drums, filled (as he explained to Trauber, the village constable) with gasoline, which would be in short supply during the approaching European war. Kiss was a tinsmith by trade, so metal drums caused no surprise.

The Handsome Hoffmann

Meanwhile Budapest police were searching for two widows, named Schmeidak and Varga, who had been missing for months. They were known to have visited the flat of a man named Hoffman, living near the Margaret Bridge in Budapest, who had also vanished. This Hoffman was a handsome, blonde man, with a bushy moustache, who seemed widely read, but was familiar to the brothel madams of Budapest as a regular and generous customer of insatiable sexual appetite.

In November 1914, three months after the war started, Bela Kiss was conscripted from his Cinkota home and within a few hours was on his way to the front; in May 1916, Constable Trauber received notice of his death in action.

The Margaret Bridge in Budapest, as it looks today. Using the name Hoffmann, Kiss lived there before he went to war.

Pickled Bodies

When, a month later, a party of soldiers entered Cinkota looking for petrol, Trauber and other townsfolk, including Kiss's landlord, remembered the metal drums Kiss had so prudently hoarded. They located seven drums inside the house, and when they drilled a hole in one of them, a nauseating smell filled the room. A chemist said it was the smell of decaying flesh. The drum proved to contain a garroted, naked woman, preserved in alcohol.

Detective Chief Dr. Charles Nagy, of the Budapest Police, lost no time in getting to the cottage at 9 Kossuth Street in Cinkota. The other drums also contained the corpses of strangled women—seven of them. In due course, the police found additional drums on the property.

A cache of letters in a locked room proved to be from women, many addressed to Hoffman in Budapest. Further investigation there left no doubt that Kiss was a "Bluebeard" killer, placing matrimonial advertisements in newspapers and living on the income of the women who answered them, including the missing widow Katharine Varga, who had owned a prosperous dressmaking business.

Nagy learned that 17 drums had originally been delivered to Kiss, and the remaining 10 were located in various hiding places, such as below the earth floor of the henhouse. Nagy finally accumulated evidence that Kiss had murdered 30 women, including Maria Kiss, and a man, Paul Bihari.

No one questioned Kiss's habit of stockpiling metal drums all over his rented property. He explained their presence by telling townsfolk that he was storing gasoline, which would be in short supply during the war.

The Search

But where was Kiss? Had he really died in battle? In Hungary "Bela" and "Kiss" are common names, and there could have been dozens of Bela Kisses in the army. Nagy received a message saying that Kiss had died in 1915, followed immediately by another stating that Kiss was in the hospital. Nagy arrived to find that this man had died, but the body was definitely not that of Kiss. It seemed that Kiss had somehow swapped identity papers with a dead man, then vanished.

The missing killer became famous. In 1919 he was reported crossing the Margaret Bridge. In 1920 a member of the French Foreign Legion reported that he believed Kiss was a fellow soldier named—not surprisingly—Hoffman. But by the time the police arrived, Hoffman had deserted.

In 1932 Detective Henry Oswald of New York's Homicide Squad (known as "Camera Eye" to the press because of his amazing memory) was certain that he'd seen Kiss emerging from the Times Square subway station, but by the time he had reached the spot, Kiss had vanished in the crowd of New Yorkers. The report of this sighting led to a rumor that the now elderly Kiss had taken a job as janitor of an apartment building on Sixth Avenue in Manhattan. Again, by the time the police arrived, he had vanished.

That, it seemed, was the last reported sighting of the elusive Bela Kiss.

A Times Square subway entrance. Was is really possible that Bela Kiss had made his way to New York, where he could live anonymously?

The Shark Arm Case

(1935)

A tiger shark

In the 1930s the people of Sydney, Australia, were fighting an unofficial war—on sharks. The climate and their national temperament meant that large numbers of Sydneyites were spending a great deal of time frolicking in the very inviting sea, with the inevitable result that shark attacks were on the rise.

The Australians reacted with a strategy of shark wardens keeping watch on the beaches and rewards to fishermen for each shark delivered, dead or alive. One of the few sharks delivered alive was a monstrous 11-foot tiger shark.

Whose Arm?

On April 25, 1935, less than a week after taking up residence at the Coogee Aquarium, the shark did something that sharks rarely do: it vomited. And in the cloud of regurgitation, before the eyes of horrified aquarium goers, floated a human arm.

Medical examination showed something even more shocking: the shark's teeth hadn't severed the arm at the elbow—it had been hacked off with a knife.

The arm was in amazingly good condition . . . considering where it had been for more than a week. Its size and a tattoo of two boxers indicated that the arm came from a man—a fact confirmed by the fingerprints. It had belonged to Jim Smith, a second-rate boxer and petty criminal.

Smith had been last seen in the company of his friend Patrick Brady, a forger, drinking and playing cards at the Hotel Cecil on the afternoon of April 7. They had then gone to the cottage rented by Brady on nearby Gunnamatta Bay. Examination of the vacated cottage showed that a mattress and a trunk had been replaced and the walls of one room scrubbed suspiciously clean—circumstantial evidence that Smith might have been killed and dissected in the cottage and then the remains removed in the trunk.

Police arrested Brady on May 16, but the apparently straightforward if gruesome case was about to take some strange twists.

Crowds pack the beach off Coogee Pier during a hot summer day in the mid-1930s.

The Second Man

A taxi driver from near Gunnamatta Bay came forward with a story to tell. A very nervous Brady had called at his house on the morning of April 8, asking for a ride into Sydney. He'd then acted strangely, keeping one hand crammed into a pocket at all times, as if hiding something. He also peered repeatedly out of the back window, as if checking for a tail.

Brady's destination was the home of Reginald Holmes, a seemingly respectable businessman who ran a successful boatyard. In fact Holmes was also a crook, secretly using his yard's speedboats to smuggle cocaine, cigarettes, and other contraband.

The police extensively questioned both Holmes and Brady, but neither would admit to anything. So Holmes was released and Brady charged with murder. Yet the charge would never stick; there wasn't even evidence to prove a murder had actually taken place—a man can survive with a severed arm, after all.

Unfortunately for the police, the aquarium owners had already killed the shark and disposed of it in the bay, removing any chance of examining its stomach for additional "evidence."

The Bizarre Sydney Harbour Boat Chase

On May 20, the investigation took another, tragicomic, twist.

That day Reginald Holmes stepped out onto his boat dock, pressed a pistol to his forehead, and pulled the trigger. But he held the gun at an angle—possibly wincing in anticipation of the shot—and the bullet bounced off his skull, knocking him bloody and unconscious but otherwise unharmed.

His knees buckled as the bullet hit him, and he fell off the dock into the water. This revived both him and his will to live. He clambered into a speedboat just as the police arrived to investigate the gunshot. A farcical four-hour boat chase ensued, weaving through the busy ferry traffic of Sydney Harbour, before Holmes gave himself up.

He confessed that Brady had indeed visited him after Smith's murder and had threatened him, outlandishly enough, with Smith's severed arm. Brady and Holmes had once been partners in a forged check scam but had since fallen out. Now Brady wanted help and threatened that Holmes would end up like Jim Smith if he held back.

Reginald Holmes led police on a long, strange boat chase through Sydney Harbour, shown above, before he finally gave himself up. He admitted that he knew Jim Smith, the man whose arm had been severed, but he swore that another man had as good as confessed to killing him.

Only Unanswered Questions

The police finally had a cooperative witness to whom Brady had all but admitted killing Smith. But on June 12 Holmes was found slumped over the steering wheel of his car, shot dead. Stranger still, he'd indirectly committed suicide. On June 11, according to author Alex Castle, he'd withdrawn £500 out of his bank and paid it to a hit man to kill him.

Brady, acquitted for lack of evidence, maintained his innocence for the rest of his life. Indeed this might be true. Holmes's evidence, like his sanity, was suspect. And Brady had no motive to kill his friend, but a local mobster, Eddie Wayman, did. Police records show that Smith was a police informer and had informed on Wayman's activities several times.

But, in the end, the stunning coincidence that the very shark that ate Jim Smith's arm was caught alive and then threw it up in front of witnesses, came to nothing. We don't know who killed Smith—or even if he was killed at all.

Embarrassed to Death

Why was Reginald Holmes so determined to kill himself? The one answer might be that he was literally mortified over the likely revelation of his criminal history, and that the scandal would destroy his respectable standing in (then) ultraconservative Sydney society.

The Riddle of the Boston Strangler

(1962-1964)

Albert DeSalvo

Between June 1962 and January 1964, 13 women were raped and strangled to death in Boston, Massachusetts, by a killer who, naturally, became known as the "Boston Strangler." The public panic and outcry eventually led to a police investigative operation similar in scope to that of the Jack the Ripper investigation in 1888—but far bigger.

The murders started on June 14, 1962, when the killer sexually molested and strangled 55-year-old Anna Slesers. Over the next month and a half the killer struck five more times. The victims were all elderly: the youngest was 65 years old and the oldest 85.

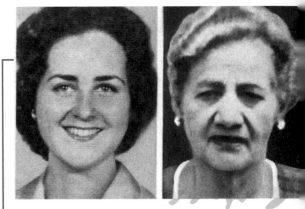

Two Patterns

After the summer 1962 flurry, there was a gap in the Strangler killings until December of that year. But when the murders began again the killer had changed his pattern.

On December 5 Sophie Clark was found raped and strangled. But unlike the previous victims, she was a young woman—only 19. Over the next month, six more women were killed in the same way as the elderly summer victims, but almost all were in their 20s.

Finally, on January 4, 1964, the killer raped and strangled 19-year-old Mary Sullivan. He had repeatedly bitten her corpse, ejaculated over her face, and left her with a broom handle thrust into her vagina. Then the killings suddenly stopped.

Boston's Gainsbourough Street, site of one of the earliest Strangler murders

An End to Killing

The rapes in the Boston area continued, however. Investigators were of two minds as to whether the Strangler had stopped killing and whether the rapes were his work, too. Bizarrely the rapist seemed to be a polite, almost gentle person; he occasionally allowed his would-be victims to talk him out of raping them and would invariably apologize to those he did attack.

The descriptions of the "gentle rapist" reminded the police of an offender who had recently been jailed for two years. He earned the nickname the Measuring Man, because, posing as a modeling agency scout, he talked his way into

Home Sweet Home

In taped interviews, DeSalvo confessed in detail to the 13 murders in Boston. He also gave investigators a life history that was both bizarre and sickening. Albert DeSalvo's father had been a brutal man who ill-treated his mother—on one occasion he deliberately broke her fingers one by one. He openly brought prostitutes into the family home, with whom he had sex in front of the children. Albert had incestuous relations with his sisters, and his childhood home was permeated with an overpowering atmosphere of sex. As an adult, he confessed, he was a man who wanted to have sex with every woman he saw, a mental outlook that led him first to the Measuring Man sex cons and later to rape.

Richard DeSalvo, left, brother of Albert DeSalvo, at a 2000 news conference in Boston. Family members of the Strangler's final victim are fighting to clear DeSalvo's name, insisting that the real killer is still free.

Five of the women whose murders are linked to the Boston Strangler. From left: Sophie Clark, 21; Jane Sullivan, 67; Helen E. Blake, 65; Ida Irga, 75; and Patricia Bissette, 23.

apartments and persuaded young women to allow him to take their measurements. Occasionally he ventured a few indecent caresses. Some of the women even had sex with him in hopes of landing one of the "modeling" jobs. The Measuring Man was a husky young ex-soldier, Albert DeSalvo. He was imprisoned for "lewd and lascivious behavior," as well as for attempted breaking and entry.

He was sent to Bridgewater State Hospital for observation. The doctors there diagnosed him as schizophrenic and not competent to stand trial. Soon after his permanent committal to Bridgewater, DeSalvo confessed to a fellow patient that he was the Boston Strangler, and the patient informed his lawyer. DeSalvo was sentenced to life imprisonment, but he had served only six years when he was found stabbed to death in his cell. His killer was never identified.

Two Stranglers?

There is now a movement to exonerate Albert DeSalvo of the Boston Strangler murders.

It seems to some that the criminal who committed the Measuring Man cons and the post-Strangler rapes was simply too "gentle" a man to be a killer. And researchers have also pointed out that DeSalvo's confessions contained many fundamental inaccuracies about details of the murders. For example he claimed to have raped Mary Sullivan's corpse. But the coroner's report states that the killer had not penetrated her.

Then there is the change in the age of the Strangler victims—between the first and second wave of murders—that some believe indicates that there was actually more than one killer on the loose. FBI investigator Robert Ressler has written that there are "so many different patterns that it's inconceivable, behaviorally, that all these could fit one individual."

A Correct Guess?

A psychological profiling team attached to the original investigation in 1962 also concluded that there was more than one Boston Strangler. They concluded that the "Summer" Boston Strangler was an embittered homosexual with a mother-hate fixation; thus his choice of elderly victims. The "December" strangler, they thought, was a copycat killer—a heterosexual schoolteacher, they surmised, who lived on his own—whose tastes were for young women. The arrest and conviction of DeSalvo nullified these theories. Yet, perhaps, the profilers may have been closer to the truth than they realized . . .

Jack the Stripper

(1964–1965)

Idendikit drawing of "Jack the Stripper"

Between February 1964 and January 1965, the bodies of six women, mostly prostitutes, were found in areas near the Thames River in England. These women met ugly deaths after living hard-knock lives. The first victim, Hannah Tailford, age 30, worked in the underground world of stag films and sex orgies. Her decomposing body was found in the water near Hammersmith Bridge on February 2, 1964. She was naked, except for her stockings, and her panties had been stuffed into her mouth.

Hammersmith Bridge

The "Nude" Murders

Soon after, the naked corpse of another prostitute showed up in the Thames. Irene Lockwood, 26, had been tiny, just 5 feet tall. All of the victims would turn out to be small women—none of them stood over 5 feet, 2 inches. Like Tailford, Lockwood had been strangled with a ligature. The next victim was found in an alleyway at Osterley Park, Brentford. She was a 22-year-old prostitute and striptease artist, Helen Barthelemy. There were a number of curious features. A line around her waist showed that her panties had been removed after death, and there was no evidence of normal sex, however, four of her front teeth were missing. Oddly enough they had not been knocked out by a blow but were forced out. There was male semen in her throat.

Here, then, was the cause of death: a penis, probably in the course of performing an act of oral sex, had choked her. The missing teeth suggested that the killer had repeated the act after death.

Helen Barthelemy

The Paint Clue

Barthelemy had disappeared some days before her body was found. Flakes of paint found on her skin provided a clue to the mystery, though, because the paint type was used in spraying cars. Clearly the body had been kept somewhere near a car factory. The "nude murders" now became a public sensation, for it seemed likely that they were the work of one man. The fourth victim—Mary Fleming, 30, found on July 14, confirmed that the same man was responsible. Her false teeth were missing, there was sperm in her throat, and her skin showed traces of the spray paint. She had vanished three days earlier.

Her body was found in a cul-de-sac, and a van was observed leaving the scene. A motorist driving past Berrymede Road, at 5:30 AM, had to brake violently to avoid the van that shot out in front of him. On November 25, 1964, another body with missing teeth was found under some debris in a car park in Hornton Street, Kensington. She was identified as Margaret McGowan, 21, and had disappeared more than a month before.

The Last Victim

The last of the Stripper's victims, a prostitute named Bridie O'Hara, 28, was found on February 16, 1965, in some undergrowth on the Heron Trading Estate in Acton. She had been last seen on January 11, in the Shepherds Bush Hotel. As usual, teeth were missing and sperm was found in the throat.

Detective Chief Superintendent John du Rose was recalled from his holiday to take charge of the investigation. The Heron Trading Estate provided the lead they had been waiting for. Investigation of a paint spray shop revealed that this was definitely the source of the paint found on the bodies. The proximity of a disused warehouse solved the question of where the bodies had lain before they were dumped. This enabled experts to establish the spot where the women must have been concealed: it was underneath a transformer in the warehouse.

Far right, police at the last Stripper crime scene. The naked body of Bridie O'Hara (right) was found behind a storage shed on an industrial estate less than a mile from where Mary Fleming had been found.

War of Nerves

Even with this discovery, the case was far from solved. Thousands of men worked on the Heron Trading Estate. The police decided to throw an immense 20-mile cordon around the area, to keep a careful check on all cars passing through at night. Drivers who were observed more than once were noted; if they were seen more than twice, they were interviewed. Du Rose conducted what he called "a war of nerves" against the killer, dropping hints in the press or on television that indicated the police were getting closer. They knew he drove a van, they knew he must have right of access to the trading estate by night. The size of the victims, who were all short women, suggested that the killer was under middle height.

As the months passed, and no further murders took place, du Rose assumed that he was winning the war of nerves. The killer had ceased to operate. Du Rose checked on all men who had been jailed since mid-February and all men who had died or committed suicide. In his book *Murder Was My Business*, du Rose claims that investigators had narrowed down a list of 20 suspects to just 3 suspects when one of them, recently revealed as a man named Mungo Ireland, did commit suicide, leaving a note that said he could not bear the strain any longer. Ireland was a security guard who drove a van and had access to the estate. At the time the women were murdered, his rounds included the spray shop. He worked by night, from 10:00 PM to 6:00 AM. He was unmarried. The case is still open, but Du Rose believes that Ireland was the murderer called Jack the Stripper.

How Many?

No one is sure just how many women were victims of Jack the Stripper. Besides the six most agreed upon, two other deaths stand out as following the same Stripper's pattern. The first was another prostitute, Elizabeth Figg, whose body was found on a Thames towpath in 1959. Gynneth Rees's body, naked except for a single stocking was found about a mile from the water. She had been strangled and several of her teeth were knocked out. Key differences are that Figg was strangled manually rather than by ligature, and her dress, though torn open, was still on. Rees, although close to the Thames, was found in a garbage heap.

Further Reading

Bataille, Georges. *The Trial of Gilles de Rais*. Los Angeles: Amok Books, 1991.

Beavan, Colin. *Fingerprints: The Origins of Crime Detection and the Murder Case That Launched Forensic Science*. New York: Hyperion, 2002.

Blinda, Lawrence. *The Big, Bad Book of Mike: Rogues, Rascals and Rapscallions Named Michael, Mike and Mickey*. iUniverse, 2003.

Bowden, Mark. *Killing Pablo: The Hunt for the World's Greatest Outlaw*. New York: Penguin, 2002.

Brackett, D. W. *Holy Terror: Armageddon in Tokyo*. Boston: Weatherhill, 1996.

Braund, Nathan, and Maxim Jakubowski. *The Mammoth Book of Jack the Ripper*. Philadelphia: Running Press, 1999.

Bugliosi, Vincent, and Curt Gentry. *Helter Skelter: The True Story of the Manson Murders*. New York: W. W. Norton & Company, 2001.

Carlo, Philip. *The Night Stalker*. New York: Pinnacle, 2006.

Castles, Alex C. *The Shark Arm Murders: The Thrilling True Story of a Tiger Shark and a Tattooed Arm*. Kent Town: AU: Wakefield Press, 1999.

Clarkson, Wensley. *The Good Doctor*. New York: St. Martin's Press, 2007.

Codrescu, Andrei. *The Blood Countess*. London: Quartet Books, 2008.

Conradi, Peter. *The Red Ripper: Inside the Mind of Russia's Most Brutal Serial Killer*. London: Book Club Associates, 1992.

Crowley, Aleister. *Gilles de Rais: The Banned Lecture*. Logan, OH: Black Moon Publishing, 2008.

Eckert, Allan W. *The Scarlet Mansion*. New York: Little, Brown & Co., 1985.

Evans, Stewart P., and Keith Skinner. *The Ultimate Jack the Ripper Companion: An Illustrated Encyclopedia*. New York: Basic Books, 2001.

Fisher, Jim. *The Lindbergh Case*. New Brunswick, NJ: Rutgers University Press, 1994.

Fisher, Joseph C. *Killer Among Us: Public Reactions to Serial Murder*. New York: Praeger, 1997.

Gaskins, Donald. *Final Truth: The Autobiography of a Serial Killer*. Starr, SC: Adept Books, 1992.

Geary, Rick. *The Borden Tragedy: A Memoir of the Infamous Double Murder at Fall River, Massachusetts, 1892*. New York: NBM, 1997.

Gilmore, John. *Manson: The Unholy Trail of Charlie and the Family*. Los Angeles: Amok Books, 2000.

Goodrich, Thomas. *The Darkest Dawn: Lincoln, Booth, and the Great American Tragedy*. Bloomington: Indiana University Press, 2006.

Harrison. Shirley. *Jack the Ripper: The American Connection*. London: John Blake, 2003.

Horowitz, Sara, and Michael Ruane. *Sniper: Inside the Hunt for the Killers Who Terrorized the Nation*. New York: Ballantine Books, 2004.

Kauffman, Michael W. *American Brutus: John Wilkes Booth and the Lincoln Conspiracies*. New York: Random House, 2005.

Kent, David. *The Lizzie Borden Sourcebook*. N.p.: Branden Books, 1992.

Keppel, Robert. *Signature Killers*. New York: Pocket Books, 2007.

Knight, Alanna. *Burke and Hare: Crime Archive*. Washington, D.C.: The National Archives, 2007.

Langlois, Janet. *Belle Gunness*. Bloomington: Indiana University Press, 1985.

Lasseter, Don. *Die for Me: The Terrifying True Story of the Charles Ng and Leonard Lake Torture Murders*. New York: Pinnacle, 2000.

Leggiere, Michael V. *The Fall of Napoleon. Vol. 1, The Allied Invasion of France, 1813–1814*. New York: Cambridge University Press, 2007.

Lindbergh, Anne Morrow. *Hour of Gold, Hour of Lead*. New York: Mariner Books, 1993.

Linedecker, Clifford L. *The Man Who Killed Boys: The John Wayne Gacy, Jr. Story*. New York: St. Martin's Press, 1980.

London, Sondra, and G. J. Schaefer, *Killer Fiction*. Port Townsend, WA: Feral House, 1997.

Lourie, Richard. *Hunting the Devil. The Pursuit, Capture and Confession of the Most Savage Serial Killer in History*. New York: HarperCollins, 1993.

Manson, Charles. *Manson in His Own Words*. New York: Grove Press, 1994.

Martingale, Moira. *Cannibal Killers: The History of Impossible Murders*. New York: Running Press Second Edition, 1999.

Masters. Brian. *Killing for Company*. New York: Random House, 1995.

Michaud, Stephen G. *Lethal Shadow: The Chilling True-Crime Story of a Sadistic Sex Slayer*. New York: Penguin, 1994.

Michaud, Stephen G., and Hugh Aynesworth. *The Only Living Witness: The True Story of Serial Killer Ted Bundy*. New York: Signet, 1986.

———. *Ted Bundy: Conversations with a Serial Killer*. Irving, TX: Authorlink, 2000.

Michaud, Stephen G., with Robert R. Hazelwood. *The Evil That Men Do*. New York: St. Martin's Press, 1998.

Mollison, James. *The Memory of Pablo Escobar*. London: Chris Boot, 2007.

Mordeaux, A. *Bathory: Memoir of a Countess*. Charleston, SC: BookSurge Publishing, 2008.

Nickel, Steven. *Torso: The Story of Eliot Ness and the Search for a Psychopathic Killer*. Winston-Salem, NC: John F. Blair Publisher, 1989.

O'Brien, Darcy. *The Hillside Stranglers*. Philadelphia: Running Press, 2003.

Olsen, Jack. *Man with Candy*. New York: Simon & Schuster, 1974.

Payne, Robert. *Ivan the Terrible*. New York: Cooper Square Press, 2002.

Penrose, Valentine. *The Bloody Countess: Atrocities of Erzsebet Bathory*. N.p.: Solar Books, 2006.

Perrie, Maureen, and Andrei Pavlov. *Ivan the Terrible*. Harrow, UK: Longman, 2003.

Pudney, Jeremy. *The Bodies in Barrels Murders*. London: John Blake Publishing, 2006.

Ritchie, Jeane, and Brian Whittle. *Harold Shipman—Prescription for Murder: The True Story* of Dr. Harold Frederick Shipman. New York: Time Warner, 2004.

Rogers, Alan. New England Remembers: The Boston Strangler. Beverly, MA: Commonwealth Editions, 2006.

Ryan, Bernard. The Poisoned Life of Mrs. Maybrick. London: Penguin, 1989.

Schecter, Harold. A to Z Encyclopedia of Serial Killers. New York: Pocket Books, 1997.

———. Bestial: The Savage Tale of a True American Monster. New York: Pocket Books, 2004.

———. Deranged: The Shocking True Story of America's Most Fiendish Killer. New York: Pocket Books, 1990.

Sebatini, Rafael. The Life of Cesare Borgia. Rockville, MD: Wildside Press, 2003.

Shepherd, Sylvia Elizabeth. The Mistress of Murder Hill: The Serial Killings of Belle Gunness. Bloomington, IN: 1st Books Library, 2001.

Smith, Carlton. The BTK Murders: Inside the "Bind Torture Kill" Case that Terrified America's Heartland. New York: St. Martin's, 2007.

Sounes, Howard. Fred and Rose: The Full Story of Fred and Rose West and the Gloucester House of Horror. New York: Little Brown, 1995.

Spurr, Wendy, and Kimberly Spurr. Alfred Packer's High Protein Cookbook. Grand Junction, CO: Centennial Publications, 1995.

Sugden, Philip. The Complete History of Jack the Ripper. New York: Carroll & Graf, 1994.

Sullivan, Terry, and Peter Mailen. Killer Clown: John Wayne: The John Wayne Gacy Murders. New York: Pinnacle, 2000.

Trow, M. J. Vlad the Impaler: In Search of the Real Dracula. Charleston, SC: History Press, 2004.

Unger, Miles J. Magnifico: The Brilliant Life and Violent Times of Lorenzo de' Medici. New York: Simon & Schuster, 2008.

Vronsky, Peter. Serial Killers: The Method and Madness of Monsters. New York: Berkley, 2004.

Watson, Bruce. Sacco and Vanzetti: The Men, The Murders, and the Judgment of Mankind. New York: Penguin, 2008.

Other Books by Colin Wilson

Aleister Crowley: The Nature of the Beast. New York: HarperCollins, 1993.

The Angry Years. London: Anova Books, 2007.

Beyond the Outsider. London: Arthur Barker, 1965.

A Casebook of Murder. New York: Cowles Book Company, 1969.

The Corpse Garden: The Crimes of Fred and Rose West. London: Pan Books, 1998.

Crimes of Passion (with Damon Wilson). London: Carlton Publishing Group, 2007.

A Criminal History of Mankind. New York: Putnam, 1984.

The Encyclopedia of Crime (with Oliver Cyriax and Damon Wilson). New York: Overlook Hardcover, 2006.

Encyclopedia of Murder. London: Pan Books, 1961.

The Encyclopedia of Unsolved Mysteries (with Damon Wilson). New York: McGraw-Hill 1988.

History of Murder. N.p.: Castle Books, 2004.

The Killers Among Us: Motives Behind Their Madness: Book I. New York: Grand Central Publishing, 1996.

The Killers Among Us: Sex, Madness and Mass Murder: Book II. New York: Grand Central Publishing, 1997.

The Mammoth Book of Illustrated True Crime. London: Robinson Publishing, 2002.

The Mammoth Book of the History of Murder. Philadelphia: Running Press, 2000.

The Mammoth Book of True Crime. New York: Carroll & Graf 1988.

Manhunt. Irvington, NY: Hylas Publishing, 2006.

The Mind Parasites. Rhinebeck, NY: Monkfish Book Publishing, 2005.

The Misfits: A Study of Sexual Outsiders. New York: Carroll & Graf, 1988.

Murder Casebook. Charlottesville, VA: Hampton Roads, 2008.

Murder in the 1930s: Colin Wilson's True Crime File. London: Robinson Publishing, 1992.

Murder in the 1940s: Colin Wilson's True Crime File. London: Robinson Publishing, 1993.

The Occult: A History. New York: Random House, 1971.

Order of Assassins: The Psychology of Murder. London: Granada Publishing, 1979.

The Outsider. New York: Houghton Mifflin, 1956.

A Plague of Murder. London: Robinson Publishing, 1995.

Rogue Messiahs: Tales of Self-Proclaimed Saviors. Charlottesville, VA: Hampton Roads Publishing, 2000.

Scandal: Private Stories of Public Shame (with Damon Wilson). London: Virgin Books, 2005.

Serial Killer Investigations. Irvington, NY: Hylas Publishing, 2006.

The Serial Killers: A Study in the Psychology of Violence (with Donald Seaman). London: Virgin Books, 2007.

The Sex Diary of a Metaphysician. Berkeley, CA: Ronin Publishing, 1988.

Strange Vanishings: Strange but True Series. New York: Sterling Publishing, 1997.

Weird News Stories. Sidmouth, UK: Paragon, 1996.

Written in Blood: A History of Forensic Detection. Philadelphia: Running Press, 2003.

Written in Blood: Detectives and Detection. New York: Warner Books, 1991.

Written in Blood: The Criminal Mind and Method. New York: Warner Books, 1992.

Written in Blood: The Trail and the Hunt. Warner Books, 1991.

Index

Credits